T0128533

EXILE
NATION

EXILE
NATION

Drugs, Prisons, Politics & Spirituality

| CHARLES SHAW |

SOFT SKULL PRESS | NEW YORK

Library of Congress Cataloging-in-Publication Data is available.

ISBN: 978-1-59376-441-8

Printed in the United States of America

Interior design by Neuwirth & Associates, Inc.
Cover design Charles Brock/Faceout

SOFT SKULL PRESS
New York, NY
www.softskull.com

This book is dedicated to the memories of two radical spirits,
Guy Herron and Roberto Venosa, who helped give me the courage to
speak truth, regardless of the consequences.

CONTENTS

One reason for the new penology is a revision in the concept of poverty. Terms like the "underclass" are now used to describe large portions of the population who are locked into an inescapable cycle of poverty and despair. Criminal justice managers *[emphasis added] now group people by various collectives based on their racial and social characteristics. Rather than seek individual rehabilitation they are oriented toward the more realistic task of monitoring and managing intractable groups. The fact that the underclass is permanent leaves little hope that its members, many of whom are in the correctional population, can be helped. Penology then stresses the low-cost management of a permanent offender population.*

—Larry Siegel,
"Criminal Justice Update," Fall 1993, West Publications

PART I
Purgatory

CHAPTER 1
Dead Time

It is 4:30 am on tier 1A of Division 5 at the Cook County Jail in Chicago, Illinois, and Donald "Frosty" Rogers stands alone in the day room, staring at the clock high up on the wall. The room has a distinct chill, and barely a sound rolls through the deck as Frosty absent-mindedly rubs the faded tattoo on his left arm, which reads, "No Mo' Pain."

He is 59, bald, with espresso-brown skin and a bleach-white beard that snakes downward from his ears to wrap around his chin and mouth. Spilling out from a sleeveless white T-shirt, his well-molded, densely packed upper body shames men half his age. He smiles a toothless grin, and to keep warm he begins to circle his arms repeatedly out before him, the fist of his right hand impacting over and over with the palm of his left, softly and rhythmically. *Thak. Thak. Thak.* Frosty hears something and looks over at the darkened security bubble. Inside the unit guard is reading yesterday's *Sun-Times*. Without looking up from his paper, the guard waves his arm, reaches over blindly to an archaic control panel, and begins pushing buttons.

A series of stark metallic pops like a row of demolition charges punctures the silence, racing around the tier as one after another the magnetic locks on the cell doors are released. A moment or two later, disheveled inmates clad in dirty brown scrubs with "CCDOC" emblazoned across the thigh and back slowly make their way from the two decks of cells situated above and below the day room. The inmates congregate around three stainless steel picnic tables and wait, heads propped, half asleep, until they hear the *clang* of the outer security door, indicating that the breakfast cart has arrived.

When the signal comes, the hungry inmates circle the doorway in muted homage to Pavlov, hoping to catch a glimpse of the day's offering. Two indolent gang-bangers in hairnets slowly begin to stack hard plastic trays one atop the other to a height of five feet, intentionally dragging out the process simply out of *schaden-freude*. Each tray has a small amount of dry cereal, a nondescript juice box, a small glop of cold potatoes, and a piece of bread.

Frosty hangs by the inner door waiting for the guard to buzz in the food so he can begin distributing it. Acrid smoke from hand-rolled Top menthol cigarettes hangs in the air, and the have-nots begin to case the haves. Hustling commences.

"I got a juice fo' a roll, juice fo' a roll," an inmate shouts. "Come on y'all, who goan gimme a square, mang?"

"Got chou, man," another says, flipping him a hand-rolled cig-arette, or "roll." Commercial cigarettes, "squares," are expensive and in short supply. The have-nots are relentless in their begging, so people are discreet about revealing their cache anywhere near the day room.

The inmate who just received the "roll" puts it in his mouth, tips his head all the way back, lights a match, and slowly connects the two dramatically before sucking smoke in deep and blowing a cloud towards the halogen lamps high above, eminently satisfied with the day's first infusion of nicotine. In a lockdown situation, this little steam valve sometimes makes all the difference in the world in preserving order.

"Only one more month, y'all," he says, alluding to the jail-wide smoking ban that will go into effect on August 15.

"Sheeeeit. This mufucka goan go live, joe," replies the one who gave him the cigarette. "Last time they tried that shit, they were takin' White Shirts hostage on Division 9. It got buck ass wild up in heah."

An old black dude who called himself "Sensei" stares down through his bifocals at a chess board and comments, "It is an inveterate habit, Grasshopper."

"A *what?*" dude says.

"Consider it a favor from the state," Sensei mumbles, while scrutinizing the chessboard.

Although they rarely discuss it, inmates are visibly disturbed by this change in policy. It is true that the administration attempted once before in the late '90s to ban smoking, and there were indeed riots. It didn't even last a month. This time, they meant business, because this time it was all about cutting back on health care costs, not because they were particularly concerned about our health. For the preceding two months before the ban went into effect, every two weeks the amount of tobacco an inmate could purchase through the commissary was halved, and tips on how not to go berserk after you quit smoking were posted on every tier.

Frosty grabs a breakfast tray and stands in the inner doorway. Next to him on the floor is a milk crate filled with small cartons.

"All right, line it up!" he shouts. "Fin Ball, then Neutron, then One Love!"

The fifty-some inmates begin to order themselves sequentially into three different groupings based upon their gang affiliation, or lack thereof. In the front of the line are members of Fin Ball, a name for the five allied gangs of the largely South Side "People" Nation—the Vice Lords, Latin Kings, Blackstone Rangers (or

"P-Stones"), Black Mafia, and Insane Popes. These five gangs bound together in the 1970s to protect themselves against the domination of One Love, or gangs from the West Side "Folks" Nation, who are dominated by the laws of the Gangster Disciples, the single largest gang in the Chicago milieu.

Sandwiched in between these two opposing armies are the Neutrons, or the non-gang-affiliated, an amalgamation of mostly white drug offenders, DUI cases, child support cases, and those blacks and Latinos who are either too old to have been part of the gang scene or who were fortunate enough to avoid it, only to later find themselves on the other side of the drug economy with a pesky habit.

One by one each inmate is given a breakfast tray and a small carton of milk, and then each heads for a specific preassigned area of the tier. Fin Ball is the largest by numbers and thus the dominant gang on tier 1A, entitling them to two of the three picnic tables in the day room. One Love sits at the remaining. They fall in like a platoon gathered for mess, have a moment of prayer, and then begin to eat. The Neutrons are left to sit on the floor outside their cells. Laconically, the inmates shovel the paltry portions of food into their mouths, finishing in only a few moments. Invariably, all are left hungry.

Less than fifteen minutes later, once all the inmates have finished and stacked their dirty trays by the door, Frosty calls the room to attention. The inmates are slow to muster, and voices echo loudly.

"On that noise!" Frosty yells. The room quickly quiets down and the inmates begin to pay attention. Frosty is joined on the day room floor by Joe "U.T." Owens, and another inmate calling himself "Celine." They stand behind him like hired goons, looking over the room.

Frosty begins.

"We know a lot of y'all come in on the new last night," he says, referring to the nightly delivery of new inmates to the tiers, which generally happens between 11 pm and 3 am. "So listen up! We ain't sayin' this shit twice."

The room is silent.

"Here's how it is on this deck," Frosty continues. "We all grown men here, so we gonna act like grown men. No stealin', no extortin', no fightin', don't *call* nobody nigger. This here is '1A.' Y'all got the best tier in the joint. We got that way 'cause we don't tolerate no boo-shit in here. We run this ourself, and the C.O.s leave us alone. So, we make the rules. You wanna fuck around on this deck, yo ass gonna get banked . . . *hard*. Everyone here is treated equal, everyone here gets treated like a man. If you need something, *ask!*"

Frosty pauses a second, then continues slower, with added emphasis. "Y'all new muthafuckas get yo ass in the shower this mornin'. You been sittin' in them bullpens for two three days now, and yo ass stink! No exceptions! Any questions?"

Hearing none, Frosty concludes with "Have a nice day." The inmates disperse and begin milling about.

The importance of at least the pretense of hygiene is important when you are in a lockdown situation with limited resources and a lot of men. The tiers are soulless old Modern structures plagued with a kind of textured and embedded filth that can never be scrubbed away. Perhaps in recognition of this futility, soap and other cleaning supplies are always in short supply, if not altogether nonexistent. Strict rules exist in order to maintain a semblance of decency. New men are mandated to shower, and all men are to wear plastic shower shoes at all times since the fungus on the floor rivals jungle rot from Vietnam. If you don't have soap or shower shoes, someone will usually provide you with some until you can work a hustle and get your own.

There is one communal bathroom space adjacent to the day room, with a row of toilets and urinals opposite a row of sinks with polished aluminum mirrors above them, nearly opaque by now. No spitting or tooth brushing is allowed in the sinks as they are used for clean drinking, and to hold cold water to cool milk cartons. The last commode is strictly for sit-down use, and large plastic garbage cans are stacked together next to it to provide the barest modicum of privacy. You clean up whatever mess you make . . . anywhere. Slack on any of the above, and expect swift and direct retribution.

Very quickly the tier becomes loud again. The television sitting high above the room bolted to a rack in the cinder block wall is quickly switched on to BET. Some inmates array themselves along the tables to play spades or dominoes or roll cigarettes. Some congregate for morning bible study with "The Reverend," a gentle and soft-spoken older man in wire frame glasses whose sole interface with those on the deck is the word of Jesus Christ; no one knows why he is in jail. Others retreat to their cells for more sleep while the new arrivals are herded into the showers, as ordered, soon to be horrified by the foul dross that awaits them in there, but so grateful for a few moments with some soap and hot water that, for the time being, it won't matter.

Before the sun has even broken the horizon, tier 1A begins to come alive, another day in the County, unremarkable, really, from any other day. Frosty grabs a broomstick—what the inmates affectionately call "the remote"—and begins to change channels on the television looming above. 1A is allowed a broomstick because it is a peaceful deck. Most other tiers, it wouldn't be such a good idea. Frosty pauses on a CBS "Special Report," which is just breaking.

"*On that noise!*" he bellows. "Y'all might want to pay attention to this shit!"

The room somewhat quiets, but it's clear no one really cares. The only shows that generally capture their attention are *Jerry Springer, COPS, and Soul Train.*

Frosty watches the coverage in silence.

. . . London rocked by terror attacks. At least two people have been killed and scores injured after three blasts on the Underground

network and another on a double-decker bus in London. UK Prime Minister Tony Blair said it was "reasonably clear" there had been a series of terrorist attacks. He said it was "particularly barbaric" that it was timed to coincide with the G8 summit. He is returning to London. An Islamist website has posted a statement—purportedly from al-Qaeda—claiming it was behind the attacks . . .

"Shit . . . Ain't no mufuckin' al-Qaeda," he mumbles.

▽

The Cook County Jail is part of the Cook County Department of Corrections, a sprawling 96-acre detention complex situated next to the Cook County Criminal Courts along California Avenue in Chicago's Lower West Side neighborhood. Most refer to it as "26th and Cal" even though the jail stretches all the way south to 32nd Street, in all a distance of nearly a mile.

The first county jail in Chicago was built in 1871 at 26th Street and California Avenue scant months before the Great Chicago Fire. That building is long gone, replaced in 1929 by what is now the oldest remaining building in the complex, Division 1. This squat art-deco structure has over the years held a fine pedigree of criminal luminaries including Al Capone and Frank Nitti, Tony "Big Tuna" Accardo, gang leaders Larry Hoover, Jeff Fort, and Willie Lloyd, and serial killers Richard Speck and John Wayne Gacy.

Between 1929 and 1995 the jail complex was expanded into 11 separate divisions that range from minimum security to supermax. Cook County is the largest single-site pre-trial detention facility in the United States (Los Angeles has a bigger overall county jail, but it is split into two separate facilities). CCDOC employs over 3,000 correctional officers and support staff and admits over 100,000 detainees a year, more than twice that of the entire Illinois penitentiary system. The reported average daily inmate population is around 10,000. The real figure, however, is quite likely higher since, due to overcrowding, it is a regular practice to put a third man in a two-man cell and have him sleep on the floor.

It is also one of the most controversial correctional facilities in the nation, referred to by inmate and officer alike as the "Crook County Department of Corruptions."

In recent years the jail has come under fire for overcrowding, violence, and, naturally, corruption. There have been all manner of federal and grand jury investigations, and plaintiff lawsuits, concerning excessive beatings and inmate deaths at the hands of correctional officers. And if they didn't already have enough bad PR to defuse, between 2005 and 2006 there were a series of high-profile escapes that received national coverage.

▼

Anyone who has had the misfortune of being behind its walls knows all too well about the violence, corruption, and squalor that characterizes this institution. Simply put, Cook County Jail is a harrowing, unforgettable experience for anyone. It is so awful that for many of its detainees a quick guilty plea and a trip to the penitentiary, even for twice as long, is preferable to staying in the County.

Or at least that was how I saw it when I was arrested in March 2005 for possession of 14 capsules of MDMA (a.k.a. Ecstasy) and was facing one year in prison.

To be fair, this was my third time in County. My first was for a month in December 1998 when I was busted for the second of three drug-related convictions I have on my record. The first two convictions came in the late 1990s, the result of nearly a decade spent in high-intensity guerrilla warfare against a cocaine addiction while in my twenties. The MDMA conviction came seven years (and really, a whole lifetime) later, following my arrest two weeks after my thirty-fifth birthday.

I had just returned to Chicago after spending most of the previous year on the road writing for *Newtopia*, an online magazine

I published at the time, and organizing for the Green Party and other related factions of the progressive-to-radical antiwar and green movements. I was back in town to face a court case I had that stemmed from an assault by tactical officers (TAC squad) of the 23rd District of the Chicago Police Department, Addison and Halsted Street station, one year before in April 2004. I was illegally stopped and searched, and ultimately beaten and arrested on false charges, by four plainclothes police officers who discovered I was connected to a local peace and justice group that was involved in fighting police corruption.

The charges against me were dismissed, and the judge who heard the case acknowledged wrongdoing by the police. From that moment forth I can only assume that, fearing a civil rights case that I fully intended to file, these cops were committed to stopping me somehow. I was watched, I was followed, and a few weeks later I was rousted and ultimately arrested for possession of MDMA by TAC squad officers from the same precinct house, one of whom I later identified as one of the four present the night of my assault.

It's important for me to take a moment here and explain that I was not using Ecstasy recreationally. I wasn't a "raver," and I didn't merely transfer an addiction from one substance to another. I was reintroduced to MDMA in a therapeutic context in 2004. Prior to that I had not taken a single dose since the early '90s.

Friends from my community in Chicago who were fellow drug war activists were also intimately connected to the Multidisciplinary Association for Psychedelic Studies (MAPS), which had done pioneering work on MDMA therapy for those suffering from post-traumatic stress disorder. Many of these friends, as well as psychotherapeutic professionals I knew at the time, helped me to see that I was suffering from a form of PTSD brought on by the effects of violent experiences in my past and my prolonged addiction to cocaine, and that some form of MDMA therapy might help me.

Although at the time there were no clinical studies available in the US, much less a regulated program of treatment (in other words, because I couldn't do it legally), I had enough information and guidance to feel comfortable—and risk—experimenting on my own. Although later on in the book I will go into detail about the specifics of the therapeutic work I did that began with MDMA and other substances and then led to more traditional therapies, it's important to understand that this was the reason I was in possession of the MDMA at the time of my third arrest, two weeks after my 35th birthday. It was a risk I was willing to take, and I do not regret it. The experiences chronicled in this book led to a complete transformation of consciousness, which would over the next four years completely change every aspect of my life.

I understand I broke the law, and many will see my punishment as deserved. The case I will make is that the laws surrounding drug use are unjust (particularly for those drugs with the capacity to heal), that the punishment does not fit the crime (and in fact does far worse damage), and that my experiences reveal that the system itself is broken, a self-perpetuating machine of dysfunction that remains in place for reasons wholly separate from either drug enforcement or criminal justice. In many ways, this book is about cognitive liberty above all—the freedom to learn, heal, and grow however you wish by whatever methods you choose, the freedom to experience life in the manner of your choosing.

After I was arrested I would spend three months dealing with my case until it became clear to me and my lawyer that, with a third conviction and a precinct house full of overzealous cops hell-bent on covering their collective asses, I could not avoid prison time.

This was a particularly bitter pill to swallow for two reasons. The first and most galling was that I was no longer a drug addict. I took great pride in that. Breaking that addiction was the hardest thing I had ever done, and I was long past engaging in any of the at-risk activities that had led to my first two arrests and convictions. The second reason was that the substances I was being punished for having in my possession had helped me immeasurably, bringing me, in a very short time, to begin to face demons that had been consuming me my whole life. I considered them my friends.

What was all the more ironic was that as I was recovering, probably as a direct result, I spent a few years investigating the drug war in great detail and had begun writing about it. I also got involved in activism trying to reform drug laws through various lobby efforts. I had been building a respectable body of work, and in that work I had been steady about one thing: Our national drug policy was absurd and had no impact on either drug use or supply. It was economics, moral policing, and social control, and it disproportionately punished the poor. I constantly argued that warehousing drug users as prisoners was a waste of public resources that were better spent on our communities, and that there were better things drug users could be made to do. The irony was not lost on me that I was now living proof of my own theories.

Thus I returned to Cook County Jail on July 1, 2005, after accepting a guilty plea and taking a two-year sentence (one year in the penitentiary and one year of parole) for—let's be clear— having a few pills in my pocket that made me want to give everyone I knew a hug. But that's an argument for later on.

I had to surrender myself in the courtroom and be led away through that mysterious back door behind the judge that the public never gets to see. As I stepped through it, I turned and smiled goodbye to my friends gathered in the courtroom for support, and I didn't take a normal breath for months. As the door closed behind me I had to put on another persona, one which I would keep until they let me out and I could go back to being myself.

I entered what is known as "dead time," or the time an Illinois convict spends in the county jail awaiting shipment to the penitentiary system, which, no matter how long it takes, does not count towards the overall sentence. It was also literally dead time in my life, *vita interrupta*, weeks and months taken from me. Though I had harmed no one and nothing, I was now part of an exile nation of American radicals, convicts, and detainees millions strong, where I would burn off my "sins" in service to the State, in what is commonly known as the prison-industrial complex.

THE GATEWAY TO THE UNDERWORLD

The first challenge of this year-long odyssey I had before me was to get through County Jail Intake and Processing, a long and exhaustive ordeal that tests the very limits of your patience and mettle. It is where you quickly have to adapt to a new reality in order to survive. Even if you've been through it a dozen times—which is not uncommon, since the recidivism rate is frighteningly high— the process is traumatic, and leaves you exhausted for days. For many, this will be the first time they will have their basic freedoms rescinded and experience the methodical cruelty and dehumanization of this kind of "factory corrections"—the production, management, and warehousing of large numbers of offenders.

Every day paddy wagons from police precincts all across this nation's second most populous county converge on the jail's receiving dock to offload their shackled human cargo into a dark and dingy chute that leads into the bowels of the jail complex.

Because of this charge, and the three months in between while my court case was in limbo, I had to go through jail intake *twice*, once when I was arrested in March 2005, and again in July when I went back into the system after being on electronic monitoring, or house arrest, a program to combat jail overcrowding. The initial arrest was on Good Friday, and I spent Saturday in the police lockup at Belmont and Western before, being transferred to Cook County on Easter Sunday. I did not see a bond judge at the Belmont and Western precinct, which had been my experience seven and eight years before, respectively. Before taking the lot of us to Intake and Processing, we were herded into a series of three dark, filthy, horribly overcrowded holding pens to await a bond hearing via closed circuit TV.

In "video bond court," detainees appear one at a time in a small room with a camera mounted on the wall above them. Meanwhile, many floors above ground and down the street in the Criminal Courts complex, a bond judge, state's attorney, and public defender discuss each detainee's fate.

The experience is uniquely totalitarian in the purest Orwellian sense, a Kafka-esque nightmare where the detainee has literally no ability to speak for himself, and it is doubtful, given the sheer volume of faces passing on and off the black and white screen, that any of us was actually viewed as a person. We were nothing more than depersonalized names and prior records next to subterranean faces distorted on an old monitor, which, from what I saw, the judge didn't even bother to look at.

Bond, if given, is determined by the category of the detainee's crime (felony or misdemeanor), the relative degree of the crime (Classes 1–4 and X), and any prior criminal history. Because of my prior record, I was given a $40,000 D-Bond, which would require me to post 10%, or $4,000, in order to gain bail. It might as well have been $4 million; I had less than $200 to my name.

A very few lucky souls with misdemeanors or first-time petty nonviolent felonies (like a Class 4 nonviolent possession of a controlled substance, my crime) will be released on an I-Bond to their own recognizance. Most will be remanded to the custody of CCDOC until they can post bail or their case is resolved one way or another.

It is important to remember, as you read what unfolds, that none of us had been convicted of anything yet, and some of those held in these conditions were in fact innocent, but simply could not post bail.

Those charged with nonviolent offenses become immediately eligible for the EMU (electronic monitoring unit) but still must spend a day or more going through Intake and Processing and anywhere from a couple days to a few weeks on a jail tier before a spot/bunk opens up and they come around to collect you. Luckily, I did qualify for EMU. Nonviolence does get you somewhere.

Each day around 300 detainees are processed in a large room deep underground beneath Division 5. The room looks as if it has not been cleaned since it opened in the mid-'70s, and the stench of smoke, urine, and vomit is at times overpowering. Along the perimeter of the room are a series of bullpens into which detainees are stuffed like chickens in a factory farm, to be shuffled and reshuffled from one to the other and back again while moving through the various stages of admission.

Only one bullpen has toilet facilities, and they are so befouled that inmates are made sick simply by looking at them. Yet, for the disproportionately large number of detainees who are addicted to heroin or alcohol, it is the only place for them when their bodies turn on them violently and provide the background music for the world's most cramped waiting room.

Detainees are led from the first bullpen to be fingerprinted and issued an 11-digit ID number based on the current year and overall number of entry (my number was 05-23995, meaning I was the 23,995th person processed in 2005). Photo ID cards are issued, which are kept by correctional officers at the individual tiers or living units within each respective division. A series of "interviews" with staff personnel determines basic personal information: name, address, employment, next of kin, and most importantly, prior record and gang affiliation if any. These, weighed against the detainee's current charge, will be used in creating a security classification of minimum, medium, or maximum, determining where you will be housed. Without explanation, I got a medium security designation, which I later discovered is given to virtually all nonviolent drug crimes.

All personal property, except for wedding rings, is turned in and any cash is collected and put on account. Detainees pray that they will see it again. Many won't. I never got any of my cash back, and a good portion of my wardrobe never made it home either.

A very precursory medical history is given. Blood is drawn for TB and syphilis, a chest X-ray is taken, and—dreaded last—a visit to the "dick doctor" for a quick and painful cotton swab down the urethra for a STD screen. You really can't fathom what it feels like to have a nine-inch Q-tip shoved into your urinary canal, or the terror it strikes into a man waiting an hour to have the procedure. I had it done the first time I was in County, in 1998, and it was worse than you can possibly imagine.

There was one ray of hope that day. Word rippled through the line that a class-action lawsuit had ended the reign of the dick doctor. Every man down that line shivering in his underwear heaved a deep, near-hysterical sigh of relief (as, I'm sure, did every male reading this). Some court had finally come to the rescue, a distinctly unfamiliar experience to most of these men, whose only association with the court system is generally punitive. The system can work, every once in a (deep cobalt, near black) blue moon. Unfortunately, it takes something as severe as a trauma-tized urethra to get anyone's attention.

In between each of these stages, detainees are left standing for hours in the bullpens. Naturally, it is unreasonable to expect anyone to stand that long, so eventually people begin to collapse onto the filthy floor, and onto the few benches along the wall, chests tucked to knees, unable to move. Regularly, correctional officers will come by and scream into the bullpens about the noise or about people sitting down. They make threats, make everyone stand up, then they leave, and the process begins all over again. It becomes this absurd pantomime, a futile back and forth of au-thority and rebellion, insurgency and counterinsurgency, stuck in an infinite feedback loop.

Contempt and disgust pours from the faces of the C.O.s and you wonder what makes them so hate-filled, before you have to remind yourself that some pretty nasty individuals have come through here over the years, and after a while it must get to everyone. Still, you wonder why they even bothered taking the job in the first place. What did they expect?

This ritualized abuse and debasement would only get worse

as I went into the prison system, a systematic brutalization of basic human rights and dignity that I faced with every turn. You couldn't even ask a simple, innocent question without running the risk of getting your skull cracked. They simply didn't care; you were like livestock to them, filthy, stupid animals that deserved nothing. It must have been what they had to think to even live with themselves. Deep inside, few humans *want* to be that cruel. Or do they?

Over time, stuck in the bullpens waiting, the men become more and more filthy and the stench in the room transmogrifies into a dull rancid taste that coats the back of your throat. That nasty taste still haunts my memories, surfacing in my dreams, like a sickness lingering.

A transsexual prostitute arrives with a large shipment of women detainees[1] from one of the West Side precincts, and the White Shirts—sergeants and lieutenants—decide he/she has to be isolated, so the men lose the use of one whole bullpen. The net result is that the tranny becomes the object of vicious, relentless abuse by both the C.O.s and the detainees, and the remaining bullpens swell so far beyond capacity that the men no longer can move.

Many hours into their ordeal, and perhaps days since their original arrest, detainees are ordered into a final bullpen so that they may attempt to make their "one phone call." However, despite popular misconceptions that everyone is entitled to a call, there is only a limited amount of time for 300-odd people to make their calls, and everyone has to share what during my experience was five working phones out of eight total.

These phones are a hell unto themselves. They are not coin pay phones, and there is no operator assistance or 800-collect numbers. They do not call cell phones, and you cannot leave a message. They are specifically designed for use in correctional institutions. They have a singular function: automated, direct-dial, direct-bill calling, which means you can only reach a number on an established landline that does not have collect call blocking, or in the case of many recidivists' families, correctional call blocking. You punch in the number you want to reach; it records your name and puts you on hold while it makes the call for you.

When the call arrives, it plays a prerecorded message that says, You have a collect call from *[your recorded name], an inmate at the Cook County Jail. If you wish to accept this call, please press "1" now. Charges are two dollars and eighty cents plus one dollar for each additional minute.*

You pray someone accepts the call, but many detainees never reach anyone.

This dearth of phone communication is somewhat alleviated once inmates are safely tucked away in their housing units. Once there they have regular access to phones. Correctional telephone services are a multibillion-dollar-a-year industry, and County inmates sometimes spend up to a year or more awaiting resolution of their cases. The phone providers are fully aware that they are the detainees' only link to the outside world. Inmates are totally dependent on them to communicate with family, lawyers, and loved ones, and it all adds up. Of course, it's not the detainees who are paying the astronomical phone bills; their families are, in effect adding another level to their punishment and creating an even further imposition of hardship, as the vast majority of detainees and their families are poor.

Perhaps the most gruesome and dehumanizing aspect of the intake process is the mandatory strip search. I lived through three different strip searches in the basement of County over nearly an eight-year period, and they were all the same. In groups of roughly 75 to 100, detainees are led into a long, narrow underground tunnel outside Intake and Processing in which a group of very large white correctional officers with fat, beefy biceps, with scalps either close cropped or bald, stand around wearing latex gloves and looking as if they would rather be exhuming the dead

than be in that tunnel with all of us. We are lined up shoulder to
shoulder along the wall. At our feet is a yellow line.

"Listen up, mother*fuckers*!" one of the thick-necks shouts.
"Pay attention, do *exactly* as I say, and this will go smoothly! Do
not talk, do *not* move unless told to! God help you if we see you
moving or talking! You do *not* want to fuck with us today!"

We are instructed to remove one article of clothing at a time.
Pants are to be held upside-down by the cuffs and gently shaken.
Shoes are to be turned upside down and banged together. We are
told that because we may, "have bugs and God knows what else
living on us and in our clothes," if we shake our clothing out
horizontally in their direction, we will not only lose that article
of clothing permanently, we will also "regret it." They make this
point *very* clear, and no one shakes his clothes.

Down the line someone suddenly vomits across the smooth
concrete tunnel floor. Before half of us are aware that he had
puked, he is forcibly dropped to the ground by one of the C.O.s,
who shoves his face in it, and orders him to wipe it up with his
own shirt. When he heaves as if to vomit again, the C.O. kicks
him and tells him he'll have to clean it up with his hands. The
tunnel fills with the stench, and another detainee breaks rank and
stumbles to a nearby garbage can. Instantly another C.O. is in his
face screaming at him, "You puke in that can, you're cleaning it
out with your bare hands!" He is forced back into line.

The process continues. Eventually, we stand naked, our
clothes in a pile at our feet, the stink of alcohol-puke drifting
down the tunnel. We are told to turn and face the wall, then to
bend over and grab our ankles. On the count of three, all are
instructed to cough loudly. This is ostensibly to check and see if
we have drugs or other contraband shoved up our ass, but the
method they employ is so easily faked that you can't help but
feel that its primary purpose is to degrade us. The percussive
thud of the collective cough echoes off the concrete. Standing

back up, we remain facing the wall, foreheads pressed against the concrete, arms above our head, palms facing outward as instructed.

"This is your last chance!" one C.O. shouts. "If you got anything on you, or in your clothes, tell us now or you'll end up catching another case!" No one is stupid enough to believe him, so the tunnel remains silent, irrespective of what anyone may or may not have on him.

The C.O.s move up and down the line picking up shoes and articles of clothing, searching through them, ripping out insoles and throwing things recklessly back down to the cold floor. Near the end of the line, mere steps from me, a large, bald C.O. finds a $20 bill stuffed deep inside the lining of a shoe, a common practice among young men in the hood who are used to being robbed. The C.O. spins the naked inmate around to face him.

"What the fuck is this?" he says, sticking the bill in the man's nose.

"Man, I forgot it was in there."

A White Shirt sergeant steps forward from behind the C.O. and, with latex gloves on, open-hand slaps the inmate across the face. "What the fuck did we just tell you!? You think you're slick? You think we're idiots?" The C.O. pockets the money and shoves the inmate back against the wall. No one dares raise his head to see what is happening. No one wants to be a witness to anything like this. But everyone knows exactly what is happening. It is nothing new.

When they are finished searching the clothing, we are given exactly fifteen seconds to get fully dressed. If we do not get everything on in fifteen seconds, we are told, we will have to leave whatever is left on the floor and it will be thrown out. Rarely do you see humans so exhausted move so fast.

One at a time, by security designation—minimum, medium, maximum, and supermax—we step forward, turn left, and are marched out in single-file lines to another row of impossibly cramped holding cells. Here we will eventually be fed a border-line-legal bologna sandwich and maybe a little six-ounce plastic bottle of some artificial juice drink while we await transfer to our living units, which can take anywhere from three to four hours.

These bullpens are even smaller than the ones in Intake, and none of us can move, stand up, stretch our legs, or use the bathroom. The benches are filled and men sit pressed together. Some are lying on the floor under the benches, making every square foot of open space occupied. It's so hot you can't breathe, and you never imagined people could smell so goddamn bad.

Now, hunger begins to set in, which is particularly egregious to vegetarians like me at that time, who had no option but to eat bread soaked with bologna slime or go hungry. I mean, I could always make an argument to eat meat, but we are talking about no meat born of nature here. We are talking about an unholy creation. After seven years of not eating meat, I feared it would kill me. So I went hungry.

When the time comes, hours later, we are dislodged from the holding cell and taken to our assigned divisions through an elaborate series of underground tunnels. This generally takes place very late at night or early in the morning.

Before being brought up to the various dorms and tiers we must make our last stop, in the clothing room, to turn in our street clothes and get issued a grey plastic property box about the size of a small trunk, a brown CCDOC uniform, blanket, mattress, and, if lucky, a "hygiene pack," which can include any combination of toilet paper, soap, towel, toothbrush, toothpaste, and deodorant, never all at once, rarely more than two or three items at a time. It will take an hour to distribute all the personal effects and store all the clothing. In that time, inmates make informal bets about which of their clothing will make it back to them. Anything leather is considered a goner.

One by one, property boxes held before us, mattresses folded on top, we begin a long climb up a narrow concrete stairwell three flights until we reach the living units, or tiers.

Each tier in Division 5, and a few other divisions like it built around the same time in the early 1970s, is made up of a large square room with yellow cinderblock walls and concrete floors, and is split into three separate levels. Cells line one half of the room on decks just above and below the day room, which is on floor level. Twenty-two cells per tier, 11 on the upper deck and 11 on the lower, making the population count officially 44, and with three-man occupancy, sometimes as high as 60.

The day room is a common area with high ceilings pockmarked by high-intensity halogen lights and a few old surveillance cameras. Three stainless steel picnic tables are bolted to the main floor. A bank of three pay phones is in the far corner. The third wall has a common bathroom and a common shower. The exit door, and the security bubble, occupy the last wall.

By the time I actually set foot in tier 1A with six other guys it's around 11:30 pm. After ten o'clock on any given night the tier is generally on lockdown and all inmates are required to be in their cells. A few members of Fin Ball remain outside in the day room to sweep the floors and keep the barter economy alive by ferrying goods between cells.

Through chuckholes—narrow vertical monitoring slots cut into the center of the steel cell doors—inmates "chirp" to each other, calling out across the tier, begging cigarettes, trading commissary food, corny crime novels, raggedy porn mags, whatever it takes to pass the time and feed the persistent hunger in your gut . . . or soul.

As we walk across the day room, calls of *"On the New!"* emanate from various chuckholes. As we pass by their cells, the other inmates scope us out, scanning for friendly or familiar faces.

"Who yo wit little nigga?" someone asks a young black kid standing next to me. *Who you wit?* is the first thing anyone asks you, because your gang affiliation, or lack thereof, is everything. This impromptu recon work is essential for all to become aware of their place on the deck. With few words, the natures of relationships are established, and a hierarchy is enforced.

"Wit dem Stones," comes the kid's reply, referring to the Blackstone Rangers gang. His hair stands a foot high after he was forced by jail personnel to take out his braids. Officially, they tell you, braids are undone because they are "gang symbols," but they don't make only gang members debraid. They make all black men do it. Ask any brother and he'll tell you it's to humiliate them, to make them look like dirty pickaninnies when they are hauled, cuffed and shackled, in DOC scrubs out in front of the court. Lookin' like that, they say, they're guilty before anyone can utter a word in their defense.

"Who got dis?" big hair asks, motioning to indicate that he is curious which gang runs this particular tier.

"Fin Ball. They got chou. These niggaz straight Vice Lords."

(*Loose Translation:* "This tier is under the control of the People Nation, mostly guys from the Vice Lords. You are safe here, you have backup.")

"Ah-aight, den. You ride?" ("Cool. Are you one of us?")

"GD, yo." ("No. I am with the Gangster Disciples.")

Realizing that he now can do whatever he wants—within the rules of his crew—and realizing he has to establish himself now on the tier, from this point on in the conversation, the youngster engages in mostly unnecessary bravado.

"You straight?" ("You got an issue with us being in charge?")

"Naw. This mufucka straight." ("This tier is peaceful and ordered, so yes, I am fine with it and we shouldn't have a problem.")

The youngster eyeballs the cat in his cell as he passes out of view, then looks over at me.

"Sup wit chou, white boy?" the kid says, antagonistically. I just ignore him. I am so thoroughly exhausted by this time that I can barely stand. All I want to do is sleep. The unit C.O. opens the various cells by hand and directs us inside, two or three at a time. My cell is on the lower deck, just under the stairs that lead to the upper deck. However, sleep is a long way off.

Luckily, the cell I'm assigned to was just turned over and stands empty, so there is no need to establish myself as the new guy with my cellmates. And since the three of us just spent all day and night together in processing, there is an instant air of levity and relief once the door lock slams home and we are left to our own limited devices. It is a strange and powerful sense of relief; you know that for the next five or six hours no one will bother you, and you can sleep.

I was lucky that last time. The two other times I had been in County were significantly harder since I was stuck in cells occupied by gang members and was forced to be the man on the floor. It meant I never had anything close to privacy, and I had to do all the cleaning, and they took what they wanted from my food tray. You don't even think about telling them "no."

This time around my cellmates were an old Irish guy named Mike who had this red bulbous pockmarked nose that made him look like JP Morgan, and this 25-year-old white kid from Idaho. Old Mike got busted while in his car buying heroin for his dope-sick girlfriend, who couldn't leave the bathroom. The kid had just moved to Chicago with his 20-year-old girlfriend to work in commercial production and got locked up for punching her in the face after gettin' lit on whiskey.

We unroll our filthy, stained-foam mattresses on our respective bunks—me on top, Mike on the lower, the kid on the floor—and we each stretch a sheet across them. Each man urinates in succession in the stainless steel toilet that sits next to the two bunks then drinks some warm, slimy water from a tepid bubbler in the sink. We crawl into bed and listen to the kid go on and on about how sorry he is for hitting his girlfriend, that he had never done it before, that he was drunk. He tells us that she was already headed back to Idaho, and he asks us how he might get her back. Neither Mike nor I say much. The kid begins to cry.

"Listen," I tell him. "It's cool that you're doing that now, in here, but don't let those other cats out there see you do that."

The kid, looking perhaps a bit too terrified, quickly wipes the tears from his face.

"What's the deal? Are they gonna try and rape me?"

"I really don't think so," I told him. You could tell he had never been in jail before. "That kind of shit doesn't go on much in the County. But these youngbloods out here, they prey on weakness. So, if you wanna eat, and you wanna be left alone, you can't show weakness. Just be cool. You'll be out of here tomorrow. Get some sleep."

"Good idea," Mike grunts. "Let's start with the light?"

The kid gets up and turns off the light. From another cell down the way on the lower deck comes another voice chirping out of a chuckhole.

"U.T.?"

"Yo!"

"*On the reach!*"

Two arms emerge from the chuckholes of two adjacent cell doors like elephant trunks snaking in and out of zoo cages, stretching out plaintively towards each other, groping blindly. One hand is empty; the other holds a few "rolls." They eventually connect and pass the cigarettes from one to the other, and the arms withdraw back into the cells.

Slowly over the course of the next half hour or so the deck quiets down as most inmates finally go to sleep. The television high upon the wall is turned to a *Jerry Springer* rerun, and the volume comes way down. Through the cinder block wall in the adjacent cell, U.T. can be heard preaching to his two new cellies about how a division between light- and dark-skinned blacks was created by white slave owners to create a persistent atmosphere of divide and rule.

". . . Thaz how they got dem Bougies, dem high yellow mutha-fuckas livin' in Massah's house who think that they better than dem field niggers, who is dark as night. And the field niggers, all they thinkin' 'bout is how come Massah like dem Bougies more? It's cuse dey be part Massah, 'cause he be fuckin' field niggers every damn night, and dey start havin' babies . . . So, right, they end up hatin' on their brother, and not on the man who is en-slaving them, because the light-skinned brother reflects the image of the Massah. And that shit still goan on today. Young boys be killin' deyselfs in the 'hood, and black folk be killin' other black folk even back in Africa . . . You remember Rwanda . . . that was the same shit. When the white man came to Africa, he favored one tribe over another, so the other tribe spent all dey time hatin' on the favorite tribe . . ."

Back in our cell the kid asks me, "Why are you in here?"

"I'm on my way to the penitentiary. I got a year for some Ecstasy."

"Jesus. How much, like a pound?"

"I think the final count was eleven capsules. A few disappeared in the booking process."

"You gotta be shittin' me?"

"Wish I was."

That's so lame! How do you *deal* with that?"

"What choice do I have?"

"Dude, I'd freak."

"Well, be grateful it's not you."

I pause, then roll over and look down at him on the floor.

"But if you don't stop beating up women, it will probably be you."

"Dude, come on, I don't *beat women*."

I didn't want to argue with him. "Anyway, it should be interesting."

"Man, I'd be so pissed."

"Find me someone who wouldn't be."

Mike begins to snore, a vicious, snorting apneac rumble, quite possibly the loudest, most phlegmy sound I have ever heard. My assessment is confirmed when a voice from above on the upper deck breaks the silence.

"Man, somebody shoot that fool!"

Sleep never really comes. I fade in and out of a sort of semi-sleep, as if I keep practicing the opening bow to a waltz, but never actually begin the dance. My mind stumbles around in circles. I think of my dog, but it makes me too sad. Of all the hard things I had to endure the previous three months, I never thought saying goodbye to my dog would be the toughest. It nearly broke me. Go figure.

There's your hardened convict for ya.

A CORRECTIONAL COSMOLOGY

There is a delicate balance to life on a jail tier. There is a class strata, an economy, and an ecosystem. Divide and Rule is the way order is kept. When inmates have to police themselves, and watch their backs, the dynamic takes on a very different character, and a certain stasis is reached. There is generally just the right mix of gangster and Neutron to keep a strange and unexpected harmony. But underlying it all is the understanding that, although County is at times the very likeness of despair, no one wants to make his stay there any worse than it has to be by being sent to solitary or by having your skull cracked by overzealous C.O.s armed with clubs and really bad attitudes. When things go wrong in County, people get hurt.

During my stay in 1998, gang members on my tier were suspected of selling various forms of contraband, so the SORT team (Special Operations Response Team), otherwise known as the goon squad, was sent in. We were all stripped naked and zip-cuffed behind our backs and made to kneel on the floor of the day room as every cell was tossed. When they located guilty parties, they beat the shit out of them right in front of us, and then hauled them off to segregation to face more charges. This type of abuse was rampant in County. Only two months later, in February 1999, SORT officers viciously beat and turned attack dogs on 400 inmates in Division 9, and then engaged in an elaborate cover-up.[2]

To maintain order and create routine every jail division has to follow a regimented schedule. In 1A we were woken up for breakfast around 4:30 am and then were required to stay out of our cells in the day room for a couple hours until around 6:30 am. Cells open at 6:30, and those wanting to go back to sleep can until lunch, which is around 10:00 or 11:00 am.

It is up to the discretion of the unit C.O., but depending on the tier, inmates can either come out of their cells, or remain inside during lunch, but not both. If they choose to remain inside they remain locked in until 4:30 pm when dinner is slated to arrive. Inmates must be out of their cells for the evening hours, which end at 9:30 pm. This staggering of inside/outside is meant to keep the inmates moving around and visible, thus reducing the various malfeasances that can occur out of sight when groups of people congregate in a jail cell or two. It is also a liability precaution meant to help minimize suicide attempts.

I preferred whenever I could to be alone in my cell reading. It occupied my mind with something other than prison bullshit and it gave me some peace, so I would try to remain in my cell during those midday hours. I would stuff my chuckhole with toilet paper rolls and slip a milk carton over the light bulb, and I would be in my own little private space for a precious while.

Inmates were no longer permitted to go to the County library in 2005 (actually, I was told library visits were done by written request only, and they never granted any requests) so the only books available on the tier were a few smuggled FBI crime novels that were so awful they made me sad (well, that and the fact that many of them had been best-sellers as well). The two weeks I whiled away before shipment I had nothing to read but this rather unabashed propaganda novel about an FBI agent hunting terrorists, "militia men," and other non-conforming sectors of American society. In 246 short pages it managed to ridicule every belief system you can think of that existed outside the Good and Evil milieu of God, Country, and Capitalism, while at the same time openly glorifying the very un-Christian merits of guns, booze, sex with your suspiciously attractive female partner, and the quick kill.

Sometimes reading is all you have to keep you from losing it. At least that's what it did for me. Over the next few months while I burned off time in the penitentiary I would read probably three dozen books, some of which I was shocked to find in a prison library, books I had wanted to read my whole life but (savor the irony) never would have had the time for in the outside world like I did while locked up. Strange blessing, in a manner of speaking.

▼

Frosty and I are watching TV. At one point he leans in close to me and says, "You know these mufuckas think you a cop?" I look over at him and he smiles mischievously, signaling to me that he does not share that opinion.

"Story of my life," I tell him, and wasn't lying. I had this problem when I used to buy drugs on the street. It's a whole different world when you have to navigate housing projects and ghetto blocks, places where often the only white faces ever seen are cops. Most of the major cities are segregated this way. As the white customer, I would slip into a virtual shark tank populated by cops, gangs, hypes, and rogue scammers, and I would have to get in and out before I was noticed by any of the above. If you think about white suburbia and their predilection to view every black man passing through their community as a criminal, it stands to reason that on the reverse end every white man coming through the 'hood is either a cop, customer, or mark.

But because I looked like I did—which is to say at the time I went into County I was clean-shaven with a buzz cut at a healthy and robust 200 pounds and not strung out—they decided I had to be a cop . . . because I looked healthy. This particular wariness and paranoia towards me, I discovered, I had brought upon myself, and then was naïve enough to think I could overcome it.

"Am I in any danger?" I ask him.

Frosty laughs. "Not now you ain't. Few months back, *sheeeit*. This place was buck wild. GD punks had this, young boys, and they were downright cruel."

He points over at a Polish kid who spoke no English playing chess with "Sensei."

"They made that man wash their clothes, their goddamn shit shorts. They were straight up looters, they took everybody's shit. Then me and U.T. and Celine and some of them Vice Lords came on the deck, and we finally had to go with 'em. C.O.s let us take care of it, I ended up breakin' their chief's jaw, and when it was over, they hauled all them muthafuckas out and put them next door. Now, it's a damn circus over there every day, and they never bother us in here."

Frosty pats me on the back. "But you came close." He laughs, and walks away.

Allow me to explain.

Asking a lot of questions is not advisable behavior while locked up. Period. Some people know this instinctively, and just keep to themselves or, if interacting, make small talk. The gang members are like that. They don't talk to anyone but each other, and they are automatically suspicious of everyone and everything. Some people learn quickly not to be nosy, others slowly, and a few the hard way. And of course some just never learn. Those people get ignored or worse. I came perilously close to being one of them.

No matter what my excuse was, whether true or untrue, I discovered there is nothing cool about writing down shit someone else is saying while you're locked up. It's simply a bad idea, and one I wish I had considered more before I did. It was bad enough most of them had never met a journalist, but as far as they were concerned, a white guy with pen and paper was either a cop or a snitch.

They were mildly impressed with me in the beginning because I got busted with what they saw as a glamour drug, one that they themselves would consent to take. And at the time, MDMA was becoming popular in their culture and they showed interest in exploring the intricacies of supply and demand. I felt like they were testing me. If I wasn't a cop, they deduced, then I must have been busted for dealing MDMA and was asking questions because I was trying to get info on other people in order to get a deal with the State's Attorney. They asked me what I did "out in the world" and I told them I was a journalist, a writer, and that I was going to write about my experience in prison. They didn't get it, or trust it. So I tried to explain to them the irony of being a drug war activist incarcerated on a drug charge, but most of these guys were short on irony and they didn't know or care what an activist was. They just wanted to know who or what the fuck I was, and whether I posed them any threat.

What confounded them was that I knew a lot about what their lives were like on the street, and about black history, and I had my own ideas on the role of race and class in the drug war and the prison economy and I tried to talk with them about it. I am willing to guess this was shit they did not usually hear other white people saying, and I spoke about it with frankness and directness, something they were also not accustomed to. I made a conscious decision to try to bridge the divisions between us as best I could by trying to let them know that, despite how really out of place I sounded and appeared, I understood them better than they thought, and had been beaten down by life just like them. Shit, we were all headed to the penitentiary, so how much better or different could I be?

They didn't go for that one bit. And it was because it was all too apparent that the big equalizer in jail is *education*. Most of the men around me never finished high school. I was the only college graduate on the tier.

Education is valuable when you are locked up because if you are smart and can perform a function for those who run or influence or protect things, you become valuable. But you also stand out like the lunatic wearing the sandwich board. Not only are most of your ideas foreign to them, but your education belies the real animosity and source of distrust, which is in the *class* difference. The white and educated are not trusted because they are the "haves."

Of course, just because these young gang bangers were largely uneducated did not in any way mean that they were stupid. They may have been living in a different reality, but they were not unaware of their circumstances. Say what you will about the moral failings of drug dealing, these kids understood market economics better than most of us. It's quite simple for them; this is a business. They have no other opportunities. They don't care if drug dealing is morally ambiguous, nor did they seem to care that they were sitting in a jail cell for it at the moment. Dealing was better than virtually all their alternatives, and jail was a necessary, and somewhat predictable, rite of passage for anyone in the game.

But more than morality, these cats understood human nature, human need, and human suffering. Contrary to myth, gang youth don't take the drugs they sell, which is usually crack or heroin. They do so under penalty of death from their own ranks. But it's not the death sentence that keeps them from turning down that path, it's seeing firsthand the daily effects of their trade, seeing people slowly decay, seeing them beg and degrade themselves for hit after hit, seeing what they will let other people do to them in order to get . . . just . . . one . . . more . . . hit. Most of them had lived through the devastation that crack wrought on a whole generation of their people, their mothers and fathers and cousins and uncles. Because of that, most have nothing but contempt for their customers. The Office of National Drug Control Policy could not have written a better prevention campaign themselves.

Frosty would later advise me to "take notes in my head" after the two gangs held an impromptu meeting to discuss me. I saw the meeting happening but had no idea it was about me until Frosty came into my cell and told me. Although they did not reach a consensus, they decided that whatever I was, they were going to stay far away from me. None of them would talk to me after that, and from that point on, the tone on the tier changed towards me markedly.

If I were anyone else, this would be a blessing. Because no one wanted to risk the chance that I was a cop or informant, everyone left me alone. For me as a writer needing material, as an investigative journalist, as an activist seeking understanding, it was a total hassle. I wasn't afraid of them, I was curious about them, about who they were as people, not as gangland mythology, and it pissed me off that I was lumped in the same category as the shithead cops who had put me in this position. Again, luscious irony . . . choke it down.

Talking to someone like U.T., however, proved all too easy. It was clear already how much he loved to preach. I suppose what made him interesting to me was the indifferent matter-of-factness with which he spoke, as if he no longer was concerned with what was going to happen to him, or what people thought of him. He exuded total acceptance of his situation, as if he no longer expected anything.

He was 45. Ten years earlier his life changed forever when he found his mother dead in her home. She had been dead for over two days, and no one had noticed. Since he was very close to her, he was unable to forgive himself for not calling her or stopping by earlier, and it shook him to the core.

"She was my best friend, the only person who ever believed in me."

He abandoned a good life with a wife, kids, and a job working as a security guard, and he hit the streets with whatever money his mother had left him. He stopped caring about anything, intent on smoking cocaine until his heart exploded. Invariably, this lifestyle led to many busts, and he began his own personal ten-year square dance with the Illinois Department of Corrections, dosey-doeing his way in and out of prison on drug-related charges.

"Politicians are no different than mobsters," he says. "They say they want to stop drugs, but they are the ones letting the drugs into the country."

Before him is a pile of loose tobacco and a pack of papers. His long tapered thumbnails furiously produce hand-rolled cigarettes one after the other, a service he provides for others on the deck in order to get free cigarettes as a commission. His ability to roll is quite a thing to behold, so everyone comes to him.

He lets his hands pause for a moment, and he looks at me, suddenly bearing deep and pronounced gravitas.

"What you need to think about is these here young boys, what this country gonna be like in twenty years. We're turning into a third world nation. Too much greed, and nobody knows shit about nothing anymore. But . . . life is indeed precious. Even those who don't think they amount to something have value."

He flips me a cigarette.

"God don't make no junk."

▽

Lane arrived on the tier three days after I did and took Mike's place in my cell after Mike was transferred to the senior wing. Lane was 26, from the West Side, and worked construction. He had spent his entire life trying to stay away from gangs and out of jail. Lane's older brother had, for complicated reasons, taken the rap for a murder a cousin had committed, and got life.

It was worse for Lane because he was in for a series of DUIs, so he was pissed because he had no one to blame but himself. His girlfriend and his son lived in the far western suburbs and Lane often had to drive out there late at night. That he chose to do so often after drinking all night with the guys on his crew was perhaps the ungallant part of his story. But Lane was one of the good guys, and he loved his son, so with dignity he accepted his punishment, 30 days in the County.

"If this is what it takes for my shorty to grow up as far away from the West Side as humanly possible, then I'll sit," he says, smiling. "Man, every time I think of that little guy my heart gets big. He's like a little man, and he don't fear nothin'."

Still, he rankled at the surrounding company.

"These West Side niggers . . . they'd leave your momma in the street to die."

He leans his head against the metal grating that covers the "window" in our cell, his hands placed before him on the sill. He breathes a long, slow exhale.

"Man, what am I *doin'* in here?"

"Seconded, and passed," I mumble to myself.

Soul and "22" shared the cell on the other side of U.T. Soul was from the same neighborhood as Lane, and the two had gone to the same high school. Soul sold drugs but was unaffiliated, and was tight lipped about how he managed to survive that way without getting clipped.

"22" was so named because he wore size 22 shoes, white Nikes with a purple swoosh that made his feet look like two pontoons. You couldn't help but giggle at them. And he was one seriously strange guy.

His real name was John. He was a six-and-a-half-foot-tall bone-skinny young dope addict with long greasy hair and a face marred by a moonscape of thick blackheads and craggy pockmarks. He was a sweet kid, but clearly his pilot light had gone out, if it had ever been lit. He was this weird kind of pathological shit-talker whose stories were lifted right out of the plots to '80s B-movies. I mean we're talking car chases and superhuman fights with six and seven cops and swallowing pounds of dope without dying. It was so outlandish you simply couldn't believe that anyone could spin such bullshit with a straight face, but he did so, with the straightest of faces.

Because of this, none of us was exactly sure why he was in jail. He spun a dozen different versions of his arrest, and never was precisely clear on what the charges were against him. And it was me they thought was a cop.

The four of us—Lane, Soul, 22, and I—formed an impromptu Neutron crew and spent most of our time together. We would eat together underneath the stairs outside our cells and trade food and cigarettes within our own little trading bloc so we didn't have to beg or trade with the thugs, which invariably came back to haunt you later.

Soul and 22 had between them an entire lockbox full of junk food and cheap tobacco from the commissary, and they were generous to Lane and me. Commissary was ordered and delivered once a week if you were fortunate enough to have someone on the outside put money on your CCDOC account. Without commissary, the stay in County is much, much harder. It's just like not having any money on the street. You get the barest minimum to survive, and you are responsible for the rest. And there's a painful gap between what most people are used to and the privation of the inmate.

As I mentioned, I was a vegetarian at the time, which meant that more often than not I went hungry. It also meant that I had food to trade. Every lunch was bologna sandwiches, so I would barter for bread, or the rare slice of cheese, in exchange for my meat. The stench of the bologna was impossible to avoid, though, and the bread and cheese would be slimy with it. I gagged it down when I could. Dinner, the only real meal of the day, was hit or miss. The food was almost always edible, but definitely nasty. It was mass-produced stuff, like beans and rice, or some goopy beef concoction. But they would often screw up the preparation and the food would be inedible. One beef and rice dish they gave us had so much salt in it people choked as they tried to swallow it.

We were all surprised on July 4th, though, because they were two hours late with dinner, but then showed up with baked chicken, an unheard-of luxury. Even I ate the chicken, and paid for it later in rancid, contorting bowel eruptions. Suddenly my enfeebled brain figured out how they could afford that much "fresh" chicken.

▼

On the other side of my cell was King, who came to Chicago from Mexico at age 15 after his uncles, in some south-of-the-border gang beef, murdered his father. They had wanted to take King and make him work for them, as a slave, as payment for his father's transgressions. Somehow King escaped and came across the border illegally. Though he says he came here to avoid gang life, that's precisely what he ended up in. When I asked him why he did it, he told me it was because he was 15 and dumped in an American city where he didn't speak the language and had no family. Mexicans base everything on the family, he said, so no one would help him get work or take him in. It was the gang, or homeless in the streets. The gang permitted him to survive; the streets would have consumed him.

King was bald with a goatee and covered in tattoos, handsome in the traditional sense. He spoke very seldom, and when he did, spoke softly, preferring to spend a lot of time working out with Frosty. It had been ten years in the gang for him, and he would talk about retiring on his own terms. I asked him how often that really happened, and he said a lot more than is talked about.

Despite this horrific past, King was surprisingly peaceful, and even somewhat playful in a childlike manner. He spoke truth to power, without hesitation, about things he had to do to survive, and you saw that he could tear you apart if he had to, which was humbling. But he was generally a gentle person. The other cats on the deck paid him full respect. No one dared fuck with him.

Unlike many of those around me, who could go off at any second given the proper provocation, King's power was tempered by the knowledge that he wouldn't ever flex it unless he had to, so just don't ever give him a reason. Mexicans, he told me, have a certain honor about their violence. They don't start something unless they absolutely have to, but if they do, they go all out until they finish it.

This was different from the way the blacks and Puerto Ricans dealt with each other. They seemed to look for trouble and were always getting into shit over pride and bravado. They had a built-in hatred that was incendiary. The Mexicans were too new to the city to have the history the other two did with each other. But they were coming so fast, soon they would be contending for power on a citywide scale. Half a million have migrated to Chicago in the last ten years alone.

King's most gracious gift to me was the jailhouse hack, a ceaseless free-floating viral infection that is like the human version of kennel cough in that it usually makes appearances in crowded institutional settings like this. It hits both the upper and lower respiratory system at the same time. You can't breathe because your face is painfully swollen and you are hacking up mucus globs the size and composition of Block Island oysters. The hack never quite goes away completely. Within days I would contract it too, probably from sharing cigarettes with him, and it would haunt me for the next month as I moved from the County into the penitentiary system to serve out my sentence.

▼

I was slated to ship out to the Stateville reception and classification center, the entry point for the Illinois prison system, on a

Friday morning. I was woken up at 3:30 by the unit C.O., who told me to "pack my shit" and be ready to go in ten minutes. I fumbled out into the day room to find Frosty sitting at one of the picnic tables, making instant coffee.

"You shippin' now, Chuck?"

"I am. Time to face the Beast."

"Shit, this is the Beast," he said, motioning around him. "You got gravy now. At least you gonna eat."

It was strange to think of a year in the penitentiary as "gravy," but it said a lot about what a shithole County was.

"When you get out, you gotta call me," Frosty said, slipping me a piece of loose-leaf paper with his name, address, and a couple phone numbers scribbled across it. "I got this idea for a play, and I want you to help me write it."

"Sure, that would be interesting," I said, not knowing if I meant it. My stomach was flopping around my innards. I had no idea what lay in store for me.

"I'm tellin' you, Chuck. I can be the next Tyler Perry. I saw that man on Oprah. He was homeless, and now he worth *ninety million dollars*! I said, shit, I got stories to tell. Lemme get some of this money."

"I know you do," I said, and clearly he did have stories, and the odds were that they would never be told.

At one of the picnic tables the Reverend was seated with one of his regular acolytes. Each had a bible open before him. They would get up like this every morning and come out to read their bibles and dissect scripture verse by verse in a way you never saw done in white churches. I have no idea whether he was speaking truth or just making it up as he went along. You never knew with jailhouse preachers.

I shuffled across the day room floor, and they both looked up at me as I passed close.

"Shipment?" Rev said.

"Yup."

"Can I pray for you, now, before you go?"

Before I could think about it my mouth said, "Sure." I figured it couldn't hurt.

Rev and his student led me down the stairs to the lower level and over into a corner where they normally held prayer circles. We three joined hands and lowered our heads and the Reverend began to pray for me, asking God to guide me and protect me and give me wisdom so that I may survive my ordeal and live to help others. When he finished, they both opened their eyes and looked at me. The Reverend continued.

"We are warriors, and we find ourselves in a time of war. You have been sent to serve this cause, and you know what we are up against, what they will do to their own people to achieve their goals?"

I nodded.

"Always remember that. Remember who they are, whenever you are faced with a difficult decision. And remember . . . all is forgiven. The past is behind you. Pay no mind to anyone who wishes to focus on that. You have a responsibility now. Your life is this moment forward."

Understand, this was the first time I had ever spoken to either of them. Even in the most benign interpretation it was clear that the Reverend had quietly been listening to me blather on about race and prison and the drug war and the government. Something in what I had said connected with him and so he spoke back directly to my heart in a way that made me believe he sensed exactly what I was feeling at that moment and wished to help quell my fears and face the unknown with dignity. However, for me, a more esoteric interpretation was self-evident as the Reverend gazed deep into my eyes, *you know exactly what I mean* streaming from his countenance. *The journey begins.*

I stood quiet, taken aback by the poignancy and eerie relevance of what he had said. It was so familiar it felt like déjà vu. Everyone in my life had been telling me that my going to prison "happened for a reason," but none of us could seem to figure out what that reason was. To write about it? Well, sure, but that wasn't only it. There was a higher reason that I was in prison, it was so obvious to me, a reason that went far beyond the banality of being caught with a handful of happy pills. It had to do with the war that the Reverend mentioned. There was a larger process going on, both within me and in the world around me, something I had sensed unconsciously for years, but had broken open only six months earlier when a combination of years of exhaustive investigation, crystallizing disillusionment, and an opportune experience with dimethyltryptamine showed me that the world I thought I had been living in was an illusion, and that I had to change my entire paradigm if I hoped to make sense of the truth. Part of shifting that paradigm, what I would later see as the fulcrum point in my "journey to truth," required me to go into, in both literal and symbolic terms, the gulag of the Empire, to understand the true workings of the machine.[3]

At that moment, though infused with a sense of rightness about my fate, I was only capable of seeing the road ahead of me in a material sense. I saw a physical place where I would be sent, where I would learn and record, where I would have to avoid physical threats, but would eventually leave, and then create some physical record from which to spread what I had learned about this place, all from the position of an "outsider." I did not yet see, nor was I able to conceive, the "insider" that belonged there, the real prison I was in, the real journey I was beginning, the real process of initiation I was undergoing, the nature of the "spiritual warrior" I was discovering, or the full breadth of the war the Reverend mentioned. Armed with only the belief that I could somehow make a difference, I set a clear intention to get through the experience safe and sound, and then I let go of my fear. It was time to go.

The security door popped loudly and a voice called out, "Let's go, shipment! Move it out!"

I hugged the two men and thanked them. Heaving a long sigh, I hopped up the stairs, ready for whatever was next.

"Hey, Chuck!" Frosty said as I stepped through the doorway, lockbox held out before me. I looked back up at him, leaning against the railing of the upper deck. He pointed to his tattoo and smiled.

"No Mo' Pain!"

▼

The moment it all became real for me—the moment I truly understood I was on my way to prison, the moment I realized I was now in a place I had never been before, and that things would never be the same again, ever, for the rest of my life—was when I was sitting on the transport bus, wrists and ankles shackled to the floor, staring down the barrel of a 12-gauge shotgun on the other side of a steel cage.

The gates to the jail complex opened and a line of buses pulled out of the complex onto 32nd Street, and were immediately swarmed by squad cars full of heavily armed SORT officers, who also provide security for the transport of prisoners.

All at once the entire correctional caravan flips on their lights and sirens and bedlam breaks loose onto California Avenue. The melee quickly zips up the on-ramp to I-55, wailing south towards Joliet. The SORT team stops traffic on the interstate, rifles in hand, in order for the transport buses to proceed far ahead of traffic in an isolated bubble surrounded by squad cars. You suddenly understand that anyone approaching the buses will be seen as potentially participating in an escape attempt and will either be run down or shot.

You realize you ain't goin' nowhere but where they take you and tell you to be. As the buses pick up steam to over 80 mile per hour the outside world looks a million miles away, passing by in a shifting stream, kaleidoscopic fragments flipping through holes in the steel security grates on the windows, and you know it will be a long time before you see it whole again. The enormity of it just pours down over you like a bath in cold concrete.

You suddenly understand you are on your own, in a whole new world, and no one can tell you how to survive.

CHAPTER 2
Hotel Hell

All cultures have their own particular concept of "limbo," purgatory, or some other form of antechamber to paradise. The word "limbo" itself comes from the Latin *limbus*, meaning an "edge or boundary." Used as proper nouns, *Limbus* describes the edge of Hell, and *Limbo* is a place for the souls of unbaptized infants and patriarchs who died before the coming of Christ, to wait for Christ to be born and pardon them. Once pardoned, they are in effect "saved" and become *de facto* Christians, and are finally granted access to eternal paradise. But the Messiah doesn't seem to come around very often, so they sit around like millions of undocumented immigrants, waiting for the next mass amnesty.

Purgatory, by comparison, is like the express line at the US-Mexican Border, the one for people with spotless backgrounds, or diplomatic cover. It's the waiting room for the already-saved, a kind of hazmat decontamination unit that scrubs off the last few sins and moral entanglements of the true believers, before they can cross the border into freedom and eternal, unencumbered bliss. What all of these places have in common is the theme of detention.

Prison is all of these things constrained within the temporal, corporeal plane. The lives of inmates exist in stasis until that time when they are released back into the world. There is absolutely nothing you can do about the outside world, or about the life you may have been living, while you are incarcerated.

Everything that you are doing in life stops in its tracks. *Vita interrupta.* Your rent and bills stop being paid, your mail stops being picked up, your phone is never answered, your email is never downloaded, your refrigerator is never cleaned out, your dog is never walked or fed. Forget about your dreams and ambitions, your plans and goals, because those get put on hold too. If you are lucky to reemerge, you are forever altered by the reality of a conviction record.

Nine times out of ten, no one but your family and closest friends, if you have them, know where you are or what happened to you. Those few people are your lifelines to the outside world, and generally are the only people to do anything for you. You find out very quickly whom you can trust and who will really be there for you. Many inmates find themselves with no one.

Prisons are situated on the fringes of civilization, isolated from most population centers and the general public, hidden away from sight in a gulag network of thousands of municipal, county, state, and federal facilities stretching across the land. Americans not only want to feel that their communities are safe, they really don't want to have to trouble themselves with thinking about the consequences of locking up millions of people, or the abuses, in all forms, that might be taking place under a system of Prohibition funded by fear, apathy, and taxes. In America, it is simply a matter of *out of sight, out of mind.*

Because of that, and because of the isolation of the prison experience, the full understanding of what it is like to be forcibly dislocated from society becomes, for many inmates, the key struggle and in the end the key transformative experience of their lives. Jazz musicians talk about "sustained intensity." Prison life is a frantic Coltrane riff that produces no sound and sucks the life right out of you. It's a negative-sum game for which there is no recuperative period. *No . . . Sleep . . . 'til . . . Parole!*

The lack of popular noise produced over our national prison system, and the underlying reasons for the apparent apathy of the public, will keep Americans from ever having a Bastille moment, which was the storming of a Paris prison that sparked the French Revolution. The American public's pervasive lack of political involvement seems to keep them from storming anything except a Wal-Mart during Christmas shopping season. Plus, since American prisons are so far away from everything else, the proverbial angry mob would have to endure a six-hour bus trip ahead of time before they could commence stormin'.

But prisoners of the drug war aren't seen by the Mainstream as political prisoners, as victims of tyranny like those held in the Bastille by Louis XVI, even though that's precisely what they are.

There are reasons for this, and most are attributable to race and class. At its core, the war on drugs is nothing more than the criminalization of lifestyle. In many regards, it is also a war on religious freedom, and on consciousness itself.

The punishment for defying the system and exerting these inherent freedoms (the ones endowed by our Creator and all) is first disability, then disenfranchisement, then imprisonment, and finally, internal exile. *Limbo time everybody, how low can you go?* When in limbo, one invariably has an entirely new understanding of *time*.

I would spend 13 days in isolation at the Stateville Northern Reception and Classification center in Joliet, Illinois, before being sent on to my prison facility to serve out the remainder of my sentence. Thirteen endless days in a brand-new, state-of-the-art, hyper-sterile, hyper-industrialized detention facility. It was "only" 13 days, I can tell myself now, four years later. But while it was happening, it was a form of torture that leaves an indelible scar on a person's soul. That is why they call Stateville "Hotel Hell."

It is a cold and sterilized form of detention, a little taste of a supermax prison for everyone. Once they process you in, and stuff you into that 6 x 10 cement hole, you don't come out again. You are on 24-hour-a-day lockdown with your cellmate, if you have one, and nothing else. Nothing to read, nothing to see, nothing to do but wait, wait, wait. And once the waiting begins, things start to go all sorts of ways inside your mind.

Thirteen days was interminable while on lockdown, yet right now I think over the last 13 days of my life and can't remember half of it. Most people wouldn't think twice about doing anything for two weeks, until it's put into the proper context. The Cuban Missile Crisis lasted 13 days. Ask anyone who lived through it to tell you what a hellish eternity it was, teetering, if only briefly, on the edge of nuclear annihilation. Ask anyone on day seven of a two-week master cleanse fast how they feel, or two new lovers separated for two weeks, or the parents of a lost child, or someone waiting two weeks for test results that will tell them whether they live or die.

Likewise, two weeks spent in the cold and dark—half-starved, without anything to occupy your mind, contemplating your past, your life, your crimes literal and spiritual, missing people you love, pondering your future as a convict, stressing about which penitentiary you will be sent to and what you will have to face once you get there, and so on and so forth—is its own particularly menacing brand of torment.

THE WAREHOUSE

The Stateville Northern Reception and Classification Center (NRC) is a shining example of the future of "factory corrections." The NRC serves as the major adult male intake and processing center for the northern portion of Illinois, which, incidentally,

contains the Chicago metropolitan area where 10 million out of
the 13 million people of Illinois live. This means that the bulk
of the inmates in the entire Illinois Department of Corrections
(IDOC) system are processed through Stateville.

Conceptually, there is little that differentiates these sorts of
hyper-industrialized prisons from factory hog farms or dairies,
including, for some, the execution at the end of the line. Both are
meant to house the largest possible number of living creatures in
the smallest possible space, using the smallest possible amount of
resources, with the barest minimum of interaction, assistance, or
interference—an automated process predicated on a complete and
total lack of compassion for the "livestock."

But whereas hogs trade for around $50 a head, prisoners garner
$30,000 to $90,000 a head. More than likely, this accounts for
the slightly better living conditions in the human prisons, and the
fact that prisoners have not yet ended up as food. And although
people can eat a big pork roast and some baby back ribs, shell
out the $21.95 and feel satisfied with the transaction, when you
blow 30 large of taxpayer money on one guy to keep him in a
cage for a while, you are left with a lot of lingering social resentment, and rather intense motivation to find inventive ways to
recoup the cost.

The NRC was constructed next door to the old Stateville
Maximum Security Correctional Center of *Natural Born Killers*
fame. Opened in 1925, the old Stateville is famous for having
a Panopticon, a type of roundhouse prison designed by British
philosopher Jeremy Bentham. Conceived in the late eighteenth
century, the Panopticon utilizes a central observation tower—a
hub—that is surrounded by a multilevel rim of prison cells. From
the central tower, guards use a series of strategically placed mirrors that permit them to look into every cell. The uniqueness of
the Panopticon is that it allows security to observe (*-opticon*) all
(*pan-*) the prisoners at once, without the prisoners being able to
tell if they are being watched. Over time, the mirrors evolved into

video surveillance cameras, and the observation tower became the security booth. The Panopticon was remarkably successful in creating a self-policing environment, so much so it was applied to the general public's life, on the streets and in shops and subways, etc.

Bentham said the Panopticon conveyed "a sentiment of an invisible omniscience." The constantly perceived presence of this "all-seeing eye" was considered a revolution in maintaining order, in that inmates (or citizens) were more apt to police themselves if they both consciously and unconsciously believed they were always being watched or recorded. The genius of the Panopticon was the ease and stealth with which it stole into the collective consciousness and set up permanent residence as a means of "fighting crime" and "protecting ourselves." The evil it bore as today's "surveillance state," where our every move is at least passively and often actively monitored and logged, is generally accepted as "the way things are," finding little resistance from any quarter.

The multi-facility Stateville complex is one of three distinct prisons in the Joliet area. Before the new NRC was completed in 2004, Illinois prisoners were processed under gruesome conditions at the now decommissioned Joliet Prison on the Joliet River. Predating the old Stateville by almost 75 years, this ancient, miserable, toxic structure was built in the 1850s and expanded upon until the 1990s. When it opened it was the largest prison in the country, and the design became a model for American prisons of its time. It was officially closed in 2004, and following the closing served for two years as the set for the ridiculous Fox television series *Prison Break*, which would debut while I was locked up, and was viewed religiously by inmates.

The new processing center is one of the largest prison facilities in the nation. Carrying on the proud tradition of Illinois penal design, the NRC has become the hot new model for other states seeking to modernize their correctional systems. The structure is immense, resembling an airplane hangar surrounded by razor wire. At 460,000 square feet it is half the size of the Mall of America. It has a capacity range of 2,200 to 2,800, twice the size of the old processing center, and the population turns over every 10 to 21 days, creating an almost perfect annual balance of 40,000 in and 40,000 out. Within the complex are eight cellblocks (A through R), each three levels high, which house inmates. Each block has a small door that leads outside to a narrow concrete pen resembling a dog kennel or the outside holding pens at Guantánamo Bay.

Since it is only a transitional facility, inmates are generally not held at the NRC for longer than 20 to 30 days unless they are sent back from another facility to serve out special "segregation" time, such as solitary or protective custody. In its simplest terms, the NRC is the place where you are officially turned into a commodity and put to some use in the prison economy. You become an inventory number, a line item on a balance sheet. You are poked and prodded and stuck and drawn, photographed and printed and tagged and labeled. Whatever needs to be done to make sure you are healthy, free of disease, and ready to work.

It is here, at the NRC, that your real-world identity is officially stripped from you, and you are given a new one.

Bound and shackled, I shuffled in as Charles Shaw of Chicago, Illinois.

Still bound and shackled, I would shuffle out as R45067, ready for a couple weeks of cold storage while I awaited shipment to my particular plantation.

IDOC has eight levels of security classification.

Level 1 Maximum Security
Level 2 Secure Medium Security
Level 3 High Medium Security

Level 4 Medium Security
Level 5 High Minimum Security
Level 6 Minimum Security
Level 7 Low Minimum Security
Level 8 Transitional Security

Although I didn't know it at the time, or what it meant in context, I was eventually designated Level 6—Minimum Security.

Throughout the intake process I found myself next to a tall, bald, middle-aged black dude with a thin silver mustache named Willie Frazier. All the way back at five o'clock in the morning, in the shipping pen at County, he sat on a bench across from me next to a Puerto Rican guy named Luis smoking Newports. He gave me a "short" off of his cigarette. He and Luis were fuckin' around a lot and seemed unfazed by the fact that we were about to be shipped to the joint.

Now in the processing line, Willie kept telling me that Luis knew one of the NRC counselors and that we should ask to be sent to "East Moline." I didn't know what that meant.

"Don't ask for *treatment*," he told me, "they only got one place, Sheridan, and there ain't never no room there, goddammit. They say you gotta wait six weeks for Sheridan, minimum. Six weeks here, in this muthafucka? Uh uh, ain't happenin'. Luis said ask for East Moline, says that's the best place to go in the whole damn system."

When the time came to speak to the counselor, she asked me whether I wanted to go to the drug treatment program at Sheridan, which had been open for only a year, but which the State was already touting as the "largest fully dedicated state drug prison and community crime reduction program in the nation." You can see just how proud of themselves they are by looking at the sobering (pun intended) press release from the opening of the center in 2004:

In addition to aggressively working to address crime and recidivism throughout all state communities, the reopening of Sheridan Correctional Center will restore more than 400 jobs in the surrounding region of LaSalle County.

"For too long, our state has led the nation in drug crime. Today, we begin our efforts to lead the nation for drug crime prevention," said Gov. Blagojevich. "The Sheridan project is about public safety. Illinois faces the highest recidivism rate in state history. Statistics show that more than half of the nearly 34,000 parolees on the street today will be reincarcerated within only three years after their release from prison. We know that drug use is a significant contributing factor in recidivism, and we owe it to our communities to take on this challenge."

According to the Department of Corrections, statistics show that approximately 60 percent of all male arrestees statewide and approximately 82 percent of all male arrestees in Chicago test positive for at least one illegal drug. In addition, nearly 25 percent of all state prison inmates are currently serving time for drug offenses, with an untold number of others who are in prison for property offenses, violent offenses or other crimes committed as a result of drug involvement.

Let's put all this backslapping by our former governor-turned-inmate Rod Blagojevich into perspective. The State freely admits that a significant (and most likely understated) percentage of the roughly 46,000 IDOC inmates are incarcerated for drug-related offenses, and yet out of a $1.3 billion budget, twenty-eight prisons, six work farms (labor camps), and two boot camps, it has taken them thirty-four years since the launch of the War on Drugs to build one—one, as in *uno*—dedicated treatment facility that can treat a *maximum* of 900 out of (conservatively) 11,250 drug-related inmates. This means that only 9% of those with acknowledged drug problems can receive treatment, a paltry 2% of the total prison population.

At the end of the Intake process I still had no idea where I was going to be sent. I was told nothing except to get back in line. I asked Willie if he requested East Moline, and he said, "Now why would I tell you to go on and ask for somethin' and not ask for the same shit myself?" Then he smiled and shrugged his shoulders again and mumbled something about Luis "hooking it up" for him. Somehow, I had a hard time going with him on that one.

After Intake we sat in a caged bullpen for at least another hour or two until they made an announcement that we were about to be taken to the cellblocks. Willie and I ended up paired as cellmates, and we fell into line together. It was a bit of a pleasant surprise, and a bit weird. I didn't know him from a hole in the wall (although, we were certainly about to be stuffed into one) and yet, we already had this perplexing connection.

They marched us along a fathomless corridor of shiny polished concrete with cellblock entrances along the left side stretching to what seemed like the horizon. Fatigue, stress, and fear of the unknown all conspired to spin out my perceptions as we shuffled along single file, stopping at a cellblock, depositing a few inmates, and moving on. The line grew smaller and smaller.

Then, it was our turn as about six or eight of us were ushered into one of the anonymous cellblocks. Willie and I were bundled into a cell on Level 2. The entire cell was molded concrete except for some stainless steel on the bunks, (single) stool, sink, and toilet. The cell was sealed behind a magnetic steel door—no bars— and a shatterproof glass window. It was lit by one fluorescent light that we could not control. There was a feed slot below the window. We turned around, and the door slammed shut behind us, and Willie and I looked at each other.

"Man, this ain't the honeymoon suite," he said, clowning. "I'm sorry, dear, they must have messed up the reservations."

I laughed, kind of.

"Well, all right then, if it's gonna be like that we might as well just go to sleep."

I let go a long protracted sigh.

"Yeah," I mumbled. "Sleep."

I crawled up onto the top bunk, laid my head down on my rolled-up blanket, and was asleep before I could finish exhaling.

I don't know what time it was when I woke up, but the lights were on in our cell and it was daylight outside. I could see faint shards of sunlight spilling in diffusely from a single window along the outside wall of the cellblock. Above my head was a vent that was pumping in cold air, and it was freezing inside the cell. I jumped down from the top bunk and shuffled to the toilet. Willie was still asleep with his blanket wrapped around his head.

After I had finished I moved over to the cell door and looked out the window. It was eerily quiet and still. I sat down on the concrete desk jutting from the cell wall and put my forehead against the glass window.

I had nowhere to go. I had nothing to do. I was in a cold and barren environment, and it felt as if gravity was pulling me into the floor. I was still so exhausted. And I was sick. I had picked up the jailhouse hack in County and now, because of the cold, it was coming on full force. I coughed so hard my head was pounding and my teeth were chattering in my mouth. I crawled back up into bed, wrapped myself inside my blanket, and went back to sleep.

CORRECTIONAL ZOOLOGY

I remember when I was a child and would go on school field trips to the zoos in Chicago. I remember feeling a palpable sense of confusion and despair as I would watch the animals in what were at the time fairly inhumane conditions. The zoos were old and decrepit in the mid-1970s, and the "natural habitat" model hadn't yet been put into practice. Most cages were cells, pure and simple, cold and hard concrete and steel cages with bars. How anyone didn't feel the animal's misery is beyond me. They would either pace restlessly, or they would sleep.

Not to beat you over the head with this metaphor or anything, but humans are animals, and all animals, regardless of how intelligent or unintelligent they are suspected to be, when removed from their natural habitat and placed in captivity, will respond in the same manner. They will either respond with agitation, or they will respond with depression. There is room for very little else when you're in a cage.

In the beginning you do nothing but sleep. Your body senses it is in a hopeless situation, and it begins to shut down. You fall into a deep depression. Throughout that first week I must have slept 18 hours a day if not more; I had only a general sense of time that was measured by the on and off periods of the light in our cell, which we did not control, and the daylight that could be seen coming in from the pen window, if we strained to look.

At first you are disoriented. You wake up and it's dark and you forget where you are, and when you do suddenly snap back to reality, you remember you're in prison and it's like being hit on the head. So you wake up only when your body has a more pressing need, like liquid in, or liquid out.

The hunger compounds the fatigue and the depression. Sure, we were fed three times a day, but breakfast was usually a milk carton and a donut, lunch a sandwich, and dinner, so many torturous hours later, was a tiny affair resembling a Lunchables box or something from some trendy crash diet. The food was better quality than we had at County, but there was hardly any of it. I calculated that I was eating only about 25–30% of what I normally took in out in the world.

Anecdotally, I heard it said that IDOC calculated how much less physical activity, and thus calories burned, the body engages in when on total lockdown, and scaled back the food portions accordingly to meet that lowered level of activity. I also heard that it was to intentionally keep us weak, and thus, more pliable. The most cynical interpretation simply said that everywhere IDOC could cut costs to line their own pockets, they did.

The hunger is what brings you out of depression into agitation. If it wasn't my bladder that did it, I would normally be awakened by the rumbling of my stomach. It would begin another absurd pantomime where I would crawl down dizzily from my bunk and sit on the desk with my head against the glass and look out to see if the food carts had been delivered. Most often they had not, and I would begin stressing.

As time wore on, and I grew hungrier and more awake, I would pace. And pace. And pace. Imagine turning round and round in a 6 x 10 foot space. By the time I saw the food cart, I would be full-on salivating. When they finally flipped open that feed slot and chucked our two food trays at us, we attacked our food like a dog goes at its bowl. We'd be done eating in a matter of two or three minutes.

Like I said . . . put any animal in a cage and it will respond in the same manner. We were being broken down, conditioned, institutionalized, domesticated. We were treated like animals, and so we began, in varying degrees, to act like them.

There's really no way to describe the maddening boredom you experience when subjected to a sensory-deprived environment for a prolonged period. You feel like you want to crawl out of your skin. You start talking to yourself and developing tics. Your mind is exploding in a dozen different directions, your emotions become all bundled together in this inextricable mass, your natural rhythms are thrown completely out of whack, and if you don't get a grip and deal with it soon, you start to go stir crazy rather quickly.

This is where humans begin to differ from animals. Humans have an additional capacity . . . for spiritual transcendence. It's a painful process, and it doesn't happen immediately, and there are many phases and stages you will go through over time. But once you surrender to it, the process can begin, and you are on your way to no longer feeling like a caged animal, even if in a cage is precisely where you are.

I hovered on the perimeter of this shift for the first week I was on ice. I spent too much time unconscious to allow my conscious mind to begin to shift, hiding in a dark, dreamless, motionless sleep, a place where my being merely floated in stasis. Nothing changed from moment to moment. I could sleep for 18 hours and wake up in the same position, to the exact same view, from the exact same perspective.

I began to verge on the place where time begins to lose all meaning, because one day is indistinguishable from the next. There was virtually no stimulus coming into the cell, and whatever stimulus I had sequestered inside my mind was still too terrifying for me to release. I was not yet ready to go inward, but I was getting close, wearing myself down moment by moment.

During my waking hours the last thing I would want to do would be to stay in bed, so I would usually sit on the desk and stare out the window. But for the air vent, which would kick on at regular intervals, it was painfully still and silent. Unlike County, which was deafening most of the day, Stateville was very quiet and gave you the feel of being underwater; everything was muffled and in lower frequencies and you felt it through the walls more than you heard it in your ears. Every few hours the C.O. on duty would walk through and count each cell, never interacting, never bothering to make eye contact. Other inmates would call out to them for something or another and they would just ignore them. A phrase began to repeat itself over and over in my head: *Persona non grata. Persona non grata.*

▼

A number of years earlier in the mid-Nineties, while I was fresh out of another stint in rehab and living in a halfway house in the Humboldt Park neighborhood of Chicago, I got a job working for the Anti-Cruelty Society as a kennel technician. In the beginning I worked the closing shift where I would feed all the dogs and cats and clean their kennels.

To be honest, it broke my heart to work there, except for the rare times when I could work the adoption center and find some of them homes. So many of the animals never made it out of the shelter, a secret the Society guarded very closely. Anti-Cruelty, despite its name, was a euthanizing shelter. What was worse was that most of the "no-kill" shelters in the city would send animals to Anti-Cruelty when their spaces filled up, thus, not actually doing the killing themselves, but leaving it for us to do.

Every day after tending to the dogs and cats I would then have to help round up the animals that had to be euthanized that night. At first, I couldn't even bring myself to go anywhere near the death room. Then, over time, I forced myself at first to watch a procedure, then assist in a few with the managers who were on duty, whose tragic job it was everyday to kill dozens of beautiful, sweet, loving creatures, which, for whatever reasons, were simply unwanted and now were too old, or not cute enough, or not the right breed, to be adopted out to a new family.

One of the managers I often worked with—a mother of four who had a house full of rescued animals—told me she rationalized the euthanasia by saying that the animals were now "with God." I didn't see it that way, and so I felt I owed it to the animals to be there with them in their last moments, to give them some final seconds of love. It was compassionate, right? It was the least I could do, right?

Wrong. As noble and selfless as the gesture may sound, it was a profoundly stupid decision for an addict newly in recovery. I was not in any way emotionally or spiritually prepared for the consequences of what I was doing, and before long something in me snapped. I continued to swallow pain after pain, until the suffering of a dying dog became for me the metaphorical touchstone connecting me to the collective despair of humanity and the wounding of my young soul. When I looked at the dogs, on some level, what I was seeing was the part of myself I couldn't hide from. In my love for them, I saw my own despair reflected in row after row of sad, caged eyes.

I went out on a binge for a few days, and when the smoke cleared, I had lost my job and had been kicked out of the halfway house, a mere month after being released from four months in an inpatient treatment facility.

It was only when I was locked in that cell at Stateville that I began to unlock the deeply repressed emotions I had about what I had gone through at the shelter, which was traumatic on a level I simply couldn't face for years for much deeper reasons than the fate of the animals themselves. The shelter experience only served to compound the malignant traumas I had buried deep within me.

Now once again, there I was contemplating the simple suffering eyes of a dog floating in my preconscious mind, these eyes that were a Trojan horse stealthily unlocking larger, deeper creatures clawing to get out of my inner recesses. I sat there in that cell endlessly bored and mind racing, tiptoeing around the psycho-spiritual avalanche that was waiting for the slightest thing to set it off.

I didn't really know it at the time, but in hindsight, I can recognize and appreciate, with a sense of awe, the clever path my mind/ soul was taking in order to achieve this very end of purging the grief it held prisoner behind my steadily darting eyes. My mind and my heart were doing everything in their power to get me to wake up and face the music. It was time to *feel*! As I got control of myself, I suddenly realized that I was not going to be able to sleep much more. I was pretty much slept out, and the natives were restless.

As the breakfast cart came around I envisioned my fellow inmates instinctively jumping to their windows in anticipation, noses leaving smudges, yelping through cell doors. Images of dogs in their cages, some jumping up with excitement, some growling, some cowering in the corner, and others just lying there listless and depressed, all of them wanting *out*. The sad eyes of a thousand scared and desperate dogs, a thousand scared and desperate convicts, besiege, besiege, and I am overwhelmed.

A quick pained sob leapt out of me and my heart wrenched down into this terrible knot and I thought I was going to collapse and have a heart attack. It was all connecting at once into this perfect storm, a thousand memories piling in, crashing the breakwaters and flooding my soul. This was the first real emotion I had felt since I had walked off the courtroom floor into custody. I went through County in an adrenal haze, and now I was finally in one place, exhausted and ensconced and awake.

The real crime here is that I was not able to truly release this massive cue ball of pain and grief I eventually forced back down my gullet. It was like holding in the worst puke of your life; I did not have the luxury to let it out. I know now, years later, that this was a critical point in my story. Yes, I managed to "get a grip," per se. But the sickness I swallowed back down went to work inside and would return later in the worst form yet, after I got out of prison, when I least expected it.

Thankfully, Willie didn't wake up when I was having my minimeltdown. I really didn't have it in me to deal with that on top of everything else. Willie slept a lot more than I did that first week, and he was a deep sleeper who snored something fierce. And farted. That goddamn prison food did a number on you. Sometimes the stink in the cell would be overpowering. Like, hideunder-your-blanket foul. It was funny for oh, about a minute. Then it just got to be annoying. But that day I was grateful for his snores and farts, if only because, ironically enough, they were serving as a thin retaining wall propping up my dignity, and allowing me to suffer in peace.

WHO LET THE DOGS OUT?

After one week they let us out of our cells for one hour, one level
at a time, to go outside into the pens attached to each cellblock.
We were marched down the walkway to the outside door, and
when they opened it, were blasted by intense sunlight and stifling
heat. It must have been a hundred degrees outside.

At first the 20 or so of us just milled around on the hot concrete,
squinting at each other as we shuffled about in a light-induced
daze, sizing each other up again, a mess of men in powder-blue
jumpsuits and white slipper shoes with disheveled hair, thick
stubble, and rancid breath. It was terribly quiet outside, no wind,
no sound, just silent heat. Just outside our pens, rising up and
stretching as far as the eye can see in both directions, is the big
wall surrounding Stateville Max. After a few moments someone
finally spoke and broke the tension. Well, shouted is more like it,
kicking off a mini-explosion of suppressed sentiment.

"God *damn* I am happy to get outta that muthafuckin' *box*!"

"Bet, yo. Dem mufuckas is crazy. I'm goin' outta my goddam
mind in there, ain't shit to *do*!"

"Man you ain't lyin', joe."

"Welcome to *Hotel Hell*, y'all."

"Anyone got a square?" Willie hollered. "Man I need a muthafuckin' squizzle!"

Tobacco was prohibited at Stateville, so inmates who were
smokers were in the first week of withdrawal. They were edgy and
irritable, despite the joy they were feeling at that moment about
what amounted to little more than moving from a smaller cage to
a bigger cage with sunlight and fresh air. So they walked around
with smiles but could often be seen gnawing at their fingers.

Eric, a blond boyish kid I met in Processing who got 11 years
for vehicular manslaughter (he ran over someone trying to car-
jack him and was convicted anyway) was housed on my level and
came outside with my group. We gave each other a pound and

sat down together with our backs against the razor wire fence, the tops of our jumpsuits unzipped with the sleeves tied around our waists.

"How you doin'?" I asked him.

"Man . . . I'm so fucking bored."

"I know the feeling."

"What have you been doing?"

"Sleeping, mostly," I said.

"Me too. I don't think I've been up for more than two hours all week. And I'm soooo hungry!"

"I know, me too."

"But I'm all right. It is what it is, I guess. I just miss my girl."

Eleven years, I thought. *My God. How is he going to make it?* I knew instantly his 19-year-old girlfriend would be looooooong gone by then. He showed no sign of it penetrating yet, though, which made sense. He had a long road ahead of him. It hurt me to think about it, and at the same time, filled me with immeasurable gratitude that it wasn't me.

The gratitude made me feel guilty as hell, mostly because I knew that if by some act of providence I was given the opportunity to switch places with Eric and give him his freedom, I wouldn't. I don't know whether that was selfishness or simply self-preservation, but the net result was the same. Despite my wanting to extend Eric as much compassion as possible, it was almost as if on some level I thought his sentence was contagious, and I fought this flight response to get away from him. I can't really explain it any better than that.

I didn't act on the impulse, though. I stayed and talked to him for a while, but the entire time I was conscious of the fact that this kid, for whatever reason, had some baaaaaaaad karma, and I had enough problems of my own with karma at the moment, thank you very much.

Willie and a couple other young brothers came and sat down with us. For a second, no one said anything, we all just looked at each other. It was a powerful bonding moment. We were searching each other's faces for support, for recognition of our own internal pain and discomfort, fear and apprehension. The fears we felt differed somewhat. Those who had never been to the joint feared the great unknown; those who had been down before feared the all-too-well-known.

"Man, joe," one of the kids said, "I just can't wait till they come around wit dem bags."

"Bags?" I asked.

"Uh huh. When you about to get up outta here they come through and slip a brown paper bag under yo cell door. That bag got the name a the joint you headed to, and it means you outta here, baby. Man, that's probably the best feelin' on earth, yo."

"So we have no idea where we are going until then?" I asked.

"Naw, joe. They don't tell us shit, you know this."

"True," I said.

There was a pause, and then Willie said, "Hey, you see that thick sistah who was workin' the deck yesterday?" He was referring to one of the female C.O.s working our cellblock. "I'm a get me some a dat," he nods.

"You out cho goddam mind," someone replied. "She don't want nothin' to do wit yo convict ass."

"Naw, I saw her lookin' at me," Willie went on. "Ole girl thought I was sleepin', but I could see she was peepin'."

"She was *countin'* yo black ass, nigga, she wasn't makin' dates!" The guys started laughing at Willie, and you could tell he was loving it.

"Y'all youngbloods don't know *nuttin'* 'bout dis," he said, then started to pimp-strut across the concrete. They all just shook their heads and waved him off.

"Yeah, ah-aight. Go on ahead and step to her like that and see what she do," the young black kid said, as he sat down next to me.

"She might crack me," Willie said. "But eventually, she gonna love me."

After a moment, I said, "I wonder where the hell I'm going to end up."

"After you get out?" Eric said.

"Naw . . . I mean, what joint."

"Shit. Me too, man."

"I don't even know what level security I got coming."

"Man, I hope I get East Moline," the kid to my right said.

"This motherfucker said that too," I said, gesturing at Willie.

"I sho did. And they gonna do it," Willie said.

"I just don't know how you think you know this," I said.

"He don't know shit," the kid said. "He's just frontin'."

"Just you wait and see," Willie responded. "They probably send White Boy there too," he said, referring to me.

"If you ain't got no violence on your record," the kid to my right said, "and you a short-timer on possession or some shit, you probably gonna go to a Min [minimum security]. East Moline is a Min, and they got movement."

"Movement," I asked?

"Yeah . . . you know . . . you get to move around, you don't have to stay locked in your cell or your day room. Aybody wants to go to East Moline, but it's small, so only like a few mufuckas ever get to go."

"It would be good to go there," I said.

"Whatchou in fo'?"

"Possession. One year."

"First time down?"

"Yup."

"Aw shit, man, you gonna get a turnaround."

"A turnaround?"

"Yeah . . . you ain't got but sixty-one days to serve, nigga."

"What makes you say that?"

"'Cause that's the way it is. Look, you got one year, right? But the law say that aybody does only half their time, so that's six months off right there. *And* they give aybody six months' 'good time.'"

"'Good time'?"

"Man . . . are you sure you belong here?" dude said, laughing.

"That mufucka *definitely* belongs here," Willie said, pointing at me. "He's got crazy ideas, wants to save the world. Don't wanna let him round the young chirren."

"Yeah, ah-aight. Whatever," the kid said, and turned back to me. "So, 'good time' is time you get for . . . you know. . . bein' good. But they give it to you ahead of time, and if you don't fuck up, you keep it. You fuck up, you do those six months and more."

"That doesn't make any sense. Half time, and six months off that, equals a year and leaves me with nothing. Why didn't I just get 'time served' and go home," I asked?

"'Cause aybody gotta get *paid*. Yo ass is worth, shit, thirty, forty stacks. And the state don't cut a check until you serve a minimum of sixty-one days. So think about it . . . it's like an assembly line in a plant. They got all these sixty-one-day-wonder muthafuckas steady goin' in and out, all year long, thousands of them, 'cause they don't got the space to hold everyone. And for every one a them, IDOC gets a check worth what it costs to keep a mufucka in prison for a whole *year*! Like I said, aybody gotta get dey money."

"Are you sure about this?" I asked.

"About what, the sixty-one days? Man . . . the one thing a convict *knows* is how much time he got."

I could be out in 61 days?

The C.O. popped out from the door to the cellblock and shouted for us to line up so that we could go back to our cells. Willie came up and patted me on the head.

"Come on, Fido. Back to your cage."

▼

The next day they let those of us on Level 2 out, one at a time, to take a ten-minute shower. I had no soap or shampoo, so I just stood in the trickling stream of lukewarm water, grateful to be out of my cell. The showers were on the upper level, and as I looked down from my stall to the ground floor I saw a newspaper that was lying folded on a chair that the C.O. was using. I hadn't seen a paper in weeks, hadn't watched the news since the London bombings, and hadn't been on the Internet in a month. I had no idea what was happening in the outside world, or how the people I knew, or who knew of me, were reacting to my incarceration.

The uncertainty of what was going on began to give me great anxiety and discomfort. One of my most highly developed coping mechanisms in the outside world was my ability to immerse myself in distraction, which for me meant the massive assimilation of information. One of the ways I was able to feel like I had some sort of control over my life was to always be aware of what was happening in the world around me.

I thought about the countless hours I spent on the interwebs, or on cable TV, or reading books, or watching an endless stream of documentaries, constantly gorging my senses on something, anything. This free flow of endorphic narcotic infobliss had been dropped to absolutely nothing in an instant. Now that it was gone, I was quite clearly in an advanced state of withdrawal.

I asked the C.O. on the way back to my cell if I could have his newspaper when he was finished, and he just laughed at me and said, "You can read?" He unceremoniously stuffed me back in my cold cell, locked the door, and walked away.

I shouldn't have been surprised, but I was. I wanted to scream at them sometimes, *I'm a goddam human being, treat me like one you Australopithecine mouth-breathing knuckle dragger! It was just some drugs, I didn't hurt anybody!* Of course, they didn't see it that way. To them, we deserved worse. To them, we had it easy, so they sure as shit weren't going to make it any easier on us. That C.O. didn't give me the newspaper for one reason and one reason alone: because I wanted it.

I was left again to stew in my anger and anxiety, furious at my inability to control any aspect of my situation, or so I perceived at the time (we, of course, always have control over how we chose to react to situations, even if we can't change them). I wanted that goddamn newspaper because my mind was screaming out for distraction. *Feed me! Feed me something or I am going to drive you batshit insane! You and I both know what I got stored away in here, and if you want it to stay stored away, you best gimme my fix!*

I realized—if only peripherally—that I was (of course) still waging the same internal war I had been waging for years. Inside me was a sea of white noise, an angry, buzzing hive of sheer rest-lessness. In the past, I pounded down the chemicals to silence the hive, and when I stopped pounding chemicals, I started pounding information, achieving the same end, albeit with a somewhat weaker buzz. Ultimately, though, information just seemed to make the hive buzz louder, because it only served to raise more questions. It was all the same. It was pounding down that which so desperately wanted to get *out*. It was all the same bingeing, with none of the purging, and so, I was ready to pop.

"Man," I fumed. "I'm gonna get these motherfuckers. Somehow."

"You ain't gonna do shit," Willie said. "You in this box right now, and when you leave this box, they just gonna put you in another one, and if you try and fuck with them, they'll lock yo ass in the smallest, darkest, nastiest box they got, and never let yo ass out."

"There are many ways to fuck with them," I said, mostly to myself.

"What, you gonna try and work some *activist* tip on them? You can't stop these people, Charles. This shit is beyond you, young man. You in the muthafuckin' joint. You talk shit, you get hit, like, wit dem big ass batons they got. You don't want that. They don't have to do nothin' for you, and you ain't got nobody to tell anyway. So go on ahead, make trouble, see where that shit gets you. You ain't got nothin' but sixty-one days to make it through, don't go getting' all up in that activist shit. All you gonna do is bring more time down on yo head. That activist shit don't never work anyway."

"Hey, come on now. You ain't got to take it there."

"Yeah, ah-aight. What worked? Tell me one thing you have done that actually changed something? Ah ah ah . . . think before you open yo mouth."

"Activism changes many things, that's a ridiculous idea. If it weren't for people like me, things would be a lot worse in this world."

"How much worse can it get for ya now, C? Look where you are. If what you have told me is true, activism got you sent here, one way or the other. The fact that you couldn't just let shit alone."

"Man, you're one to talk! If your story is true, you're in here for the same reasons I am!"

"I'm not sayin' this to appear better than you, child. I'm sayin' this to show you we all end up in here 'cause we can't leave *somethin'* alone."

DOWN GOES FRAZIER! DOWN GOES FRAZIER!

Living in a confined space with another person, particularly a stranger, is a difficult process. Neither of you is going anywhere, so whatever happens, you have to deal with it, right then and there. It requires a tremendous sense of patience, something I simply did not possess at that point in my life. You have to eat, sleep, talk, and shit with a person no more than four feet away from you at any given moment. It is a forced intimacy greater than what most couples have to face out in the everyday world, and so if it doesn't click on some level, it can immediately go very bad, and end up in a very dark or dangerous place. A significant portion of the fights, injuries, and deaths that occur in prison are between cellmates, as I would soon learn.

Willie and I had it OK. After being semi-comatose for the first week, we mostly spent the second week talking endlessly about our lives. But we had our moments, boy. Willie had managed to smuggle a single hand-rolled cigarette through the entire intake process, and the day we were allowed outside Willie finally found a match from one of the other guys. He was intent on smoking it when he got back to the cell. I was adamant against it.

They had warned us that if we got caught smoking it would mean solitary and more time on our sentence. The cells had highly sensitive smoke detectors inside the intake vents, and when triggered they would shut down the entire cellblock's air system. We knew every time someone was smoking by the abrupt way the system would shut down, followed by an alarm, followed by C.O.s storming onto the cellblock to haul the offender(s) off to solitary. It had happened three times already, and I was not about to get into any more trouble. Willie wouldn't have any of it. He was going to smoke that damn cigarette whether I liked it or not. You can't imagine the fear and rage it brought out of me. He was fucking around with my freedom.

We argued and fought with each other for an hour, getting all up in each other's grills, shoving, taunting, tearing each other apart out of sheer frustration with our situation. This was in no way atypical. You could hear other cellmates arguing or fighting from time to time. Invariably, others would egg them on by shouting out their feed slots. Any hint of violence drove some of them into a frenzy. As each day passed, more and more of our animal selves emerged.

Aside from this blowup, and some minor bickering, what made Willie and me see eye-to-eye and cohabitate well was that, beyond all the surface differences, at our core we were the same. We both had a powerful thirst for justice, were proud, impulsive, rebellious, fiercely independent, and pathologically averse to abuses of power. We just expressed it in very different ways.

Although he prevaricated for most of the time we were confined together, Willie eventually revealed that he had been convicted of assaulting a cop. The story he gave is that he was playing pool in a bar on the corner of his block, and out the window he saw a TAC[4] squad car pull over to the curb and two TACs jumped out and began rousting a friend of Willie's.

Willie watched from the window of the bar as the two TACs starting roughing up his friend. He got angrier and angrier, and finally got up and went outside, and began shouting at the TACs to leave the guy alone. Naturally, they took issue with anyone challenging them, so they told Willie to get up against the building and asked for his ID. Willie refused. When they grabbed him, he fought back. Big, big mistake.

They beat his ass, pepper-sprayed him, and *then* arrested him. He was charged with assaulting a police officer, and they hit him with a possession charge to make it all stick. Willie claims the possession charge was bogus, that the cops put a bag on him. This of course is entirely plausible, and a regular practice for the Chicago Police, particularly the TAC squad. They had pinned a bogus case on me a year before I ended up in prison. Most people never get the chance to fight it like I did, and few ever win. Most are fucked. For the few who do win in court, as you will see later with what happened to me, the police rarely, if ever, roll over and take it.

What was not in Willie's favor was that he had a legitimate crack habit, and you can't have a crack habit and not somehow have it contribute to your difficulties with law enforcement. Sure he was a first-time offender, but that didn't mean that crack hadn't ruled his life as well. Whether the bag was planted or not, Willie had to face both the case and the knowledge that he had an addiction. He was far more accepting of the former than he was of the latter.

As far as he was concerned, he didn't have a problem. So, naturally, his prison was many-layered, most of it hidden from view. I suppose you could say the same about virtually any one of us, but anyone who knows addiction knows what kind of fetid dungeon it is. The environment is far more hopeless, and so, the prospect of release seems dimmer, to put it mildly.

Still, Willie wasn't no hype.[5] He was one of the functional addicts. He had been doing cocaine in some form or another most
of his life. He told me he was introduced to it at age 12 when he
found a small box full of it in his grandmother's dresser, which she
would nip at throughout the day.

"She caught me messin' with it and said, *Boy, don't be gettin'
into that shit, it'll make ya mannish!*"

He had worked for over 25 years as a trucker, and he loved his
job. You could tell because his whole demeanor would change
when he talked about it. He loved the driving, he loved his 18-
wheel semi with the satellite/DVD player (which he said cost
more than his home), he loved seeing the country, and he loved the
people he would meet along the way.

"Now, you gotta remember, when you in the South, you gonna
get yer *vittles*. You don't eat *food*, you eat yer *vittles*. And boy is
them vittles *good*! Them peoples is nice to ya in the truck stops
and they looove to eat, boy. And they eat *good*. I got places
mapped out all along the way, I get me something different in
each one so I got somethin' to look forward to in each city and
stretch of highway . . ."

It was a charming kind of boyish enthusiasm, which, because,
of course, we're talking about Willie here, would invariably back-
slide into something like . . .

". . . and after dinner I get me a couple bags and trick off with
a ho in the back a mah truck! *Schwing!*"[6]

Still, he made trucking sound so good that I began to consider
doing it myself. At that point I didn't know what my future held,
but I can fairly say that I had a very cynical perspective looking
forward. I was convinced my record was going to prevent me from
ever having another "decent job." So I picked his brain about it.

"They hire convicts, C, lots of 'em. One of the few jobs a convict can get."

"Why do you think that is? Isn't that generally the mark of a
shitty or dangerous job?"

"Sometimes. And yeah, drivin' a truck can be a pain in the muthafuckin' ass, especially when you have to drive in the East, in the cities. And diesel keeps gettin' more expensive. But it's like this: everything in this country—every piece of food and every appliance and every piece of clothing and every muthafuckin' thang—it all get delivered on a *truck*. They make it easy, 'cause they need drivers. They always need drivers. Them trucks never stop."

He had a house in the suburbs he bought with his second wife, a house in the city he bought with his first wife, and a few kids and grandkids between the two. He also had a girlfriend. Despite his habit, he was able to keep it all together, which is probably the single most dangerous rationalization an addict can keep in his pocket.

He would tell me about his routine. He would drive for a week, come home, drop money with the ex-wife, visit the girlfriend, and then go home to the wife. He had a "study" in the garage of his house in the suburbs where he would "play my Xbox and take my *schwings*." He told me about an elaborate pipe he had made out of a socket wrench (crack users are generally MacGyver-esque creators of paraphernalia). Each time he talked about another "bell-ringer" he took on his socket pipe, he would somehow let it slip that he hid his use from the Missus. When I challenged him on that, he got indignant.

"I pay the muthafuckin' bills, I give them someplace to live and they eat good, and as far as I'm concerned, I can do whatever I want with my own time."

I, self-righteously, would argue with him. "You're an addict in denial. You're smoking crack in your house and messin' around on your wife. How can you justify that?"

"What, you ain't never done that? Come on, now."

"I've never been married," I said, almost embarrassed that I would equivocate so lamely. But something about it drove me crazy and I couldn't let it go. No, I hadn't ever been married. But I had cheated, and I had deceived, and I had lied, like everyone else who got involved with that shit. What I wanted was for him to *admit* it, admit he had a problem and that what he was doing was "wrong."

In hindsight, it was such a blatant projection on my part, and Willie knew it, which was why he never backed down. I was no better than he was; in fact, in many ways I was a lot worse, because when I was using I was never able to keep it together like he did, I was a binge user. And in the worst of times, I stole for my habit, something that in Willie's morality ranked far worse than anything he had ever done, a very interesting distinction when you compare it against what he next told me.

THE GREAT BETRAYAL

The other major topic Willie would often talk about was the Vietnam War, the defining experience of his life. He spoke about it in such a frank and disconnected manner that it was unsettling. He would describe in gory detail the operations he would go on, how he went about crawling through the jungle disposing of Viet Cong.

When he talked about, for example, gutting another human being, one after the other, he spoke as if he was talking about fixing a car. He went into the mechanics of how to grab the victim (from behind, underneath the jaw), the place and manner to enter and exit the knife (across the throat first, to prevent screaming, then from the bladder to the sternum to eviscerate), to what he did to the bodies afterward (generally cut off ears or fingers). He talked about the insanity of the "body count" policy that the Pentagon operated, where after a firefight every dead enemy body had to be accounted for and reported back to HQ, so that it could then go on to be reported on the evening news back in the States.

There was no remorse in him that I could detect, but that's not to say none existed. His approach was to infuse it all with humor, to laugh about it. Sure, he talked about the atrocities that were committed, but always within the context of "They were the enemy, you did what you had to do." Everything was justified because it was war.

When he talked about some of his kills, he actually seemed to get excited, or if not excited, proud. So although there was this relatively smooth dude sleeping below me who most times seemed to "get it," it didn't take a rocket scientist to establish my lingering conviction that the trauma he experienced had served to shape the rest of his life. Was his crack habit a result of Vietnam? Who knew? He wouldn't talk about it.

There was one aspect to his story, however, that I had never heard before. It was about life in Chicago after Vietnam. The conversation began while we were talking about the role of the CIA in drug trafficking, something that the black community is quite familiar with but that goes almost unspoken in the Mainstream. Willie talked about the easy and ready availability of high-grade heroin while he was in Southeast Asia on deployment. At one point up to one-third of all active servicemen in the theater of operations were addicted to this heroin, which was grown and processed by the Laotian Hmong peasant army, who were backed by the CIA. The heroin was often processed in Thailand or Taiwan, both nations allied with the United States (the KMT, the Taiwanese military, largely controlled the heroin trade through the Chinese Triad network). The CIA in turn flew planeloads of this opium and refined heroin out of Southeast Asia in a contract airline called Air America. It was everywhere he went in Southeast Asia, Willie said, and it was everywhere—the same heroin—when he got back to Chicago.

This, of course, didn't surprise me. I had known this part of the story for a while. In fact, when I first learned, in the late 1990s, that the crack I was able to find on any of a thousand street corners in any major city was first brought into this country by a network of Nicaraguans and Colombians working with the CIA and distributing though street gangs, it sparked something in me, gleaned across the edge of the massive canyon of injustice I had welled within me, and sent me down the rabbit hole. I had to know how, why, more. How could I be considered a felon for using a substance my own "government" made readily available? There had to be more to it. Uncovering this intentionally buried history became the Rosetta stone that drove me on.

The staggered release of the Nixon tapes over the years revealed much of the thinking behind that administration's decision to launch the War on Drugs. It wasn't just that Nixon called drug abuse "public enemy number one" in the speech that launched the war. Behind that rationale lay the truth: because of the high levels of addiction among US troops, Nixon and the Pentagon brass feared a massive wave of crime and insurgency from disaffected veterans as all the GI Junkies came back to the States, hungry for a fix. Beyond that it is obvious to anyone who takes the time to look into the issue that the heroin so essential to quelling dissent in Vietnam and financing secret operations throughout Southeast Asia was intentionally distributed in the American ghettos by the same CIA/Mafia network that brought the drugs into the country. It was during the same time that inner cities were exploding in riots that began with Newark and Watts and intensified later in the wake of the King assassination—there were 37 major urban riots between 1964 and 1968—and militant Black Nationalist groups like the Black Panthers were gaining in strength and numbers and scaring the ever-lovin' shit out of Middle America. The extent of this fear at the time cannot be understated, even in the face of what now appears to be a total whitewash (pun painfully intended) of that portion of our national history.

The heroin, like crack would become 14 years later, was a means of chemical pacification. It accomplished a number of goals all at once. It numbed the populace and pacified revolutionary behavior. It provided an entrée for more and more police presence in the black community, and was a pretext for doing an end run around constitutional protections. It also acted as a powerful corrosive agent, eroding the social cohesion of the community, turning one against the other in what would later become somewhat offensively labeled "black-on-black violence."

Willie agreed but took it a step further.

"You gotta understand somethin', C. The government wasn't half as afraid of a bunch a pissed-off niggas from the ghetto smashin' windows as they was about all of us highly trained killers coming back from the 'Nam to find out ain't no jobs, the neighborhood's gone to shit, and they won't even give us the damn VA care they promised us. You see, they had no problem turning us into killers, because we went and did they dirty work for them. But they didn't know how to shut us off when it was done. And they was enough of us to fuck they shit up good."

"Whatta you mean, revolution?"

"Revolution? Man, ain't nobody ever wanted that shit fo real but some punk ass white kids who came into the 'hood to work with the Black Panthers. Niggers didn't want no revolution, niggers wanted jobs and houses. Naw, muthafucka, I'm talkin' *armed robbery*. I'm talking we had gangs of military-trained niggas knockin' off banks and shit."

"Why?"

"Whatchou mean, why? 'Cause we didn't have shit, and the government that turned us into what we was just washed they hands of us. We was takin' back ours. Warn't nobody waitin' to give us shit, so we had to take it. Man, why do you think there are so many homeless vets? You think vets prefer to live in the streets? Naw. It's because we got hung out to dry. We were the most dangerous force the US had ever created, and now we were loose in the streets. And people wonder . . ."

"So how do you feel about it now?"

He paused.

"I think we gave up too soon."

I WOULD LIKE TO USE MY LIFELINE PLEASE

One night a C.O. came around with a telephone and allowed everyone to make one call from our cells to one pre-approved phone number we provided during intake. The only number I was able to get through to was my friend Bryan Brickner, a fellow author and activist in Chicago. He was a trusted advisor, and a dear friend. I let him know I was OK, albeit going a bit stir crazy.

"Are you writing it all down?" he asked me.

"Not yet. I don't have access to pen and paper." I looked up at the C.O. standing outside the cell listening to my conversation. I looked him in the eye, smiled, and said, "I don't suppose there's any way I can have some paper and a pen, is there?" He just looked away, so I went on with the conversation. "I had some in County and began to take notes and interview a few people, but it didn't make me the most popular guy."

"Do you still have those notes?"

"Yeah. Ironically, the prison staff doesn't seem interested in them at all. They give you a folder with all your prison paperwork, and you have to carry it around everywhere. So for now, I got a lot of time on my hands, if you know what I mean, they don't let us do anything here, we never leave our cells, 24/7."

"Not even to eat?"

"Nope. It's like we're in quarantine, literally. All we have is time, so I write in my head and repeat it over and over. I figured out this way of tagging conversations with key words so I can remember the full scene later, like shorthand. Just the ways in which I have to adapt my process alone would make for a fascinating story."

"That's got to be a good way to keep your mind occupied, then," he said.

"Sadly, my mind has no trouble occupying itself. As far as I'm concerned, this is the productive option. The other is that I 'sit here and think about what I have done.'"

"Maybe that's not such a bad thing."

"Hey, come on, I'm the 'innocent' one here."

"No, Charles. You're not innocent. You're guilty. You know that."

"I know, I was kidding."

"Were you, though?"

Silence.

Bryan continues. "The laws may be unfair . . . ridiculous even. They may even be unconstitutional, but they are laws, and you broke them. Don't blur the difference between the two; it makes all the difference in the world. When you're 'innocent' it's all about you. Being guilty, but claiming the law is unjust . . . well, that's about the issue, not about you."

"So why do I still feel this overwhelming need to defend myself at every turn?"

Bryan laughed. "You'll be OK," he said. "You're on a journey, but not one you can't handle. Look at how all this has unfolded for you. You have such an opportunity."

"I gotta hand it to you, Bry. That's about the rosiest assessment of the penitentiary I have ever heard. Almost makes me feel like you'd appreciate the experience more than me. I can have a car at your place in ninety minutes."

"No, this is your trip, man."

The C.O. was motioning for me to give him the phone, so I told Bryan I had to go, and that I'd call him once I got to my prison facility.

The phone made the rounds of the cellblock for the next couple hours until everyone had had a chance to make a call. After the C.O. left the deck, the fellas started chirping to one another. It was something pretty amazing to behold. Echoing across the cellblock you would hear the sounds of one dude calling out to another dude he clearly knew, who would answer from another part of the cellblock. Then the first would relay the substance of the call back to the second. Often they talked in code, intentionally not wanting to be understood by others.

It quickly became apparent to me that there were enough guys from the same community locked up on the same cellblock—just one of eighteen—to have a group conversation, to talk about the same people in the outside world. In other words, it was becoming ever clearer that the bulk of the feedstock for this prison machine was harvested from only a few densely packed, relatively homogeneous neighborhoods.

Phone calls can also cause inmates to become unglued, particularly if the call is unpleasant. An hour after the chirping died down some guy on Level 3 above us began to freak out. He began screaming to be let out, screaming that he couldn't take it anymore, and pounding on the door. It went on for over an hour. Although he could hear him the entire time, the C.O. ignored the dude, until his cellmate started calling for help.

"Hey, y'all need to come do somethin' about this muthafucka! How long I gotta listen to this bitch scream?! I think he fuckin' himself up! *Hallo!!*"

Eventually the C.O. shuffled across the floor, climbed the three flights of stairs, and plodded down the aisle to their cell.

"You don't shut the fuck up you're both goin' to seg!" he shouted. "Is that what you want?"

The guy having the meltdown didn't seem to care, or was too freaked out by whatever was going on to realize he was about to be sent into complete isolation. He was in that totally irrational state where he just wanted *out*, and kept shouting at the C.O. So the C.O. slowly plods back down to the bubble, calls for backup and a White Shirt, and the process repeats itself, except this time with five C.O.s instead of one, and the White Shirt doing the talking.

"We're taking you out to segregation. Are you going to go peacefully or do we have to restrain you?"

His response was muffled, but a second later she says loudly, "OK, back away from the door then and put your hands on the wall."

We heard the door being unlocked, followed by some rustling and minor commotion, and then a moment later the entire crew comes marching down the stairs with the guy in the lead, handcuffed behind his back, looking *scared*, more scared than I had seen anyone since being locked up. Something had gotten to him.

"That mufucka snapped," Willie said, shaking his head as he watched the group of C.O.s walk him off the block.

Everyone snaps, eventually. The weaker ones, like this guy, snap early on in the process. Others snap at some point while doing their time and end up in seg, the "mental health" unit, the hospital, or dead. Some snap later on in life. That usually lands them back inside, or on the streets. At the very least, it leads to shattered opportunities, families, and lives.

Now, take any creature and isolate him like Stateville does, and it simply accelerates the snapping process. After two weeks, despite nearly all of us having a cellmate to talk to, we were all in various stages of extreme mental distress, going out of our minds with boredom and claustrophobia. For many, there was nothing else to do but endure the mental torment of their crimes, or their lives.

Imagine what it is like for those locked in pure solitary confinement, all alone, for months or years at a time? This is the fate of those held in Supermax prisons, like the one in Tamms, part of the IDOC (Illinois Department of Corrections) system. Supermax prisoners remain in their cells, alone, for 23 hours a day, many with no means of distraction. For one hour a day they can move around by themselves in a small enclosed concrete pen.

The incidence rate of severe trauma and mental illness *caused* by that method of incarceration is staggering. To many, this type of imprisonment is a hell worse than execution, but it's hard to find a great deal of public compassion for people sentenced to a Supermax prison since the crimes that get them sent there are usually the most heinous. Opposing the death penalty is a much easier moral argument to make, because it involves the taking of life, and more importantly, state-sanctioned execution. Sentencing a man to madness for his crimes, however, exists in a morally vague space that is simply easier to ignore than contemplate.

Perhaps what got to that dude on Level 3 was what gets to everyone who's locked up sooner or later, the irrational panic and paranoia that come with the eventual realization that your life depends on those people in uniform on the other side of the door. *If there was an emergency would they let me out?* It's like the fear that sometimes overtakes people on commercial airliners in mid-flight when they suddenly realize they are 30,000 feet in the air hurling at 500+ miles per hour in a thin aluminum tube with no escape if things go wrong.

These may seem like ridiculous and irrational fears, and on the surface they are. But something about them becomes very real once you're actually locked inside and realize there is no way out but for someone to physically let you out. And because so much of the process is mechanized, and the doors and windows are sealed, if the power shuts off or something breaks, no fresh air will circulate and within minutes your cold cell will become stifling. Even the air is regulated in prison, and there's a certain helplessness, an absolute dependency that comes along with that. Unless you've been in that situation, it's difficult to comprehend, much less contextualize, the fear.

I had the unfortunate experience of reading Stephen King's *The Stand* at a very young age, and the most harrowing aspect of the story that stuck with me through the years is the passage where a character is abandoned in prison after a plague kills 99% of the planet, and slowly he begins to starve and die of thirst. This haunting theme would resurface for me once or twice while in Stateville in a series of post-apocalyptic dreams I had, one, in which Willie was trying to eat me out of madness and starvation, from which I woke up screaming. It would become real and acute

two months later in the penitentiary with the arrival of Hurricane
Katrina.

THE ROAD TO DAMASCUS

It has been said that the human mind can find significance or symbolic meaning in anything if that is what it is looking for. Many
people dismiss synchronicity as nothing more than one's mind attempting to attribute a pattern to an opportune coincidence or
the intersection of random events. If this unlikely series of events
somehow brings you to some form of epiphany, it is dismissed as
the work of your unconscious. If something—a message, a sign,
a symbol, a person, an opportunity—appears at just the right
time, its significance is dismissed as projection or wish-fulfillment.
Rarely does the rational-mental type ever believe in a power that
is greater than themselves and that exists beyond their compre-
hension. The smarter they think they are, the more fervently they
will defend their position that nothing has any meaning beyond
what we ascribe to it.

At this point in my life, mystical understanding was entirely
beyond me. I was raised a lazy Catholic, became an "atheist" when
I was in college, and up until January of 2005 was pretty much set
as a secular humanist, with the scientific orthodoxy as my religion.
Then, in January of 2005, I had a life-changing experience that
made me acutely aware of a higher order of things. It's too complex
and distracting to go into the specific details of the experience at
this time, but I do describe it later. Know that this experience completely changed my mental paradigm and unwittingly set me off to
wander over the next few years into the realm of spirit.

So, with that context in mind, understand that, to me, it was no
coincidence when out of the blue one day, while Willie was sleeping,
a strange old man appeared on the cellblock dragging along a small
laundry sack and asked me if I "wanted anything to read?"

Are you fucking kidding me! I almost jumped through the glass.

Arbitrarily, it appeared, he reached inside the sack and retrieved two thin paperback books that he then slipped through the feed slot. They were two Evangelical Christian study guides, one for the Gospel According to Paul and one for the Book of Corinthians.

Are you fucking kidding me?

Caveat lector. Christianity is not my thing, and Evangelical Christianity is definitely not my thing. But I was so grateful for *something* to occupy my mind that I figured I'd just see what it was all about, so I started reading the book on Paul.

Saul of Tarsus, who would later become Saint Paul, is considered one of the three most important figures of early Christianity, along with Saint Peter, who was the first Pope, and James the Apostle. Paul is considered the single most important voice in the New Testament, yet although he is named as one of the Apostles, Paul never actually knew Jesus. In fact he loathed Jesus and was an avid persecutor of early Christians. He was known to roam around with a gang of thugs and beat up unsuspecting Christians before turning them in to the Romans and Sadducees for payment. Not a nice guy.

One day as he was riding his horse along the road to Damascus, Saul of Tarsus was knocked to the ground by a powerful light through which Jesus spoke to him about his persecution of Christians, basically calling him out on his shit. *Saul, Saul! What is with all the aggro and the freakin' dra-ma? You ain't got no love for ole G-Sus? Why you dousin' me with haterade, dawg?*

The long and short of the experience is that Saul, humbled by the encounter, has a full conversion. He changes his name to Paul and, until Pat Robertson comes around two thousand years later, becomes the most bellicose and bombastic missionary in the history of Christianity. His specialty was writing letters to the various ruling bodies—Romans, Corinthians, Galatians, Ephesians, etc.—exposing their crimes and hypocrisies and "crucifying" them publicly. These letters make up the bulk of the New Testament. Through his efforts, the church grew in strength and numbers, eventually taking over the Empire, then most of the world, and pretty much everyone knows the rest of the story from there.

Here is why I believe it was no coincidence that, of all the things I could have been given to read, I was given a book about Paul. I immediately identified with his story because I too was a strident non-believer who had a life-changing experience that made me aware of the existence of "God." This revelation changed my whole reality and set me off on my own "missionary" path to spread the hidden gospel of our postindustrial world.

Like Saul, I had been a persecutor of those following the "wrong" way. Politically, even though I believed that I was working on the side of justice, I demonized those not sharing my values or worldview. I engaged in demagoguery and I fostered oppositional dynamics of fear, distrust, and anger. I played on people's sense of outrage, or paranoia, or their own unresolved inner conflicts, exploiting every conceivable intellectual and emotional angle in order to find a pathway into their consciousness and upset the apple cart of their reality.

But after this divine awakening in January of 2005, I changed. Although I was no closer to understanding the nature of the Divine, like Paul I was trying to convince people that I had been wrong all these years. I felt compelled to preach what I felt was the right way, the way of unity, even though at the time I had no idea what "unity" was, what it looked like, how it would come into being, or what it meant in relation to myself.

I felt like it was my purpose in life to expose hypocrisy whenever I could, even if it meant opening myself up to constant ridicule. I was cursed to perpetually keep it real, pathologically compelled to tell people that the things they say, think, or do might be wrong or the cause of suffering for others. The people in my life didn't know what to make of my political conversion except that they didn't much care for it. I was OK to those around me when I was railing against Republicans, but the minute I began saying that they were no different from us and that the differences between us had been manufactured to keep us perpetually divided and at odds, most thought I had gone daffy.

Reading that book about Paul gave me the strength to follow through with a commitment I had made to myself to let this prison experience transform me, a commitment I had made to transform my entire life, and stand behind the transformation. If you look through the veil of what Christianity became under the reign of the Catholic Church, back into the original teachings of Jesus—the light-being that tried to bring us a message of universal love and compassion—Paul's conversion seems that much more significant.

Although I had yet to tap into that field of universal love, I knew that I had been given an awareness of "God" that became the touchstone for my new journey, and so, like Paul, I was setting off into uncharted territory, with really shitty credibility, but enough faith and drive to persevere. If I could just maintain my passion and my faith like Paul, then perhaps I could make a difference by *being* that difference.

Paul had once written, "The profane do not have spirit, they are creatures of baser instinct." The "profane" to Paul were, on the surface, the unconverted masses, the denizens that Jesus would have gathered up into a flock, the lepers and the prostitutes and the criminals and the poor. Today they remain the same, the discarded segments of society that end up in the ghettos and rural wastelands, the streets and the prison systems. What resonated with me was the understanding that without a conversion to one's higher self through some form of purification, through some major self-reckoning, we would continue to operate from a place of fear and division, of "other-ness," and we would remain trapped in the vicious cycles of violence and imperial domination that have ruled life on this planet for the last 10,000 years.

I finished the book on Paul in less than a day, unable to sleep or wind down my brain. I had been trying to quell the white noise sea between my ears, but something was telling me to let go. So over the next few days I would remain in a quiet space, slowly reliving whole sections of my life that had been stuffed away, understandably, as a coping mechanism. For the first real time in all my life, I began to own the memories, and own responsibility for much of what I had done.

I also began to dream deep, complex, weaving archetypal narratives where contrition and redemption were central themes. Whereas I could not scream or cry in my waking state, I would purge grief in my dreams, only to have it haunt me upon waking, lingering throughout the day in a residue cloud of sadness that fogged up the interior of our cell.

After some time my mind kept returning to one specific memory that had retained remarkable significance over the years. This took place more than 20 years earlier, in the summer of 1984, when I was an irascible 14-year-old upper-middle-class feedbag from the suburbs. My parents, thinking that it would teach me discipline, sent me to Outward Bound wilderness survival school. I spent my summer canoeing through the boundary waters area of northern Minnesota and southern Canada. After a number of weeks in the wild with our two guides and the other teens in my "brigade," we came upon a remote lake deep inside the Canadian border. Each of us was deposited at regular points around this huge lake, out of view of each other, with nothing but a tin cup, journal, bug net, and sleeping bag. We were told to survive on our own for four days with no food or fire.

By the third day I had entered that non-ordinary state of consciousness that often accompanies fasting. I had hyper-awareness of my surrounding environment as well as a somewhat novel awareness of my own internal process. I was managing the experience fairly well until I began to hear loud distant rumblings like thunderclaps or explosions. They came one after another after another, in fairly regular intervals, for about an hour.

Now you have to remember, if you are able, that this was 1984, dead center of the Reagan years, and we were still in the Cold War with the Soviets. I was a kid who was raised under the ever-present specter of total nuclear annihilation, what they called Mutually Assured Destruction, or fittingly, MAD, because the entire idea is totally fucking insane. For those of us who lived it—my generation and my parents' generation—it was like living with permanent dread. Teenagers like me were inundated with propaganda about the Cold War like *Rambo, Red Dawn, Rocky IV, War Games, Top Gun*. The year before I went on Outward Bound ABC broadcast *The Day After*, a television movie that imagined what the aftermath of a nuclear war would be like. I was 13, and it freaked me the fuck out.

Staring across this vast lake listening to the distant rumbling I was convinced that the world was ending all around me, and we—a handful of teenagers like in *Red Dawn*—had been spared only because we were in such a remote location that was hundreds of miles from the nearest target, which would have been Minneapolis. I was in the grips of pure mortal terror, as this was the first real existential crisis I had faced in my life.

I began to panic. I paced around my little area, ripping chunks of skin and nail from my fingertips (a miserable stress habit I have had my entire life), uttering these weird, whine-like wails, repeating *oh no oh please oh no oh please oh no oh please . . . God!* Please God please God! Eventually, I was able to calm myself down enough to grab my journal and begin writing. What poured out of me was a mixture of deathbed confession, battlefield conversion, and the inevitable bargain I begged the Creator, or whatever was up there, to make with me in order to spare us from annihilation.

Perhaps strange, perhaps not, but certainly telling, was that this all came out framed as one gigantic *mea culpa*. The only God

I knew of at the time, as a Catholic, was one that judged and condemned, and I had been sent to Outward Bound (and was being sent to military school in the fall, my mother reminded me daily), because I was "bad." I was a bad kid who deserved punishment, and my little 14-year-old brain had decided that God and my mom had had a kind of Parent-Teacher conference and decided that I was so bad that I was going to be thrust into the midst of a nuclear holocaust.

So I begged for forgiveness and absolution, a stream of consciousness borne out of fear that bleated *Yes, I am bad, I am bad, I'm sorry, I never meant to hurt anyone, I never meant to hurt anyone, please, if only you spare the world, I'll be good, I promise, I'll do whatever my mom says, I promise, just PLEASE LET ME OUT OF HERE!!!!*

Although my life at 14 was complicated, I certainly had never hurt anyone in that context, and I did not require divine absolution. I was materially comfortable and isolated from much of the hardship of the world, but our home was a place of conflict, and we were not happy people. My mother was violent, hyper-controlling, and terribly abusive. My father, who was a much more deferential, lackadaisical, people-pleasing personality, was always working, always on the road for his job, and never there to defend me. When he was around, he mostly wanted to be left alone, and would occupy himself in projects that would consume his time (like the futile weekend war against nature being waged on suburban lawns across the nation, as legions of beleaguered Dads try to hold back four billion years of grass evolution with a ragtag army of gas-powered mowers). My parents' marriage dangled precipitously.

Although I was clearly intelligent and had plenty of academic aptitude, I constantly challenged my teachers' authority, and had the attention span of a tweaking gnat. The stress and anxiety over what was going on in my home bubbled over into my behavior at school, and as a result for most of my childhood I was more or less a social outcast who was constantly getting harassed, beat up, or ridiculed. I had no real long-term friends because I never stayed in one school for longer than two years, a pattern that would have a profound affect on my ability to form lasting relationships later on in life. The community in which I lived was very conservative, and very white, and people like me stuck out like a bad rash on a nude beach.

Beneath the Pleasant Valley veneer was a treasure trove of skeletons and demons. I was secretly dealing with the consequences of being sexually abused for a number of years by a neighbor boy five years older than I was. He had started out as my hero, and then just perved out on me and a couple other boys in the neighborhood, manipulating us into individual and group situations.

Yes, I can see now that I was healthy and ate well and had a lot of "stuff," but I did not have two critically important things in my life: love and trust. From my purview, my life pretty much sucked, yet despite all that, I begged God to please send me back to the sadistic comforts of that fucked-up world over the post-apocalyptic nightmare that I was certain was unfolding all around me. At the core of it all was my deepest fear: that I would be left *alone*.

My intention in bringing all this up is to shed light on the fragile state of my psyche at that time, which would not strengthen in the coming years but, instead, would career towards disaster. At 14, while convinced the world was ending, I begged for forgiveness, not because I really deserved it, but because I didn't know what else to do. In the end my whole bargain with God was really a reflection of how I felt about myself; I was what was "wrong." This belief would plague me in the coming decades and would directly contribute to landing me in that prison cell with Willie Frazier.

But let's get real. I was a child. I was still innocent. I hadn't actually done anything "wrong" in life. I was sheltered and controlled in all directions. What did I really have to be sorry or penitent for? My worst transgressions were innocuous teenage rites of passage.

On that day in the wilderness I didn't know my mother was the way she was because that was all she knew, because she had come from even worse violence and abuse, which was why she beat me and was incapable of showing affection, because that was what she had been taught by her parents. But 20 years later in that prison cell I sure did know what had happened to my mother, and so, I had to ask myself how much longer I was willing to blame her for how I was and hold onto the pain of the past.

Likewise I had no idea at 14 that my father was always hustling because our profligate lifestyle demanded it, and that when he had a nervous breakdown it was not only because he was trying to shield us from the consequences of bankrupting us, but also because he had been lying for so long he had forgotten what was real and began believing the lies. But since then he had suffered greatly, so when would I ever forgive him for what he had done?

It would be decades before I understood that the education system was institutionally incapable of handling the "non-traditional personality," since its sole function is to create a condition of conformity and standardization. Those of us who were eccentric, unique, gifted, troubled, or simply different were punished. We were labeled "learning disabled" and were segregated from other children, as if what we had was contagious (which it probably was, since ideas *are* contagious).

And although I had no control over a boy so much older and stronger than we were, who took advantage of our trust and awe in him, I wasn't the first person to suffer such a fate at such an age, and I wouldn't be the last, nor would it be the last time I would find myself the victim of sexual assault.

As I reflected on these traumatic events, which had become the demons driving my madness, for which the drugs became a temporary respite, and for which I still sought healing, I had to ask myself: How much longer I was willing to play the victim? How much longer would it be before I took responsibility for my part in all of these things? Because I had nothing to do but sit and think, and I had finally stopped resisting.

Now I began to see the larger patterns that had dominated my life. What I needed to face was how the experiences of my past affected my life in the present. I had to accept that, although I was not responsible for much of what was done to me as a child, I was completely responsible for how I chose to respond to it as an adult. For most of my adult life, my response was chaotic, and my behavior shameful.

Of course, there was no Armageddon in 1984. The explosions I heard in the distance were the result of loggers detonating tree stumps. I would go home to resume my life, quickly forgetting the bargain I had made with God, and meanwhile my life became worse than I could have ever imagined, as I was soon to be subjected to unspeakable brutality when I entered military school. So, for the child that I was, there would be no Saul to Paul conversion. Neither the vast Canadian wilderness nor the Chicago suburbs to which I returned led to Damascus. Twenty years later, at 35 years of age, I had much to repent for. I had made many, many bad choices in my adult life, and they had all come full circle.

In the intervening years since that first crisis, I had, of course, lost my way. I descended into the darkness and depravity of addiction and post-traumatic stress disorder, and I lied, cheated, stole, fought, and caused untold misery to my loved ones. Despite everything my mother had done to me, she was still my mother and I had put her through hell too, as I had also done to all the women who dared to love me. Strewn behind me was the wreckage of more than two decades of broken friendships, relationships, and opportunities. I had already been busted twice and managed to avoid prison. Three strikes, under most circumstances, and you're out.

Even though my life was in a totally different place now, and even though I still believed that no one deserved to be locked up for what they put into their own bodies, and even though

I came from good intention and wanted to "save the world," I was forced to accept that I was in prison now because of my karma. I had been blazing through life in a fog of defensive anger and self-righteous indignation, seeking out justice at every turn without ever taking a moment to stop and reflect on the fact that there were scores of people out there who sought justice, karmic or otherwise, for the things I had done to them. I had not taken the time in life to properly atone for my transgressions, to get right with myself and my Creator, and so I was now in prison to sit and think, to remember all the things I never got caught doing, and for the spiritual crimes for which I refused to hold myself accountable.

I finally accepted—two decades in arrears—that things would never ever go back to the way they were, before my real innocence had been lost, and that home was long, long gone. There is a reason "innocence" is synonymous with "virginity": you only get to lose it once, and your world is never the same once it is gone.

Hotel Hell was, in every respect, a personalized prison, custom made for the particular torments of our individual psyches. If I had any hope of redemption, I would have to quietly accept my punishment with dignity, and navigate my way safely through the rest of my prison experience, and try, in any way that I knew how, to make something of it once I got out and was able to resume my life. I knew, at the very least, that if I did not take this on now and own it, eventually I would be back in this cold and miserable concrete cell asking myself yet again, *Well, how did I get here?* But of course, I would know why.

It was time to stop fighting and get real. Ultimately, I held the key to my own heaven and hell, if not the grey steel door a few feet away. Now, all that mattered would be how I would move forward.

Two weeks earlier in the county jail I had stood in a circle with the Reverend as I was awaiting shipment to Stateville, and he told me to leave the past behind, that it no longer mattered, that there was only this moment forward. I embraced his words. I was ready to be in prison now. I was ready for whatever came next.

VAYA CON DIOS—THE SEQUEL

Around two o'clock in the morning of my 13th day in Hotel Hell, a C.O. came onto the cellblock and began slipping brown paper bags under certain doors. When she stopped at my door she looked at me and said, "Shaw?" I nodded yes, and she slipped the bag under my door. I snatched it up and scanned it for the name of my prison. All I saw was my name and IDOC number.

"Put any personal belongings in that bag, and grab your bedding."

There was no bag for Willie. Although he forced a smile, you could tell he was not happy. The door popped open. With my sheet and blanket and brown paper bag in my arms, I turned around to look at him.

"I guess this is it," I said. "Thanks, Willie. Take care of yourself."

"You take care now too, C. And remember . . . when you down there . . . *listen*. Don't talk so much. Not every brother is as understanding as me. You wanna write a book, listen to what niggas is sayin' to you."

"I'll get in touch when I get out," I said, as I walked through the door.

"Yeah, do that. We'll go get some *vittles*."

The C.O. closed the door on Willie. He moved over to the window, and for the first time I got to see him like they had been seeing all of us this whole time, pathetic animals locked in a cage. Willie shrank back into the cell as he waved goodbye.

I spent the better part of the next morning sitting in the bullpens waiting for the fleet of transport buses to arrive that would take us to our respective prisons. One at a time, by facility, they began to segregate us into separate pens, chaining us together:

Big Muddy, Logan, Pontiac, Menard, Shawnee, Vandalia, Jacksonville, the list went on. Finally, after nearly everyone had been assigned to a prison, the few remaining inmates, of which I could count myself, were told that we were being sent to East Moline.

I really began to believe that someone, or something, was definitely looking out for me.

CHAPTER 3
The Sweet Moline

I

Nestled among the trees on a prime hilltop just east of the Mississippi River in the Quad Cities area, you will find the East Moline Correctional Center (EMCC). You may think "nestled" a strange verb to use while describing a prison, and normally I would agree. With the exception of maybe Alcatraz, which is closed, prison plots are generally not known for their idyllic vistas. You're more likely to find them intentionally segregated from the larger population centers, surrounded by cornfields, desert, badlands, or swamp, looking flat and boxy and relatively nondescript but for the tell-tale razor wire fences and guard towers.

The history of how East Moline became a prison, however, begins in a slightly different milieu more than a hundred years ago when this particular hilltop complex opened as the Western Illinois Hospital for the Insane. Set high above the noise and smoke of what was then a bustling turn-of-the-century river port, the hospital was situated inside a calm and picturesque campus with ancient, massive trees and a bloated creek, a pacifying setting for those acutely on edge.

Eventually renamed the East Moline Mental Health Center, the hospital closed in 1980 and the complex was sold to the Illinois Department of Corrections, which converted it into what they call a "Level 6 minimum-security prison." By some grace, the calming grounds left a unique legacy; East Moline is the only facility in the notoriously vicious Illinois prison system with a "free movement" policy that allows inmates, at regularly scheduled times, to freely move about certain approved areas of the grounds.

Because of its setting, the movement policy, and the prison's uncharacteristically low incidence rate of violence, EMCC is known to all as "The Sweet Moline." If you had to go to prison in Illinois, this would be the place you'd want to end up.

Keep in mind, this is still the *joint*. It is still filled with some bad men, serious thugs, the bulk of whom are not graced with a sense of patience. The potential for something really bad to happen exists at every moment. The motivation to stay out of a worse place does influence behavior, but as my story will show, East Moline is anything but a safe place.

Most of the inmates at East Moline come from two groups: first-time nonviolent short-timers like I was, who are perceived as low escape risks; and certain long-timers who are coming to the end of their sentences. Long-timers are perceived as an even lower escape risk, and East Moline is meant to serve as their transitional facility; it's the closest thing to a social environment, let alone free movement, that many of them have seen for perhaps decades.

According to IDOC stats, East Moline maintains an average daily inmate population of 1,100, generally broken down demographically in the following manner (which I was able to confirm by sneaking looks at the daily "count" sheets distributed to the C.O.s): on any given day there are roughly 700 black, 250 white, and 150 Latino inmates. The official capacity of East Moline is only 688, making it overcrowded by some 37%. The average age of the inmates is 34, and the average annual cost per inmate is around $20,000, which is at the low end of the range reported by IDOC. On the other end of the spectrum is the Supermax prison in Tamms, where inmates spend 23 hours a day alone in their single-man cells. There the annual cost per inmate is around $90,000 a year.[7]

As is the case with every facility in the IDOC system, the prison in East Moline is an essential part of a local economy that has seen better days. Historically, Illinois prosperity was powered by the twin-engine economy of manufacturing and agriculture. Year after year the state ranked among the highest agricultural producers, and the great central metropolis of Chicago was the hub where raw materials were bought, processed, packaged, and shipped around the world.

The Quad Cities—Moline and Rock Island, Illinois, and Davenport and Bettendorf, Iowa—is a sprawling metropolitan area of 400,000 that spreads along both sides of the Mississippi River three hours due west of Chicago. For most of the 20th century the region supported a thriving agricultural and industrial economy specializing in the manufacture of large-scale farm equipment. All the titans of that industry had plants in the area: International Harvester was in Rock Island, Case IH and Caterpillar were in Bettendorf, and John Deere was in Moline.

Over the past 40 years, however, those economic engines corroded badly. Beginning in the late 1970s, shifting conditions caused by foreign competition led these manufacturers to close down their operations in the Quad Cities. Deindustrialization emptied out most of the Rust Belt cities of the Midwest while Big Agribusiness firms like Cargill and Archer Daniels Midland consolidated the bulk of midwestern family farms. In the last 50 years alone the number of Illinois farms shrank by more than 60%, dropping from 200,000 to under 76,000 and still falling.[8] This precipitated a period of significant decline throughout the

Midwest in which population, land values, and per capita incomes fell sharply. The region was also hit hard by the closing of a number of military bases following the end of the Cold War.

With the passage in the 1990s of international trade agreements like NAFTA, the symbiotic relationship between Chicago industry and Illinois agriculture largely faded. Chicago forged ahead with a new postindustrial economy while the rest of the region was left behind. Although efforts at revitalization were made throughout the last two decades, prosperity has not yet returned to the Quad Cities and scores of other rail stop towns throughout the Rust Belt, where you now find prisons.

Unable to find decent jobs, and unwilling to take what's left, many of those left behind in the transformation to a global economy— what writers like Noam Chomsky and Christian Parenti have termed "surplus labor" or "surplus population"—turned to the two sides of the War on Drugs for economic sustenance: drug dealing and criminal justice. Cops and prisons, drugs and guns, McDonald's and Wal-Mart . . . these were the replacement economies America had to offer in her postindustrial age if you couldn't get a college degree and become a (generally white) white-collar professional. With so many people needing work, not everyone got to choose which replacement economy they would end up in.

The rural prisons built during the prison boom of the 1980s and 1990s were end products of the War on Drugs that produced hundreds of thousands of jobs in economically depressed regions. Between 1990 and 1999 a new prison opened somewhere in rural America every 15 days, so that by the end of the decade, the US had the largest prison system in the world and had imprisoned more black people than South Africa ever did during the apartheid regime. With drug arrests representing around 60% of the total annual arrests in Illinois, and around 110,000 nonviolent drug offenders passing through the Illinois correctional system every year—most of whom come from the Chicago Metropolitan

Area—a new dependent link between Chicago and rural Illinois was forged: urban prisoners, rural guards. What they all have in common is that they are poor and uneducated.

In these downstate communities the War on Drugs is a godsend to almost anyone who can get a coveted prison job. When you get down to the local level, people aren't thinking about a global drug economy; they're trying to feed their families. Yet even if they too are poor and hungry, they don't see themselves as living in the same situation as poor people in the inner cities. Prison jobs are sold to the public not just as an escape from the go-nowhere service economy but also as a noble public service, a job where you can wear a uniform with the American flag and kick ass if necessary.

My friend author/activist Bryan Brickner grew up in Scales Mound, Illinois, not far from the Quad Cities. He puts it this way: "In those kinds of towns the mentality is, *We're helping out, we're housing the criminals of the state. We're providing a good and necessary service and we're risking our lives to do it.*"

Bryan comes from a farming family, and he served in the army during the first Gulf War. He's seen firsthand the transformation of rural Illinois after farm consolidation, the emergence of bedroom communities, and the closing of military bases. Most people moved away. For those who remained, IDOC later came knocking, offering economic panaceas in the form of prisons.

Of course, sometimes the panacea turned out to be poison. Nowhere is that more evident than in the village of Thomson, Illinois, just down the road from Scales Mound, the most recent site of IDOC prison construction. Back in the late 1990s, facing some of the highest unemployment rates in the state, Thomson was wooed into building a $140 million maximum-security prison. "The main reason we built a prison," Village President Merri Jo Enloe told me back in 2005, "was because everyone needed a job."[9]

The prison was to deliver 750 permanent jobs and millions in economic development grants and service contracts. The state borrowed the money to build the prison and to upgrade Thomson's roads, rail crossings, and water systems in order to serve the increased demand. Tax incentives permitted the Village to bolster their population count by adding the eighteen hundred future residents of the prison, which is not a bad deal when you learn that the Village receives $110 a year per resident from the state as a reimbursement on taxes paid. This action alone would have increased town revenue by 61% by adding another $198,000. You know you're in a small town when your entire municipal budget is under half a million dollars. That 61% increase would be a veritable windfall, and was mighty enticing.

Frankly, the only resistance to the prison was racially motivated. When you interview a town's highest elected official, the last thing you expect to hear the person say—particularly in this day and age, and even more so, on the record—is, "This is a predominantly white area, and there was a lot of objection to minorities coming through the community, particularly from white transplants from the Chicago area who felt that the prison would bring to our community the kind of people they were trying to get away from by moving out here." Her statement encapsulates so much of the generalized racism that drives Illinois society and its politics. The people of Thomson did not want black people coming through their town, period.

Never one to miss an opportunity to exploit prejudice or fear, in response the state promised increased funding for the Thomson Police and the Carroll County Sheriff's Department, despite a very low crime rate. As if to justify the expanded law enforcement, miraculously, an unsubstantiated rumor began to cycle through the community that "drug trafficking" in the area would increase because of the prison. The net take for Thomson? More concrete and steel, more badges, and more guns for a sleepy little farming town. This is, to the letter, how the War on Drugs has worked for the last 25 years in communities all across America.

Despite all this outlay and rigmarole, the new Thomson Correctional Center never opened as planned in 2001 because the

State of Illinois, facing a $4 billion budget deficit caused by the dot.com recession, couldn't afford to operate it, so it sat empty for the entire decade. Many residents went into debt or bankruptcy either starting or upgrading their local businesses to meet the increased traffic that was expected to come though the Village, and things only got worse with the economic collapse of 2008. Then, in late 2009 the Obama administration announced that it was considering moving detainees held at Guantánamo Bay to Thomson, and that the prison would hold military tribunals for "enemy combatants." The announcement released a maelstrom of Republican histrionics about a wave of jihad descending upon Chicago, but in the end the Obama administration won out. Thomson would become Gitmo in the Heartland.

But Thomson residents received a double slap in the face when they learned that they would not be eligible for most of the prison jobs—since they would have to be filled at the federal and military level—and that neither foreign nationals nor "enemy combatants" held in detention can be counted on the tax roles.

In 2002, facing the same budget crisis that was keeping Thomson closed, then-Governor George Ryan closed the 141-year-old Joliet prison and attempted to close the prisons in Sheridan and our very own East Moline. He was met with fierce resistance from elected officials and the union representing correctional officers. Former East Moline Mayor Jose Moreno sent Ryan a letter in April of 2002 in which he wrote that closing the prison "is a touchy and important issue," adding "we cannot afford to lose these jobs." In the end, both facilities remained open, Sheridan got a multi-million-dollar retrofit to become a drug-treatment facility, and millions more were spent on the new processing center in Stateville.

When Ryan's successor, the now-disgraced, cartoonishly corrupt Rod Blagojevich, faced the same budget gaps in 2003, he also tried to close older prisons in Pontiac, Vandalia, and St. Charles. As with Ryan before him, state lawmakers stepped in and blocked Blagojevich's attempt for the same reason: jobs. Then, in early

2008, Blagojevich announced his plan to close the old Stateville max prison and transfer all the inmates to the unopened Thomson facility. While it was clear that the inmates would be transferred, it was not so clear whether the correctional staff would join them, and Blagojevich was not exactly forthcoming. The plan was dropped and the issue rapidly faded into the background after Blagojevich was indicted on fraud and corruption charges and forced from office.

Pat Quinn, the former lieutenant governor who inherited Blagojevich's mantle only to face even greater deficits than any of his predecessors, opted to try to release 1,000 nonviolent offenders rather than close any prisons. Political opponents immediately resorted to fearmongering, the primary tool of prison politics and criminal justice policy, shrieking the expected, "He's letting dangerous criminals loose on our streets!" Quinn, fearing the dreaded "soft-on-crime" curse, which is political suicide, ultimately bowed to pressure after only 170 inmates had been released. To make their point clear to him, state lawmakers introduced a bill codifying into law a mandatory 60-day incarceration for every person sentenced to time in IDOC, even those with good time credit and time served—those Quinn wanted to release—ensuring prison time for all petty nonviolent offenders regardless of circumstance. Since then, the population of the Illinois prison system has set a new record high every week, with no end in sight.

II

On the day I arrived at the East Moline Correctional Center— July 20, 2005—the Quad Cities (along with most of the nation) were broiling under the hottest temperatures since the 1995 heat wave that killed nearly 600 people in Chicago.

We left Stateville NRC early in the morning in a row of buses with no windows and no bathrooms, cuffed and shackled to each other and locked to our seats. We would be on the road for more than seven hours of decidedly uncomfortable travel. From Joliet we headed south some three hours to the Logan Correctional Center in Lincoln, Illinois, a medium-security facility hidden inside Illinois Railsplitter State Park, an island of trees two miles off I-55. At Logan we disembarked to switch up the buses, a security procedure meant to thwart breakout attempts, you depart Stateville on one bus and arrive at your prison on another without anyone on the outside knowing a switch was made. We stood on the blacktop in our thick bright yellow IDOC transfer jumpsuits in the near 100-degree heat for almost an hour before we were allowed to urinate into a bucket. We were then loaded onto our new bus to head northwest up I-74 to the Quad Cities, a ride of another three-plus hours.

I was shackled to a quiet young brother named David Leftridge who was serving three years for selling marijuana and possessing a handgun. In front of me was a young white brother named Robert Smith, who we would later call "Smitty." He was shackled to a smart-ass little punk named Thomas Ephraim who they called "Li'l G." He was just over five feet tall and couldn't have weighed more than a buck twenty soaking wet. He got 18 months for possession and unlawful use of a firearm. He was four months shy of his 18th birthday, and after knowing him for only a few hours, I knew this wasn't going to be his last trip inside the razor wire.

Behind me was Frank Root, one of the very first guys I met on this whole odyssey. Root, Willie Frazier, another cat named Melvin, "Big Mo," and I all shipped out from Cook County together and ended up warehoused on the same storage wing while at Stateville.

Frank was in his thirties with close-cropped receding hair and a goatee that wrapped around his mouth, forming a natural frown. Frank was one of the first people whose name I learned. You try to make connections when you can, however you can, particularly in those early days when you don't know what lies ahead and you're just trying not to feel alone. Now, here we were headed to East

Moline, our third bus ride together. As the only two white guys of roughly the same age on this shipment, after seeing each other this much, we figured we were meant to know one another.

Root was an Irish kid from the Bridgeport neighborhood of Chicago who had gone to music school and was trying to make it as a rock guitarist. He lived with his Italian girlfriend from Berwyn who worked at an advertising agency and, from what he told us, was just about done with him 'cause he spent most of his time hunting down bags of dope, which eventually got him two years for possession and retail theft.

I started calling him "Smokey," owing at first to how much he bitched about wanting a cigarette when we weren't permitted to smoke, and then to his prodigious consumption of tobacco when we were. He needed that nicotine too, boy. Smokey done got himself a *nasty* dope habit, and his nerves were shot. He got arrested while hooked, went through the acute phase of withdrawal (the sickness) in Cook County—which is a hell I have seen firsthand, but thankfully, never had to experience—and went through the secondary stage (severe anxiety and agitation) in his meat locker at Stateville. He was just beginning to feel better when we arrived at East Moline, more than a month after his last dose.

Smokey shared a cell at Stateville with a young Latin King who had recently been shot a few times in the abdomen and as a result had a colostomy bag. On the way to East Moline Smokey described in agonizing detail the intimate operations of his cellie's lower intestinal tract, particularly the interface between the last few remaining inches of his colon, which protruded from his abdomen, and the clear plastic tube and bag that eventually collected his waste products, which he would then have to dump out in the shitter. We all wondered aloud, *why do they make the bags clear?*

Affixed to Smokey was Thomas Clemon, who called himself "Pee-Wee" even though he was big enough to rip arms from sockets. Pee-Wee's complexion was deep, deep black and he had a Louis Armstrong smile that lit up his whole face. He was 42 years old, and had 12 shorties by a number of different women. Pee-Wee was kind and gentle and almost completely illiterate. He got busted buying a bag of dope, which he admitted he used sometimes, and got three years on his *first offense*. David, who was shackled to me, used to joke that Pee-Wee got such a harsh sentence because he was so black he absorbed the blackness of others around him like a wormhole in space sucks in light. No white judge could abide that level of concentrated black power.

Having had no sunshine or a decent meal for weeks, we were happier than pigs in shit to be out of Stateville, out of lockdown, and out into the sunshine and air and the company of other human beings. It was an interesting head check. Throughout the bus multiple conversations about East Moline were filling the air. David told me his older brother was there now, but that he hadn't spoken to him since he had been locked up. Now we can spend some quality time together," he said, half-sarcastic. "Moms is definitely proud."

The bus pulls into the town of East Moline and begins to climb the hill where the prison is situated. We can see glimpses of it out the front windows through the silvery blur of a razor wire fence running the perimeter of the property. Unlike the bulk of Illinois prisons, East Moline is surrounded by a quiet, unostentatious residential neighborhood, mostly because the residential district grew up around the old hospital before it became a prison. As the bus shoots past these modest homes I catch a flash or two of a person outside and I wonder what the locals feel about the prison. What are they thinking, if anything, as another busload of convicts goes flying by? Do they watch as we pull into the gate? Are they afraid of us? Do they even see us anymore? *Wait*, I think, as they blur out of sight, *I'm different, I have a story!* Embedded in my telepathic entreaties is my true sentiment: *Don't judge me.*

At the gate, the doors retract and the bus slowly advances through the checkpoint and pulls to a stop at the receiving bay of an old split-level modern building. Two-by-two we hobble off the bus. The sunlight and heat are intense and the grounds are quiet. Out the bay door, across the driveway and up a short hill, is the hundred-year-old three-story stone building that housed the original insane asylum.

One by one we are uncuffed and de-shackled and told to sit in a few rows of folding chairs. The jumpsuits do not breathe, so even in the shade the heat is fast getting to us. The C.O.s from Stateville scoop up all the cuffs, shackles, and waist belts and clamor back on board. They back out the gate and are gone, the drone of the engine and transmission fading fast, melding into the high-pitched whine of a legion of cicadas and the percussive rattle of dry leaves dancing across the pavement and high in the massive, water-starved trees that surround us. With no one talking or otherwise making a sound, these are the most peaceful and pleasant few moments I experience in months, losing myself in the hypnotic sounds of nature for the briefest of time until the calm is shattered again by the sounds of men.

A tall skinny white assistant warden with a mustache strides into the room and stands before us. "Gentlemen," he says, "you're at The Sweet Moline. You don't know how fortunate you are. Don't fuck it up."

He checks us in one at a time and then we are led across the grounds to the cafeteria, known in prison parlance as the Dietary Unit, so that we can finally eat. We mount the hill and the grounds come into view. Facing eastward is a big field that serves as the center of the campus. To the left is a fence line that runs for about 100 yards before taking a 90° left turn where another collection of buildings from at three least distinct architectural eras stands. Behind the fence are woods.

To our right is the original hospital building, and behind it a good 50 yards down a path is a modern cell house structure; next to that is the Dietary Unit. We can see the distant tops of trees falling away in a steep decline on the back side of the prison grounds. We look at each other, squinting in the heat and bearing semi-restrained expressions of relief; the place doesn't *look* so bad. Of course, we had been there less than an hour, so what had we really seen?

Lunch had already been served, so we were the only inmates in the Dietary Unit at that time. The room is surrounded on three sides by tall glass picture windows, with a southern view that looks out across the Moline Valley. There are long rows of cafeteria-style picnic tables. Below us down the hill a bit rises the smokestack of the power plant, and the industrial laundry facility that is part of Illinois Prison Industries, the for-profit arm of IDOC.

Up high on the wall, in plain view of all, is a sign . . .

"SIT DOWN WHEN SHOTS ARE FIRED!"

Reading that precipitates another one of those *Toto, we ain't in Kansas anymore* moments. *Shots? Greeeeeat. The sign would probably be more helpful if it read . . .*

"TRY NOT TO SCREAM OR SHIT YOURSELF WHEN SHOTS ARE FIRED!"

I'm so overwhelmingly grateful to have a whole plate of food in front of me that I eat so fast I get crushing heartburn within minutes. We are hurried out of the Dietary and taken over to the modern-looking cellblock that stands behind the original hospital building. This structure houses the largest number of inmates. It was built in the early 1980s just after the place became a prison, as part of the initial expansion efforts, and it certainly reflects the architecture of the times. It was designed in the shape of a four-story cross or plus sign, with an enlarged center that serves as the stairwell while the four radiating arms make up the four cellblocks called Wings—A, B, C, and D—each comprising a two-story right angle that makes up one quarter of the cross. Like the Dietary Unit, the front half of the building opens to the top of the hill, and the back half drops away dramatically along the slope, like the edge of a castle abutting a cliff.

We enter the building and descend four flights to B Wing, which is for new arrivals. Once we are buzzed inside, the C.O.

tells us that we are restricted to the unit and will be gathered up tomorrow to "complete our orientation," which includes turning in the bright yellow jumpsuits for prison blues and getting whatever living supplies they deem sufficient. Within three days we will all be assigned to our permanent cells somewhere in the prison complex, but in the interim we are each assigned cells in B Wing, and I end up in the far corner cell with David.

Three-quarters of B Wing is for permanent housing assignments, so most of the inmates milling around us are already into their evening routines, which is difficult to pick up on. To make it worse, the heat has turned the cellblock into a convection oven, and while most inmates are walking around in shorts, we are still in our hot bright non-breathing yellow jumpsuits, so we really stand out as fresh meat. It is loud as hell, only one shower works, the water fountain is broken, and although there are sinks in our cells, the water from the tap is god awful. We have no supplies of any sort, not even a cup to drink from, so David goes out to try and work a hustle with some of the cats on the unit who might know his brother.

Naturally, the first thing Smokey does is fan out in search of a cigarette. I go to look for him and wander down to the lower level where I find him standing in a corner. He waves me over to a cell occupied by a big white guy around my age who has sleeves of old green tattoos and a long ratty mullet. In the cell with him is a young white kid with close-cropped hair who can't be older than 21. As Smokey and I are standing there talking to them, the kid says, "How many of us came in with you guys?"

"I think there were about thirty," I replied.

"No, man, how many *white guys*?" the kid immediately corrects.

For a second I'm not sure I heard him right. Without missing a beat Smokey replies, "seven." The kid and mullet guy look at each other and shake their heads. Then mullet guy says to Smokey and me as he's handing him some tobacco, a cup, and a towel, "This is for you . . . don't share any of this with the niggers.

They'll be all over you for it, though, so you gotta hold your ground." I say nothing, just slowly back away while Smokey stays and talks to them.

I suppose the honest thing to do would be to admit how shocked I was by their bigoted comments. I don't consider myself naïve—I certainly didn't then—but it had been a long, long time since I had been in the presence of that kind of brazen racism. I felt like I was listening to my grandfather. What I did not know at the time but was soon to discover was that this sentiment not only existed in 2005 but was institutionalized. It would come to dominate my experience at East Moline, at one point threatening my life. It would also become the vehicle by which I would have to confront an even deeper level of disillusionment than I already felt about the society in which I lived and from which I had now been officially disenfranchised.

III

Later that evening the rest of the B Wing inmates went outside on the grounds. New arrivals were not given "movement"—the ability to leave your housing unit—until we were moved to our permanent housing assignment. We milled around our corner of the wing inside those infernal jumpsuits, the tops of which we had unzipped and tied around our waists. The air was stifling. There was one big industrial-sized floor fan recirculating hot air, and none of the breeze it created reached my corner cell, where it was nearly 15 degrees warmer than the rest of the wing. It was unfit to spend any time in, by any standard, and no human being would willingly choose to remain there.

That first night on B Wing was one of the most uncomfortable in my life. It was like trying to sleep in a sauna; our cell was easily 110 degrees with no airflow whatsoever. We couldn't sleep, could hardly breathe, and were stuck to the mattresses as the moisture slowly seeped out of us. My head pounded and my muscles cramped with dehydration, excruciating sensations. I might have panicked, had I the strength, because I couldn't imagine how I was going to survive this for long.

Out of sheer exhaustion I passed out for what couldn't have been more than an hour. I rapidly imploded down into a dark whirring dreamscape, where I found myself paralyzed on my back and smothered as if I were being waterboarded. I woke up thinking I was screaming but it came out more like choking. David was awake below me and kicked the bunk.

"You straight, Chuckie?"

It took only a fraction of a second for me to completely wake up and remember where I was.

"Yeah. I can't breathe, though."

"Sheeeit . . . open your mouth then," he laughed. He kicked the mattress again. "What's the problem, inmate? Our luxury accommodations not good enough for you?"

"Mother's *ass*, it's *hot*!" I moan.

"Man, please. You ain't never lived in no projects. It got like this every summer. It gets so goddamn hot up in dem mufuckas it'll melt the black off ya like a chocolate-covered peanut. Thazz right. That's why I'm so light-skinned. Shit, I used to be darker than Pee-Wee, but all that shit done melted off by the time I was ten."

We both laughed.

"Naw, I'm bullshittin'. What really happened is I got in trouble a lot, and my Moms was always threatenin' to 'smack the black' off me. As you can see, mission accomplished."

"You're pretty clever for a convict."

"We get that way from time to time. Anyway, you'll know what I mean when you meet my big brother. He's blackalicious. He don't look a thing like me."

It was quiet for a moment but for the droning whir of the fan outside on the tier, and then David started freestylin' . . .

I got in trouble a lot
and it was always hot
In the penitentiary,
It's always this way,
It's proper hot today.
I wanna go away, yo
Make a play, yo
Stay away, yo
From the penitentiary.

"Wow," I said. "That's really awful."

"It *sho* is," he laughed. "I don't know nothin' about no rappin', joe."

"No you don't. It's a good thing you're not loose on the streets committing violent rhymes. You're guilty of at least nine counts of illegal use of syntax."

"Yeah, ha ha, motherfucker. I guess now is a bad time to tell you I'm getting' some air blowin' on me from this here window above my head."

▼

The next morning I was moved to a three-man cell on the third floor of the old hospital building, which was called Building 10. My room was known as "the bubble." It was enclosed in glass directly behind a security booth no longer in use. It was a big room, and there was a set of bunk beds in one corner and a single bed in the other. The windows looked south over the Moline Valley. I was told by the C.O. to take the empty top bunk.

About an hour later I met Bryce Krause, my cellmate and the resident of the bottom bunk. He was just shy of his 45th birthday, and he had received 43 years of prison sentences in eight bits over the course of his life for armed robbery, retail theft, obstructing justice, drug possession, forgery, burglary, and aggravated battery of a police officer. He had done time in most of the maximum-security joints in the system and was currently working on a six-year bit for a 2004 burglary conviction.

Krause was a white supremacist and had been a chief in one of the Aryan Nation gangs. He was, as one would expect, a big mean-looking Caucasian with the obligatory close-shorn head. Additional accoutrements were a six-inch-tall "WHITE PRIDE" tattoo across his abdomen and a swastika on his right forearm. He had blue eyes and ruddy red skin and yellow/brown teeth. He was about the most menacing-looking motherfucker I had ever met, and as our situation together unfolded at The Sweet Moline, I would come to consider him one of the worst human beings as well.

But on that first day he was relatively friendly. He joked about the "rent" on my bunk being negotiable, and he reassured me, once I told him what my sentence was, that I'd be out within 60 to 90 days.

"They got too many people in here and a line stretching halfway across the state to get in," he said, and then repeated what everyone else had been telling me: "Bro, you don't know how lucky you are to be here, and they ain't gonna keep you a minute longer than they have to."

Krause told me our third cellmate had been put into segregation the day before I arrived because he got into it with someone on our floor and they ended up throwin' down right there in our cell, right where we were standing. Both guys earned themselves a transfer to a higher-security facility and another year tacked on to their respective sentences.

"So watch it," Krause warned. "This cell has a tendency to make people punchy."

He then launched into the usual litany of questions meant to figure out who I was and what I did "out in the world." I told him I was a journalist and activist, and before he really knew a thing about me, he began, in a sense, pitching me his story and asking if I would help him when I got out, which he assured me would be in 61 days. He pulled a stack of papers from his lockbox and showed them to me.

It was a paper trail of his attempts to get treated for Hepatitis C. Krause shot drugs most of his life and, as he put it, "stuck it to enough dirty women to get it that way too." By the time I met him he didn't look so good. His torso was round and distended from the inflammation to his liver, and his skin was ruddy and greasy. He also smelled pretty foul.

"You gotta understand," he began in the clipped long "a" accent that is characteristic of the white working class from the southern areas of Chicago, "people are *dyin'*. IDOC won't give us no treatment cause it costs too much and the Feds won't fund it needer. They'll give money for fuckin' HIV for the fuckin' fags, but not for Hep C for us normal people. They ain't even tellin' guys if they have it."

He told me what kinds of treatment were and weren't available. He said he wanted interferon and a combination of other drugs he had heard worked better than those he was taking. He claimed he was always sick, and had lost his sex drive, which he didn't mind given the circumstances, but that he hadn't had an erection in months and that wasn't normal.

"This all started once Wexford came around."

"Who's Wexford?" I asked.

"Not who, what. They got the health care contract."

I told Krause I wanted to take a few notes and asked if he had paper and a pen, which he did, doling me out a sheet. I knelt on the floor before my lockbox and used it as a desk as I scribbled out "Krause . . . Hep C . . . Wexford . . . Interferon . . . '*People are dyin'!*'"

Pittsburgh-based Wexford Health Sources is America's third largest correctional health care company serving 90,000 inmates at more than 100 facilities in 13 states. They have an extensive record of lawsuits in Alabama, Florida, Illinois, Michigan, Mississippi, New Mexico, Pennsylvania, and Wyoming for shady business practices and substandard health care in the prisons. Interestingly enough in a 1999 Pennsylvania case a former medical director at Wexford sued the company, claiming he was fired because he disagreed with a plan to begin treating Hep C with an experimental and unproven drug—in effect, using the prisoners as guinea pigs.

In 2004, amidst a rash of controversy, Wexford was granted a $114 million contract to provide health care to IDOC. The *Chicago Sun-Times* reported that this came about mere days after Wexford contributed $10,000 to then-Governor Rod Blagojevich's reelection campaign. In July 2007 former IDOC director Donald Snyder was indicted for allegedly taking $50,000 in illegal kickbacks to hand out state contracts to favored companies during the previous administration of George Ryan, $30,000 of which came from Wexford lobbyist Larry Sims.

Krause complained about Rod Blagojevich, who, after becoming governor of Illinois in 2002, unable to close any prisons, immediately slashed IDOC's budget, citing the $4 billion state deficit as his rationale. Krause claimed the food quality had taken a nose dive alongside health care. This was not surprising since Aramark, the international food service leviathan, held the contract.

Headquartered in Philadelphia, Aramark has approximately 240,000 employees serving clients in 18 countries. Publicly traded since 2001, they pulled in $12.4 billion in sales in 2007 from food and hospitality services for businesses, schools, stadiums, hotels and resorts, and senior assisted living. They also manage large facilities, provide a vast array of uniforms and work apparel, and have contracts for food, laundry, and uniforms at 475 correctional institutions. Aramark's record is almost as scintillating as Wexford's. For two health-based companies, the level of sickness attributed to their products and services is staggering.

The $10 million IDOC contract "awarded" to Aramark in 2000 was a sole-source, no-bid deal. Aramark has been accused of fraud and over-billing, driving up state budget deficits, poor service, and poor treatment of workers. Their worst transgression (considering the nature of the hand that feeds them) appears to be serving tainted food to schools and universities. On two occasions rodents and worms had been found in school lunches. Here in Illinois, Aramark paid more than $3 million to settle a 2004 class action suit charging they defrauded approximately 50 school districts in the state by accepting national school lunch program food donations from the USDA without reducing the cost for the schools, which was in violation of federal law and the district's food service contract.

If the food is bad in the schools, one can only imagine what it is like in the prisons. The list of Aramark's prison indiscretions spans correctional systems in Illinois, Texas, Oregon, Tennessee, New Jersey, New York, Missouri, and Florida. However, tales of bad prison food shock no one, so it's a waste of space to even make that a story point. What's interesting is the number of scandals in which Aramark finds itself embroiled.

In the same case that brought indictments against former IDOC director Donald Snyder and John J. Robinson, a former lobbyist, Senior Vice President for Aramark, and Undersheriff of Cook County (take a moment to drink in all those luscious conflicts of interest), pled guilty in July of 2007 to federal charges of mail fraud relating to alleged kickbacks paid to Snyder. While Aramark contracts were not implicated in the indictment, Robinson did obtain correctional food service contracts for Aramark from Illinois state and local governments. Connecting the dots on that one does not take a Herculean measure of aptitude, and one is hard-pressed to differentiate between the criminals in prison blues shuffling around the yard and those in business suits running the show.

Krause blamed Blagojevich for everything wrong with IDOC, which was a wee bit of hyperbole and misplaced blame. Blagojevich may have been the smarmiest politician in recorded history, but he was small potatoes as far as political corruption in Illinois goes, and there was plenty wrong with the prison system long before Blago showed up. Krause swore up and down that Blago's predecessor, George Ryan, was good to the prisons, because inmates ate better and had more programs and health care options. That didn't surprise me. It was only 2005, but most people had already forgotten that back in 2000 Governor Ryan emptied Death Row and put a moratorium on the Illinois death penalty, reigniting the global debate on capital punishment.

Ever since the death penalty was reinstated in 1977 in Illinois, 12 death row inmates had been executed while 17 had been exonerated and released, giving Illinois the highest rate of overturned capital convictions of all 38 states with the death penalty. Ryan later commuted all the state's pending 167 death sentences to life in prison after finding out that most of the cases appeared to have been built upon falsified or suppressed evidence and confessions elicited by torture. Many of these illegal police activities and fraudulent convictions dated back to the 1980s and implicated former Chicago Police Chief John Burge, a reprehensible character if there ever was one, and Chicago mayor and Democrat powerhouse Richard M. Daley, who had been serving as Illinois Attorney General.

Ryan's decision to empty Death Row earned him a nomination for the Nobel Peace Prize and a federal indictment for corruption on unrelated charges, a prosecution Ryan insists was politically motivated both to silence the newly reinvigorated movement against the death penalty and to protect Daley. Like in Blagojevich's case, the petty bribes and corruptions that eventually landed Ryan 6½ years in federal prison were measly offenses (often committed by others unbeknownst to Ryan) compared to what the rest of the state's political body was up to on a regular and systemic basis. The 75-year-old Ryan is scheduled to be released sometime in 2012, if he lives that long. Later, I will discuss the ongoing attempts over the years to bring Burge to justice. And the former five-term Mayor Daley remains the most powerful man in Illinois.

IV

Every inmate at East Moline receives a work assignment. Krause worked in the maintenance and grounds department.

"It's a choice job, bro. The guy who runs it is a good old boy so there ain't no shines workin' with us, just our own. I get to pick who works with us, so I got my ride[10] Bob transferred there."

Bob was Robert "Cockeyed Bob" Schranz, a former IDOC correctional officer who was doing a three-piece (three-year sentence) for burglary. Krause and Schranz had met in the early 1990s at the old Stateville max prison when Krause was doing his first bit for armed robbery and Schranz was a C.O. Schranz would supply Krause and his White Power boys with whatever they needed from the outside world, and from what they told me, they hooked up many a caper together once released. Their entire lives revolved around drugs and prison.

Cockeyed Bob was manic. He never shut off. He was constantly wound and spun, twitchy and stuck at maximum volume, forever animated, doing bits, telling jokes, and relentlessly fucking with people. Sometimes he would make you laugh so hard you thought you'd puke, other times he was so annoying you wanted to throw him off the roof. There was definitely something off about this cat. When he stared straight at you with those dark beady crossed eyes, he looked totally psychotic. You just knew his central processor had been fried a long time ago.

These guys epitomized the worst types of recidivist criminal (and the fine line between cop and criminal), the kind of violent, diseased, drug-addled sociopath who, by his very existence, keeps drugs illegal, Republicans in office, and the Fox News Channel on the air. They were the veritable *casus belli* for the whole "tough on crime" ideology, the kind of junkie that would stop at nothing to feed his habit, the kind of convict even the reformers, myself included, claim should be behind bars. And here's the irony: despite a public that is inculcated with news reports of black-faced criminals, and a massively disproportionate percentage of black inmates in all 50 states, this type of incorrigible career criminal is almost exclusively white. If you removed all those incarcerated for only the strict low-level sale or possession of drugs, most of your young gang-bangers would vanish.

This point becomes more salient when you begin to understand the dynamics of prison drama. Serial offenders have spent so much time being socialized in a prison setting that it's the only way they know how to function. Most of the brothers who are slangin' dope are like hourly employees of a huge corporation—if they get popped then they go do their time, keepin' the drama low, so they get out alive and get their asses back to work. The ones who don't know anything but prison are the most dangerous.

My rapid descent into their dark and twisted reality began as I spent the next two days, July 22 and 23, inside Building 10. During those two days all outside movement was canceled due to the ongoing heat wave, so we were restricted to the deafening, sweltering housing units. This would happen another nine times during my stay at East Moline, as the summer went on to record 30 days over 90 degrees. It made for some seriously cranky convicts.

On July 24, 2005, months into a journey that began with my arrest in March, I finally began a daily journal scribbled on a quarter-inch-thick stack of old dot matrix printer paper that the library used for book inventories. What follows is reproduced directly from those handwritten pages with minimal alterations—except for certain entries that were coded to avoid writing down anything that either was incriminating, could be misconstrued as incriminating, or could directly lead to my harm. Those details I entered later following my release. This way, without the softening or sharpening touch of revision and reflection, the rawness of the experience unfolds in real time.

DAILY JOURNAL
JULY 24, 2005

Early in the morning I walked into the day room and found this 22-year old bald thick-necked white kid named Slade talking to a few other guys about needing to write a letter to his State Rep so he could try and get transferred to work release. It seemed to really intimidate him, so I offered to help. He looked at me like I had just asked to screw his sister, so I quickly explained that I "wrote for a living" and could probably help him sound pretty good. His response was to shove a few papers in my face, claiming they were transcripts from a writing or communications course he had taken. "I know what I'm doin', look at this," he kept saying. When I looked at the draft of his letter it was clear that he did not. I offered again, and he told me once again that he knew what he was doing and he "ain't no idiot." I told him it didn't matter to me, I was just tryin' to help.

We dosey-doed back and forth for another few moments before he handed over a piece of paper and a pen and said, "Let's see what you can do." I wrote out a draft for him, which he read. He didn't say anything, but he looked me over a few more times, then packed up his papers and split.

Later that night after lights-out I was lying at the foot of my bed trying to read by the dim light coming from the hall, and Slade came walking by with a broom and started sweeping the day room. He saw me reading, walked away, and then a minute later returned with a small desk lamp. He opened our door and handed it to me.

"I need that back soon," he said, "so read fast."

I thanked him and he brushed it off, saying, "We take care of our own."

Who, or what, is "our own?"

JULY 25, 2005

It is a rare occasion when any of the inmates watches the news, but whenever the topic of terrorism arises the racial divide becomes quite noticeable, and quite partisan. Almost without exception, white inmates are pro-military, pro-US, and viciously anti-Muslim. Older black inmates, particularly if they are veterans, don't trust anything they hear and regularly call what they see on TV bullshit, often times yelling "shit" at the screen to the effect they believe the government is behind it. It gives us a lot to talk about. The young black inmates couldn't care less and are largely oblivious. They're only interested in hip-hop, sex, drug dealing, or gang-banging. That gives us little to talk about.

Most, if not all, of the white C.O.s are fanatically patriotic. All across the complex are posted faded newspaper clip-outs from the days following 9/11. "We Shall Never Forget!" "God Bless America!" etc. etc. Maybe they think because they wear a "uniform" they are also part of the same paramilitary cadre as cops and firefighters. I wonder if they have any idea that the government they so zealously defend shipped their lifestyles overseas to cheaper labor markets and left them nothing but this shitty prison job and a cheap poly-blend uniform.

The white C.O.s express a great deal of ignorance and bigotry, and they do it with such galling arrogance. It's *so* clear how much they hate us. Most of them buzz their heads and roll up their sleeves above their biceps and wear Revos like they are in the Special Forces. I'm fairly certain they are unaware how ridiculous they look. They pomp and strut and if you dare look at them, they'll rip you a new asshole and call you every degrading name in the book. They are constantly trying to provoke inmates into losing their cool; they seem to get a perverse thrill out of it. You can't imagine how hard it is for me to keep my mouth shut.

Not surprisingly, the black C.O.s are a lot cooler than the whites. The black guards just seem to chill and wait for their shift to end. I don't know whether they got hustles going with brothers on the blocks, or they just don't believe in being assholes, but they actually spend time talking to inmates.

▼

I was hanging around with "Smitty," a friendly and intelligent 25-year-old Downstate kid who is in for cooking meth. Probably should qualify that. Yes, cooking. Yes, it was meth. There ain't much else to do in rural Downstate Illinois. But it's important to understand that Smitty was only cooking small amounts for personal consumption. Yes, meth totally sucks and perhaps he should not have been doing it, but he wasn't dealing, and he knew what he was doing, and he wasn't endangering anyone else but himself. Smitty got busted because he got turned in by someone who got picked up for some other charge and ratted him out to save his own ass. I realize I may be alone in defending him, but I'm of the opinion that he deserves defense, and that this case highlights yet another vaguely defined grey area into which people disappear, invariably ending up on the down side. Perhaps this is just another projection of my own shit.

Smitty and I were talking about prison culture—the day-to-day life of being incarcerated, the different ethics and value sets that direct life inside—and he made a really interesting observation.

"The basics of gratitude, honor and selflessness . . ., the stuff the outside world takes for granted, are alive and well inside here. When you got nothin', you're grateful for whatever you can get, 'cause you know it took a lot to get it. You gotta have honor in a closed society like this, or else you got nothin'. You don't steal other people's shit, you don't talk shit, and you don't conspire, unless you got good cause, and everyone knows whether you have good cause or not 'cause everyone knows your business. And when you got to rely on other people for your survival, you learn to be selfless first, 'cause you never know when you're gonna need them to have your back. It's a serious reality check. And for as tough as all these bangers are, I have never seen so many cowards and hypocrites in all my life. You and I are basically racially blind, but in many of the white guys' eyes, we are worse than 'niggers' since we tend to gravitate to the black guys.

"And beyond the pettiness of their racial fears, most of the inmates behave like teenage girls. How superficial is the shit in here? They all dress alike, eat the same shit in the same way, and do the same stupid shit day in and day out. Dude, you got called a 'fag' by nearly every guy on this floor because your shorts didn't hang down low enough. They told you if you didn't want to get your ass beat, you better find another pair of shorts! And God forbid you and just one other person are in the shower, the third guy who walks in will automatically assume you were sucking each other's dicks. It's totally ridiculous."

Smitty shrugged in exasperation. It amused him. He conveyed such a sense of calm that it really helped me lighten up for a minute.

"These are little bitches in here," he said, and popped out a huge toothy smile.

We both laughed hard. It was probably the first time I had laughed in weeks, though I found myself looking over my shoulder as I was doing it.

JULY 27, 2005

The resentment of the long-timers for us short-timers or first-timers is palpable, even though we don't have any control over where they send us. One of the guys that work in the library told me, "I've seen you sixty-one-day wonders go through here *thirty times* since I first got transferred here, and it took me five years of ass-kissin' just to get myself transferred here."

Yesterday, that kid Slade came into our cell with a bunch of other cats who had all done some max time—these guys were serious bruisers—and Slade said to me, "I think all you little pussy-ass first-timers should have to go to The Pit (the nickname of the max prison in Menard, Illinois). I *guar-an-tee* you will never go back to the joint again."

I pointed out that it hadn't seemed to stop him from coming back. He didn't say much to that, so I tried to explain to him that *most* people in the Illinois prison system, particularly these days, are more like me, petty nonviolent offenders, than him. Most have no concept of violent crime, much less the brutality of the max joints. This seemed to be lost on him. Violence is all many of these guys have ever known, particularly the group of serious recidivists that tend to gravitate to inmates like Krause and Cockeyed Bob. They definitely don't know what to make of me.

They see me reading and writing and watching the news and bitching about politics to anyone who will listen. And they got hip real quick-like to my gingerly dropped suggestions of tolerance, though I stray far away from hot-button issues like race or homosexuality, particularly with these boys, since they are all avowed White Power. They tease me about it, but so far have generally left me alone. They do tell me I should praise God I'm in a min joint, because if I had been sent to a max, "You'd be our fuckin' house maid in a dress cleaning our cells and sucking our dicks, and we'd have already taken all your shit," Krause tells me, his breath stinking of pinto beans.

It's chilling to hear. I sometimes experience these surges of panic and anxiety. I know it is only because I am here that I am spared that hell, and I *do* often find myself thinking about divine intervention, particularly since I landed here at The Sweet Moline. Smokey is not so lucky. Because he's from Bridgeport, and he wants to hang with these guys, they've already started the initiation process and are regularly pounding on him. Not to hurt him, just to "toughen him up," although it sure as fuck looks like it hurts to me. They see Smokey as weak, a spineless, shit-talking junkie, which is exactly what he is. But since he's a racist white kid from Bridgeport, he gets a pass and gets to be in the club, albeit as the combination punching bag/mascot. He has no real value to them; in fact, he's a parasite, always begging tobacco or whatever. At some point, they are going to make him justify his continued presence, which invariably means servitude.

My value—education and literacy—may also be why they don't fuck with me too bad, since I hooked Slade up and promised to help Krause with his Hep C treatment once I got out, but you'd never get them to admit it. In those few one-on-one moments I have had with them, they seem naturally curious to learn things. In a group, however, education suddenly becomes a weakness, something to taunt. There is virtually no individualism here; it's antithetical to the gang ethos. You can only imagine what it is like for me. I'm a fucking freak of nature to these cats. I think part of the reason they haven't really fucked with me yet is that I confuse them. They can't know too many other people like me out in the world, where I'm sure they see a hundred Smokeys a day.

Smokey ended up hating me pretty quickly probably because every time he would offer some bullshit excuse for why his life was the way it was, I would simply show him that it was his choices, decisions, and lack of will to change that landed him in prison. He seems pathologically incapable of taking responsibility for anything in his life. Everything is someone else's fault and he's always the victim. It's clear he hates himself; the loathing just slides off him like melting skin.

Smokey jumped on the bandwagon and made a few snide comments about my education, the usual class-based stuff. I can just see the resentment dripping off his face; somehow now he's convinced himself that I'm more responsible for Smokey being in prison than Smokey is. I really would pity him if he didn't disgust me so much. I saw his true colors the day we arrived when he went from hanging out with me and Smitty and David and Pee-Wee to following around the white supremacists like an abused puppy, talking all the same racist shit as them. I was totally flabbergasted; it really came out of nowhere. But there it was.

I mean, maybe it's me that's sounding naïve now, but what kind of person chooses to hang around a bunch of quasi-simian rednecks who want nothing more than to beat him from sunup to sundown? Carl Jung would have had a field day with Smokey.

JULY 28, 2005

Today was very strange.

Edward Yancy, the East Moline Educational Director, summoned me to his office. I had no idea who he was or why he wanted to see me.

I asked a few brothers who had been around East Moline for a while who he was and what it might be about. They all laughed and made comments like "Yancy lookin' for a new boyfriend." I pressed for more information, but the only other thing I was told was that it was probably "because I had to get my GED." I was royally confused, more so because no one else that arrived at East Moline with me seemed to get this request.

"When I saw your file I just had to talk to you in person. Boy, what the fuck are you doin' here?" was the first thing Yancy said to me.

He was short, black, and middle-aged with horn-rimmed glasses. He spoke boisterously and with authority, but it came from a different place than force. Yancy, clearly, was a smart dude. His office was lined with books on progressive politics and history, and he had this vibe of someone who expected more.

Apparently, Yancy had been around East Moline since the early '80s. He explained that as educational director his job was to make sure that every inmate had GED certification before he was released. He said he used to be in charge of actual educational programs, but they had mostly been eliminated over the years. "But if you got family that want to pay for it, you can get a correspondence degree." The fact that I had a BA from Boston University made me rarer than a dog that practices reiki.

Yancy was looking at me with what I could only describe as a mix of amusement, skepticism, and fascination. He said that my file was "very interesting" but declined to tell me what was in it. He did, however, ask me about my work as a journalist and probed deeper into my beliefs and motivations. I explained to him how only a few months before I got to East Moline I had published a number of articles on the drug war and the prison system, with a particular focus on IDOC.

But as the words were coming out of my mouth, I was suddenly overcome with the feeling that I had just made a terrible mistake. I didn't know where this cat was coming from, nor why I was trusting him when I shouldn't have been, and I really started to feel like a schmuck. He asked me what happened in my case, how I got locked up, and I told him the story, the whole story.

Yancy paused a second, just staring me down in silence. Then he laughed and said, "You know, you are one seriously stupid mother-fucker, doncha?" I had no idea where it was going, but I was convinced that it was headed in a bad direction. I said nothing.

"As you probably have guessed by now, Shaw, we don't get a lot like you around here. So I had to take time out of my very busy schedule, which I cannot spare, to talk to you, because I needed to let you know that you fucked up. Do you see how you fucked up?"

I explained that yes, I had full awareness of my fuck-uppage, and that I had already taken time to think about it, and had much more ahead of me.

"Well, the problem is, you don't even belong here! You're taking a bed and $20,000 of tax money from the good people of the proud State of Illinois—not to mention my precious time—from someone who deserves to be in here and needs my services."

"I'm more than happy to offer my space to someone else," I said. "I can be ready to go home in five minutes."

He laughed. "I wish I had that power, but I don't. I don't have any power around here."

Yancy paused again, cracking some sunflower seeds on his desk and popping them into his mouth. Then he gave me a smirk that I just couldn't figure out.

"So, you know about all this shit, right? How rigged this game is? You know, right?"

"Of course," I said.

"Knowin' that, how did you ever let yourself get sent up in here?"

"Part of me thinks it was my fate," I replied. "Karma."

"Karma, huh? Hmpf. Well, lemme tell you 'bout Karma. In 1983, right around the time I started working for IDOC, right before the whole crack thing went crazy and the drug war really got cookin', there were thirteen prisons in this state. And they were full of some truly dastardly sonzabitches. Today, there are twenty-eight! And they are full, and there's more comin' every day, except, they aren't necessarily dastardly sonzabitches anymore. Look around you, man. You've seen this place. You see they got enough of *our* people locked up in here, so now they're coming after you and yours. They didn't really hurtcha by sending you here, they just embarrassed you a little. Gave you one year so that they can walk on out to the public and say, *Racial profiling? Warehousing the poor? Nossir! We got us some white folk up in hyeah too, some college-educated white folk!* What I'm tryin' to say to you, son, is that they don't care anymore. This is a business, and now they're lockin' up *everybody*. You *should have known better*."

I did not expect him to be so frank, and I really did not expect myself to be seeing eye to eye with him. He was as qualitatively different from the rest of the IDOC staff as you can get. Still, knowing that did not prepare me for what I heard next.

"Shaw . . . we need more advocates out there tellin' folks what's really goin' on in here. And if you're in here, you're wasting that opportunity, and your responsibility. This little bit you got now is your free ride. You're here for a reason. You need to listen and you need to *observe*. You need to learn, and you need to take this knowledge out of here. Hopefully I can help prepare you for when you leave here, because you won't be totally changed. You'll be wiser, hipper to the game, more aware of your surroundings and your situation. But you're still going to need to change. You don't realize yet how selfish you are going to need to be to stay out of here, and also how *selfless* you will need to be at the same time in order to put yourself and your future on the line for this message. I know that's what you are thinking too, but there ain't no heroics in this shit. People will not love you for doing this. They will revile you. You just gotta always remember that you're fucked up, and so long as you do, you'll stay humble. It don't matter how many old ladies you help across the street or babies you take care of or how much you preach that you're harmless, when you touch the right nerve out there, you'll be more dangerous than any of the knuckleheads in here."

Yancy said he wanted to talk to me more. I asked him if I could get a work assignment teaching one of the classes or tutoring, like I did in County back in '99. He said he'd check it out.

As I started to walk out of his office he said, "Shaw, you're in a very exclusive club now. Martin, Malcolm, Mandela, Mahatma . . . they were all prisoners."

"Man, I think that's stretching it a bit. None of them were crackheads."

"Don't you be so sure. Before they became who we understand them to be, Malcolm loved that cocaine, and Mohandis loved that opium pipe. That ain't the point, son."

"It's just that enough people have accused me of having delusions of grandeur that I'm not sure this is the healthiest way to go about this."

"Great men are made by great deeds. It don't matter what came before. Don't let it weigh on ya. You will not be coming back here because God gave you a mission, son, and my job is to see that you carry it out. Now get the fuck out of here."

It wouldn't have been half as weird if the Rev back at County hadn't told me I would be meeting one of "God's messengers" who would help lead me through. This shit is off the hook. Really? I don't know what to make of it, but it's definitely doing a number on my head.

Did I mention things were getting weird?

The first book I check out from the library is Ralph Ellison's *Invisible Man*. I don't know why I was so drawn to it, since I had read it in college, but I felt this overwhelming compulsion to read it again. And you are not going to believe what I found when I started reading:

> Perhaps the sense of magic lay in the unexpected transformations. "You start Saul, and end up Paul," my grandfather had often said. "When you're a youngun, you Saul. But let life whup your head a bit, and you starts trying to be Paul—though you still Saul around on the side." No, you could never tell where you were going, that was a sure thing. The only sure thing. Nor could you tell how you'd get there—though when you arrived, it was somehow right.

How am I supposed to take that as a coincidence? I mean the hair is standing up on the back of my neck.

Be careful what you ask for, you just might get it.

▼

I just met Rich, my new cellie who took the last bed in our three-man. He told me he just got transferred up from Shawnee, after serving 10 years—his mandatory half—of a 20-year sentence for home invasion and attempted murder. He gets out in March of 2006, so he's here to "transition." He's a big, big ole country boy from Downstate. He's never seen the Internet, and it's clear he has no clue how the world has changed since 1994. It blows my mind.

Rich also believes first-timers like me should not be able to come to East Moline. "What the hell do y'all learn from comin' here? Nothin'!" I told him I learned plenty. I learned I wouldn't be coming back, that was for sure, and wasn't that the point?

While I am talking to Rich, Krause is telling Smokey not to apply his academic good time—extra time off your sentence for people who complete GED certification—to his sentence but instead "save it for your next bit." I am totally flummoxed by that kind of thinking, and I think they heard my jaw bounce off my mattress because they all paused a second and looked at me.

What the hell do they want from me? This is pure, unadulterated self-defeatism! First of all it convinces me that Smokey will be back, but it also gives credence to what Rich was saying: small-time drug users shouldn't be allowed to come here. Well, I say violent motherfuckers like him should have to prove they have been rehabilitated (however that can be shown in a system that offers virtually no rehabilitation). They shouldn't expect to come here just because they didn't kill someone while doing their bit. I have listened to these guys, and I can tell you without even being here a week they are anything but rehabilitated. I am willing to bet a non-essential organ like my gall bladder that every one of them will go back to a criminal lifestyle once released.

I started to make a class argument in my head about how I thought Krause and Cockeyed Bob and Rich were trying to keep Smokey in their "criminal underclass," but then I realized, wait a minute, Smokey *is* a slimeball and maybe they see that too and realize he will more than likely become one of the 60% who re-enter prison within three years of their release. Maybe they knew better than me that Smokey was hopeless, and that I was a hopelessly naïve idealist.

Then again, misery do love company, don't it?

JULY 29, 2005

It was just about yesterday, almost a month into my bit and a full week into the routine of The Sweet Moline, that I began to lose my shit for the first time. About ten minutes ago I had a serious H.A.L.T. moment (Hungry-Angry-Lonely-Tired: a popular acronym in recovery culture, signifying a high probability of relapse) where I had to stop and get it together to avoid crying or snapping. Had I given in to either, I would have been in some serious shit. I was so, so lonely for my friends and family and for just one substantial conversation. It was beginning to make me angry. The adolescent pettiness of Krause and Cockeyed Bob and Smokey and Slade was driving me crazy!

I went to find Smitty instead. I barged into his cell bitching my ass off about the rednecks and how close I was to snapping, and he was totally cool and offered sympathy and understanding. It took me a minute to realize, though, that something was really eating him. He was always smiling and now he was *pissed*.

I asked him if everything was OK, and he showed me a letter from his girlfriend that had just come in today. When Smitty got busted, they charged his lady along with him and as a result she is now serving time at the women's prison in Dalton. Smitty swears up and down she had nothing to do with his cooking and I believe him.

It gets worse. Smitty's girlfriend was four months pregnant when they got arrested, and their baby will be born behind bars and could potentially be taken away from them by the State. No, she was not using, she and the baby are perfectly healthy. This is why Smitty is desperate to show IDOC that he's serious about getting into the drug program. He's 25. He deserves a chance to prove himself.

"Shit, man, this place may not be the worst, but it's still *prison*. There are still razor wire fences and guns and bars and seg. And this place . . . this place is more of a mental prison. This place tests your strength and integrity. Can you rise above the convict mentality? Can you create positive change? Be an individual? I think that's harder."

Smitty paused, looked at the letter, looked back at me, ruminated. He was struggling.

"We have to be here for a higher purpose, don't we Chuckie?"

"That's how I live with it," I told him. "But by believing that, it means that I subscribe to the belief that there's somehow something special about me, and every time I start thinking that there's something special about me, I end up in a situation like this."

"You've never been here before. Nothing about this experience is who you really are as a person."

"I don't know. Is that true? The laws may be unjust, but I still broke them. And I could say all those things about you as well."

"Were Caesar's laws unjust?"

"Not to Caesar. And he had the Praetorian to enforce them. All I got is a big vocabulary and a dog with huge ears."

"Chuckie, this place is definitely our Damascus road. We gotta put the past behind us. We gotta hang on to that and not let the rest get to us. We're not like these guys, we're not *malleable*. That's why the White Power boys leave us alone. They're afraid of us. They know they'll lose any kind of rational argument, and all they have is brute force, and they can't use it here without screwing themselves too."

I told Smitty I didn't think for a moment they were afraid of us. They were afraid of getting shipped and getting more time. But push them far enough, and they'll snap. I was seriously freaked out about that.

"How you and I act out there in the world," he said, "calm and nonviolent, that's how they have to act in here. Don't worry, you won't have to fight."

It didn't do much to assuage my fears. Maybe the White Power bloc would leave me alone, but this was not a happy place. There were about a thousand other cats in the joint who I just might happen to cross paths with on the one day they decide to lose *their* shit and I just happen to become convenient collateral damage.

But if I were honest with myself, I would have to admit that what I am most afraid of is *me* losing my shit and mouthing off to the wrong dude. In my world, people generally don't fight, so people feel free to mouth off to anyone they want, opting to beat them up intellectually or psychologically. These cats don't play that shit. They hit first and reach for the dictionary later. It's so ingrained in me that it's often unconscious, and although I am reminding myself now as I write this, I fear for the first moment I forget.

▼

Rich and Krause were talking in the cell this afternoon as I was lying in my bunk reading. Rich was showing Krause his photo album and letters from his family. At one point he pulled out a large bound photocopied book that looked like one of those Kinko's specials.

"This is my family history," he said, flipping pages proudly. He stopped on one page and pointed at it hard. Krause smiled approvingly. "The Klan marches on," Rich said, holding up a page that displayed a photo of some of Rich's KKK descendants gathered for a lovely group portrait. "I got my granddaddy's hood and robe at home in my closet," he says, without irony.

My stomach flipped over.

Krause pipes in, "Yeah, you know, you gotta fight for your own. These fuckin' people are tryin' to take away all our traditions."

I wasn't sure who "these fuckin' people" were, but it was obvious he was defending the Klan and I was so disgusted I hopped down and left the cell, not knowing if they registered my disgust, but hoping they hadn't in the interest of preserving peace. But man, it was seriously hard to contain myself. It's beginning to get David Lynch–style surreal living with these cats. I just cannot believe people like this still exist. Yet there they are . . .

Later, when I came back, the whole White Power crew was in there, and Krause had his pants down around his thighs like how all the brothers wear them, and he was goin' on and on with "Yo, Joe! Deez my niggaz!" The whole herd of these cracker organ sacks were snorting and guffawing and giggling like preschoolers. Then Rich says, "Yeah, they are a whole different breed, aren't they." He paused a second as if he was in deep thought, then said, "Goddamn baboons!"

At that moment I think I felt more alienated and alone and utterly irritated than at any other moment in my life. I started thinking about Krause's Hep C and I said to myself, *You know what, fuck him, let him die. A man with that much hatred in his heart deserves to be sick and suffer. It's probably part of his punishment, why the fuck should I help him?*

But then I started thinking, *He's a human being, he's got a terminal illness, and he's being denied care, and no one gives a shit about him, is that fair?* A voice asked me how could I ever hope to effect real change if I judge and perpetuate the same animosity and divisive behavior? Knowing that change begins in the human heart, what has really changed? What was the right thing to do? What would a humanitarian do? What would Jeebus do?

▼

I ran into David in the yard where we usually hook up at least once a day, and I told him about what had gone down earlier in my cell with "KKK Hour." As I unfolded the story I could see the shock, astonishment, and then hurt on his face, and I began to wish I hadn't told him. It was one thing to hear that shit myself; it was something else entirely to repeat it to someone at whom those hateful words were directed.

But David seemed to shake it off and said, "I just pity those people. You can't have nothin' but pity for them, 'cause they pitiful. Shit, they tell us, go back to Africa, go back to where you came from. And I'm thinkin', shit, you the motherfuckers who brought us here, put clothes on us, put Jesus on us. Y'all ain't even from here either. You got no more claim on this land than I do."

I have been contemplating requesting a move, but when I think about it, I realize there is so much more I can learn simply by listening and observing. Lord knows there is much more I could learn about patience and self-control and keeping my mouth shut in the face of a great deal of anger and disgust.

I admire David for the same reasons I admire Smitty: both are open-minded *individuals* who judge people on their actions, not their appearances. Both love their children and want a better life for them. Both honestly want to change their lives, and their actions bear that out. Both are more interested in talking about life with me than screwing around with all these convicts, and both of them are generous to a fault, even when things are scarce. It shocks me that they are both only 25 years old.

I know, in some strange jailhouse way, that both of them look up to me, but it's hard for me to see myself in that role. Yet the infantilism here defies description. Krause and Cockeyed Bob are little more than a pair of emotionally retarded teenagers, and that's clearly a consequence of their lifelong addictions and incarcerations; they have yet to grow up. By spending most of their time on the inside, the system keeps them from ever being able to assume most of the responsibilities of adulthood. If society really wanted these guys to mature, they'd make sure they have jobs and some kind of support community when they get out of here, instead of $20 in gate money and a promise to "See ya soon!"

Last night something else dawned on me as I was sitting there on my top bunk observing them (I honestly think they forget I am there sometimes, and other times I know they are seriously hamming it up because they have an audience). They behave and interact remarkably like a middle-aged married couple. When you consider their attitudes towards women—which is to say misogyny *in extremis*—and the fact that they have never had either a healthy relationship or a family that gave two shits about them, it's pretty clear they find themselves able to love one another when the rest of the world would likely find them despicable.

They spend all their time together, and that's the only time either of them laughs or smiles. They feed each other, share belongings, and constantly make gay jokes about each other. You don't need a master's in clinical psychology to figure that one out.

Still, they'll never act on it physically. They constantly joke about homosexuality: "Hey, in the joint you do what you have to do to get by." I don't think they realize how much unspoken validation they give the idea. Like David, I pity them. For all their brute strength, they are hypocrites and cowards.

▽

The library has become my personal sanctuary. I was really surprised to learn they even had one, much less one with real books and an interlibrary loan program. From what I'm told, this is the best library in the whole IDOC system. Virtually no one uses it. Big phuckin' surprise, right?

There are typewriters available, but the process of writing all of this by hand helps make each thought more brief and deliberate (the carpal tunnel hurts like hell, though, and I haven't written by hand in any extended sense since college). This gives me something to think about every day, a time to withdraw into my own mind (albeit, a strange and challenging landscape) and contemplate what is happening around me. It gives me a chance to slow down and make sense of things, but also to remind myself why I am here. Being relatively alienated from the usual social dynamics of this place has helped me remain more objective, and hopefully that will show. Sometimes it's just good to write out that which plagues your mind moment to moment. It makes the ideas more tangible and real.

▼

Krause, Cockeyed Bob, and The Klansman (my new nickname for Rich) were in our cell listening to the radio *really, really* loudly—I think the song I walked in on was "Radar Love"—and I was suddenly struck by an eternal vision of Hell spent with these cats listening to bad classic rock, a kind of redneck *No Exit*. I attempted to read, but they didn't give a shit. In fact, I felt like they were getting a big ole charge out of seeing me grow increasingly annoyed, albeit in as subdued a manner as I could muster. At one point this U2 song came on—"Pride"—and when it was over, The Klansman turned off the radio and Cockeyed Bob goes, "Good fuckin' music, but that fuckin' Bono guy is too political. They'd be better if he wasn't so political."

Against the impassioned counsel of my conscience, who was screaming for me to let it go, I asked Bob, "What does 'too political' mean?" My conscience could have lived with just that, but not with what I said next. "And what do you know about politics?"

I heard my brain say, *Oh no you did-int!? I'm outta here! You're on your own, pal*, and my mouth—now running on the back-up system that was almost exclusively powered by my ass—continued on with, "He works on poverty and AIDS in Africa. Is that political?"

Bob simply scowls, and then walks out of the cell to go punch Smokey, who was walking by looking for a cigarette to bum from someone. But The Klansman pipes in and says—he actually says this . . . with his mouth . . . and, I imagine, at one point, the connivance of his brain:

"AIDS is God's way of saying there are too many niggers in the world."

"That's lovely. Thanks for offering that," I responded.

"Well, tell me if I'm wrong?"

"You're wrong," I said, and then left the cell again for a while before I said something worse. When I came back in later just before dinner to get my blue shirt, Cockeyed Bob was back in our cell and he asks me, "What do you know about AA?"

"Alcoholics Anonymous?"

"No, dickweed. AIDS in Africa!" Then he starts cackling like the inbred twit he is, like that was the funniest thing he had ever heard in his life.

Bob sees me annoyed as hell and asks me, in a baby voice, "*What's wong?*"

I respond, "I'm just shocked there are still people like you in the world."

Bob noticeably changes his tone and walks right up into my face. "*We're* your people, ride." (He calls everybody "ride.")

"You are most definitely *not* my people. I have nothing in common with any of you."

I walked out again to go to get in the chow line and see if I could entice my brain back into my head. As I was standing there fuming, I realized it had taken me less than ten days to shatter whatever peace existed in my cell, and I have this sneaking suspicion they are going to make my life a living hell.

AUGUST 1, 2005

I was expecting a lot of hostility from the White Power bloc, but they're being strangely quiet this morning. They're watching me wherever I go, particularly when I am kickin' it with any of the brothers. I know they don't have the stones to say all that racist shit to these guys' faces, but it seems pretty clear they are worried if I am telling the brothers what they are saying. That's what it's like in here. Except, frontin' a racist script ain't no minutiae. It'll get you killed if it gets to the wrong person in the wrong way. I'm beginning to see the power dynamics at play here. The fact that the whites are outnumbered almost three to one becomes very clear whenever the race card gets tossed in a game of prison spades.

▼

There are essentially two main topics of discussion between inmates that I have noticed: crimes they pulled off in the world, which includes all the voluminous tales of drug use and drug dealing, since almost all inmates are here on drug charges; and stories of life in other prisons, since the recidivism rate is so astronomically high, at around 60%. Many if not most of the inmates here have done multiple bits, particularly if we're talking about the white inmates. There is virtually no talk of getting one's life together or changing one's habits. Most simply pine for their release date so that they can go out and do it all over again. When asked, most simply say, with a certain resignation, "What else are we gonna do? There ain't no jobs. And who would hire us anyway?" You hear it said a lot: *That X on our backs is a motherfucker. It don't never wash out.* I like to refer to it as the "Scarlett C" hung around our necks.

I have to admit to periodic denial of it because I still hold out hope for myself. For most of these men, however, this is as good as it is ever going to get. Only in here do many of them have status or work that gives them dignity. And this is a profoundly undignified place, so you can imagine how so little dignity goes so far and means so much. It's a shame too because there is so much untapped talent here that society has simply forsaken. Out in the world, these men are nothing. So many simply give up . . . understandably. As horrible a thought as this is, with the rate prisons are growing, soon there will be a need for permanent inmate staffing, as the "criminal class" is exploding. By 2020, given current trends and policies, there will be around 6.5 million Americans in prison, and upwards of 20 million or more on some form of correctional monitoring. That's equal to the entire population of the Southern California megalopolis stretching from Santa Barbara to San Diego.

What is the most dismaying is that rather than show any interest in learning more about how they are exploited, and perhaps getting organized to change their situation, the inmates are too wrapped up in the minutiae dividing their lives: racism, drugs, pop culture, violence, materialism. Perhaps that's the part I should be least surprised by. The system maintains the status quo for precisely this reason. I'm having to face the fact that my disappointment may be more about my own expectations, and I'm beginning to suspect that maybe what everyone is saying about me being idealistic may have some merit after all. The Weathermen went into the ghetto believing in their heart-of-hearts that if they could just turn the Black Man onto Chairman Mao, they would wake up and smell the oppression, and get all up in Whitey's ass. But the Black Man didn't need no bourgeois white kids to teach him about oppression, he lived it day in and day out. Maybe these cats already know they're defeated, and they're just scrambling around for what's left, in which case, who's really the ignorant one?

▼

I may have spoken too soon regarding any sort of amicability between my cellmates and me. Shortly after dinner I returned to the cell to find Krause and The Klansman there.

Krause immediately confronted me.

"Bro, I told you not to fuck with my TV and I hear you got those fuckin' colored boys in here watching my shit. No way, bro, my shit ain't for entertaining the niggers! So now it's off limits. And God help you if I hear that one more of those shines was in here!"

I looked back and forth between the two of them, and I realized what was going down. Earlier in the day me and The Klansman were watching CNN on Krause's TV, and Tremaine, Smitty's cellmate and one of my homies, came in for a minute to grab me before dinner.[11] He sat down while I put my shoes and shirt on, and watched a minute or two of TV before we both got up and left. This confrontation between Krause and me was about the fact that I dared to have a black man in our cell, never mind that there is an endless cavalcade of execrable White Power rednecks hangin' around.

Once again, I was flummoxed. I just turned around and walked out of the cell, where I ran into Tremaine again. He could tell I was really upset. I began to explain what had happened, and in the process I referred to The Klansman as "the fat one." Just as the words were leaving my mouth—*way* too loud—I turned to see Smokey hovering in the background. He made a beeline into the cell to tell them what he had just heard me say.

I went back into the cell a minute later to grab my ID, and found Krause, The Klansman, Cockeyed Bob, Smokey, and Slade all in there. Immediately The Klansman says, "I have a name, don't I?"

"What?" I said, trying to ignore him.

"My name is Rich, not 'the fat one,' fucker!" His tone shot up so fast that it made my heart leap. I looked over and saw Cockeyed Bob moving in front of the door to prevent me from leaving. Man, I can't tell you how fuckin' scared I was lookin' at all five of these really pissed off motherfuckers ready to kick the shit out of me.

"Man, what difference does it make to you?" I said. "You called my friends niggers and shines and baboons." Silently I continued, *and if you only knew what we really call you.*

Faster than I had ever seen a six-foot-six, 270-pound man move, The Klansman leapt out of his bunk and charged me, effortlessly catapulting me backwards into the wall at high velocity. I thought half the bones in my body had broken. It hurt so bad I couldn't even form words.

"I oughta pound the shit out of you!" he growled, and meant it. There was such malevolent hatred in his face that I suddenly had absolutely no problem understanding that this was a man who had been locked up for attempted murder.

"I call you by your name, you call me by mine, got it?" he spat.

Not only was it lost on him how much he disrespected me with his racism, but I also knew he was just waiting for me to say something so that he could unload on me. Krause then jumped in and said, "You know, bro, no one buys your bullshit around here. We don't know why you can't just be yourself."

"This is myself, this is me, and it's not bullshit," I said, meekly. "And it's not my problem if you don't believe me. I really don't give a shit."

Krause leapt up from his chair and closed in fast so that the two of them had me wedged in a corner. Krause was my height, six one, and about 250 pounds of solid rock. There was absolutely nothing I could do. I had one good arm (I had destroyed the other in a kickboxing match), and if I tried to fight all five of these guys, there was a very good chance I'd never walk out of my cell again. I was bracing myself for the pain. It infuriated me to feel so helpless, humiliated, and weak, but what the fuck could I do? These were four of the biggest nastiest dudes I had ever met, and, of course, Smokey's pathetic ass. Krause continued his tirade.

"You're living in a fucking fantasy, some crazy idealistic world that doesn't exist. Don't you get it? These fucking niggers will take everything from you! They'll stab you in the back and take your shit . . . *everything* . . . and your own won't help you. They'll disown you out of *shame*! Your fucked-up world doesn't exist. This is the real world. I know, I been fightin' these animals my whole life. You're fucked in the head, you need to go see that shrink doctor and get you on some meds, bro, 'cause you got serious issues."

I took a breath after what seemed like years. The two of them seemed to ease up slightly.

"Look, man," I began, "I'm real sorry you had that kind of experience, but it hasn't been mine. I don't share your views or your values. But I don't tell you how to think, live, or act, and neither should you be telling me. I don't need or want your protection from people I have no problem with in the first place. If you don't want people in here, just say so. But don't accuse me of disrespecting your shit."

Krause lurched forward. "You disrespected me be bringing niggers into my cell to watch my TV!"

It suddenly became clear to me that this was all about forcing submission from me since I did not or would not offer it willingly. They were pack animals enforcing their alpha hierarchy, and I would not join the pack. So they were going to use the law of the jungle on me to teach me a lesson. Brute force was the only weapon they had. In many respects, it was all they had in life. I had been facing this at every turn throughout my entire life. Everywhere I went, people, places, and things tried to control what I said, thought, and did, and when I didn't capitulate, they responded with violence, and punishments like this. I don't know what was crazier: that it kept happening, or that my response was always defiance.

Here I was a heartbeat away from the worst beating in my life, and all I could say was . . .

"We're just from two different worlds."

Krause said, "What, are you part nigger, is that it?" I explained to him that, yes, I came from a mixed family, but that no, I was not mixed myself. They all looked horrified and disgusted. They would never "get it," ever. It was really clear by now. I believe the same thought crossed their minds about me. We just differed on what "it" was.

Krause looked around at the other four, and motioned his head towards me. I knew what was coming.

"We gotta tax ya, bro," Krause said, and then they came at me.

As fast as it started, it was over. I got hit a few dozen times in the span of about ten seconds, half of it landing on my back and the back of my head as I collapsed to the ground, my ears ringing, the wind sucked right out of me, pain exploding from every extremity. Then they all moved out of the cell lightning fast, leaving me there on the floor gasping for breath.

I eventually gathered my senses and went outside with Tremaine to find David and Pee-Wee and tell them what had happened. As soon as I stepped foot outside I spotted the gang of five watching us. They followed me and Tremaine to see where we were going and who we were talking to, and if it looked like I was telling people what happened. They wanted to make sure that what happened in the cell, stayed in the cell.

AUGUST 2, 2005

It's as if nothing happened, like I was a child that was disciplined, and now am expected to carry on as before, without making the same mistake again.

This morning Krause and Cockeyed Bob were talking about the famine in Niger that was being reported on CNN. Krause says, "These faggot Liberals wanna make us think it's our responsibility to take care of these fuckin' animals . . . that they're repressed or regressed or whatever the fuck they mean. Fuck that shit, these people brought all that shit upon themselves. Just like their *cuzins* over here. They got no one to blame but themselves. If they knew how to grow food, they wouldn't be starvin'. If they weren't lazy and would work, they could buy food."

I was reading, and trying to ignore them, but I could feel them both looking in my direction, expecting me to say something. I said nothing. I didn't even look up.

AUGUST 3, 2005

Prison tends to redefine how much value or importance you attribute to the everyday things in your life. In the absence of that which most people take for granted—food, a private bathroom, the ability to talk to your loved ones—your emotions tend to swell over seeming minutiae.

Case in point, my living situation and the backward-ass insanity of my cellmates and their crew (who consider me equally, if not more, backward). It's oppressive now. Imagine having to live in close quarters with two people you absolutely despise, through and through. Krause is rotting from the inside, and it's noticeable. He stinks, and makes the room stink, and every day it gets a little bit worse. He also chews tobacco, Skoal, and there are these foul-ass spit cups everywhere that reek.

Conversely, The Klansman is obsessive about hygiene and primping (for who?) and showers every day and uses gobs of hair gel and male body spray. I believe he is even more dangerous than Krause. Krause may be the worst human being I have ever met, but he's not irrational. He's cold and calculating. The Klansman is a psychopath, and anything can set him off. That's what I really fear now, having already seen (and felt) it for myself.

It's been over a month since I had any contact with the outside world, and the uncertainty and isolation is starting to get to me. I was feeling pretty angry and depressed, but it was a helpless anger because there was nothing I could do about what was causing it. I can no longer handle spending any time in my cell, redneck circus that it is, so I hang out with Smitty and Tremaine in their cell, or I go to the library, whenever they decide to open it. Sometimes I run or lift weights, but man it's been *hot*. The whole area around here is yellow and brown and all the grass and trees are wilted and withered, making it look like the Depression-era South, like the tableau in *O Brother, Where Art Thou?*

Smitty is always able to rejuvenate me, and we always have great conversations. He's a good kid. I really hope he stays out of trouble. I think he will, if he's able. He's smart enough to figure out a decent future for himself. He and David are the only two I have any faith in. The rest . . . way too much against them, and no desire to change themselves.

I was in Smitty's room when mail call came and I *finally* got my phone clearance (permission to use the phone) and two letters, one from my mother and one from Natylie Baldwin, an activist friend from San Francisco who wrote-for *Newtopia*. Smitty elbowed me and said, in his funny, perma-grin way, "See how things change?" I *finally* got on the phone and talked to the two "Brians"—Allemana and Brickner—for about an hour each (not being very respectful of the rules, but not really crying about it either) so that they could then download some of my experience to our readership and the activist contingency. Brian Allemana is *Newtopia*'s webmaster, but more than that, he has been a true friend. I can't even begin to thank him for everything he has done for me during this whole ordeal. Without him and Edie[12] and my sister I don't know where I would be. As I talked to my friends I slowly began to remember who I was, what I was doing, that people cared for me and missed me and were awaiting my return.

I thought all day about talking to Edie and hearing my dog whine and bark in the background. I couldn't even admit to myself how much I missed her because it depressed me too much. I had written her a letter an hour before I got my phone clearance that reflected how lonely and frustrated I felt, and perhaps inadvisably, had said some things that I probably should have spared until I saw her again in person, but had been weighing on my mind since Stateville when our whole five-year relationship was replayed in my head, this time with a depth and clarity that made me heart-sick for the grief I had caused her. I *needed* to hear her voice and to hear my dog bark . . . to remind myself that it would all end and I would go home, even if only for a while before I would have to move on and let them go.

In so many ways I struggle with all the kindness and sacrifice Edie has shown me. Part of me questions whether I deserve it, knowing that I can never give her what she wants. She, more than anyone else, has taught me the meaning of family and uncon-ditional love; even through this, she's been there for me, going above and beyond whatever duty to which she feels obligated. I feel I can live my whole life and still never repay her a fraction of the kindness and generosity she has shown me. The absurdity of our situation hangs over us like a world gone mad and malevolent, two people who love each other dearly, who have a bond like no other, and yet cannot remain together because they are too incompatible and their paths are leading off in two very different directions. Sometimes I see our time together as an indulgent limbo, an ever-expanding rotary exchange that we circled and circled, refusing to exit off into our respective futures. That day still looms, inevitable, painful, but necessary.

"I've said goodbye to you too many times," she told me, "and each time it killed me. I can't keep doing it."

After trying all night to reach her, right up until the point that I almost got walloped by the C.O. on duty for lingering, it dawned on me that her phone company probably has a correctional block (a function that prevents calls from correctional facilities) and she would need to set up a separate billing arrangement in order to be able to receive my calls. I would hear the phone ring, and then she would pick up, and I would begin to hear her voice, and then it would cut off. It was *cruel*.

I may only have a year sentence, and may only spend a few months locked up, but when you're stuck in here, and you see how hard it is to communicate with the outside world, you realize how much you are at their mercy, and that at any moment any number of things can happen that could keep you here much longer, or worse, transfer you to another facility, without anyone on the outside knowing.

I went to bed angry and sad. It was as if we had passed each other in El trains headed in opposite directions, waving frantically but unable to hear each other, and powerless to stop the trains. It was one of the many small mental torments of prison that they never tell you about, being constantly *denied*, and having your expectations repeatedly shattered.

The next morning I was devastated to learn that Smitty had been transferred to the drug program. In a flash I was left alone on the deck. He [Smitty] was my only friend on this deck, and now he was gone. It hit me hard, and all day I was morbid and angry and sad and deflated. I wrote my mother another of those letters that I probably should have saved for when I next saw her, but I knew she needed to hear how much I loved and appreciated her, and that I was OK. Shit, I damn near broke down when I had to board my dog at a kennel, I can't imagine how it must be for my mother having her eldest son in *prison*. This is the same mother who at one time harbored fantasies of me being President or a Supreme Court Justice or corporate CEO. If it wasn't fair for me to be here, then it was doubly unfair for her. She and I had lived through too much for a letter to touch, but it was critical that I let her know not to worry. She had had enough worry in her life, that was for damn sure. So I told her to stay strong, even though I didn't need to, and I told her my cellmate Krause was probably the worst human being I had ever met, and that I was reading two Gore Vidal books, and that I loved her very much.

The rest, as they say, was squeezed in between the lines.

AUGUST 4, 2005

"Pancho" Ruiz lives on the same deck as me, in a cell down the hall. He's 47 years old but looks like he's pushing 60. He's a junkie. He did his first bit back in 1977, and has put on a lot of mileage in between. He is three weeks into a two-piece for possession, probably his sixth conviction.

We spent a couple hours this morning sitting in the day room talking about the Spanish-American War and the history of Puerto Rico, his birth home. Back in the late Eighties when Pancho was doing a bit in Shawnee (max prison) he met a bunch of cats from the FALN (Fuerzas Armadas de Liberación Nacional), the Puerto Rican liberation army, or "terrorist group," depending on who you are talking to. They taught Pancho about his Puerto Rican heritage, and what US foreign policy is *really* all about. Pancho talked about the sinking of the *Maine* in Havana harbor, the value of the sugar cane trade and how it had been exploited by successive empires, the Statehood movement, and Ferdinand Marcos's private island north of Hawaii.

"I loooove hiiiistory," he said, dragging out the long "i" in the manner that is characteristic of the Puerto Rican dialect found in Chicago. "It makes me feel like I'm part of something bigger than all this shit."

Pancho found out three weeks ago that his woman of 27 years, the mother of his many children, had died while in the Lincoln Correctional Center for Women, another facility in the IDOC system. She had been locked up since December of 2004 on a heroin charge. Pancho was quick to explain.

"I'm the junkie in the family. My lady, she was sick. She had bone cancer, and she was always in so much pain. I taught her how to take dope for the pain. We couldn't afford to treat the cancer, but a bag a day we could do, you know. It helped. She got locked up because she was in bad pain one day and I wasn't around to get her dope for her, so she went out to get it herself. She didn't know nothing about copping no dope on the street."

They told him she had died of a heart attack, the second of two she had suffered in a week. Pancho found out about the first heart attack while he was in the bullpen at 26th and Cal waiting to see a judge about his possession charge, for which he had just been picked up.

"I went before the judge and said, 'Your Honor, I just found out my wife is very sick and they told me she may not live. I need a continuance of a month to take care of this. I need to see her and be with my kids.' The judge offered me two years and said, 'Mr. Ruiz, the offer of two years is for today only. If you do not take it, the next offer will be six years.' Like he was selling me a car or something. And he wasn't playin' around. I had to take it. I had no choice."

While he was in County waiting to be shipped he received word
she had died. His family had put together enough bond money to
get him out, had the judge just given him that one-month continuance, but it was too late. To make the situation all the more
profane, Pancho was not allowed to attend her funeral because
he and his lady had never been legally married. 27 years and a
house full of children and grandchildren and it was as if they were
nothing to each other. Now, he was solely responsible for the care
of his son, who had been paralyzed in a gang shooting, and his
grandson, who Pancho and his lady had raised themselves. And
he still had a year left to do.

"This whole thing has got me so fucked up in the head. She
was my best, best friend. I can't sleep anymore. I know it's really
going to do a number on me when I get out. That's when it's really
going to hit me. She made me promise I'd take care of the kids and
grandkids . . . you know, because of her cancer. She knew she was
going to die. I promised her I would, on my life. Now I'm in here,
and I can't do nothin'."

He paused and looked out the barred windows across the
grounds to where the Mississippi flickered in the morning sun
and the distant bluffs of Davenport lay shrouded in a deep haze.
His eyes tightened and a faint grimace crossed his face, like the
jagged tip of some deep emotional lava dome piercing the crust of
his soul. Smoke from a never-ending stream of hand-rolled cigarettes poured out of his nose and lips. His stained fingers trembled
slightly as they held on to what was left of the butt.

"They told me it was a nice funeral."

▼

Things are going completely out of control.

Earlier this morning as Krause and The Klansman were gone
at their job assignments, I caught Smokey in my cell working out
and listening to The Klansman's radio. I told him he knew the
rules, that he shouldn't be in our cell without one of us present,

and he told me that he "had permission." I told him he didn't have *my* permission, and I didn't want him in there, so dangle, yo. He left, then came back and said he wanted to "talk to me." I told him I didn't have much to say to him, and left it at that.

He came back into my cell another three times at moments that I was out of the cell, in the bathroom, or talking to someone else. When I caught him the last time, I had had enough. The C.O. was making his rounds, heard us arguing, and asked what was going on. I told him I didn't want this guy in and out of my cell when no one was here. The C.O. asked Smokey why he was going in my cell, and Smokey said, "Krause wants me to stir his beans while he's gone."

You see, Krause and Cockeyed Bob cook pinto beans in a hot pot every day, and make these disgusting burrito-type concoctions with the beans, hot sauce, and processed cheese spread. Every day without fail. Then they spend four or five hours farting their asses off and giggling like eight-year-olds. Now, true to form, they had made Smokey their houseboy.

Well, the C.O. on duty was a serious redneck who let the White Power boys do whatever they wanted, so he told Smokey to take Krause's hot pot into his own cell, and he told me to "stop whining like a little bitch." Smokey, meanwhile, makes a bee-line down the hall into Cockeyed Bob's cell, and a second later he and, shockingly, Krause (where the fuck did he come from?) emerge and come at me hard as the C.O. walks away laughing.

I told Krause I didn't want Smokey in the cell alone, that I didn't trust him, and that I knew that if anything turned up missing or whatever, I'd get blamed for it. I told him it was a risk I did not want to take.

What I didn't tell Smokey was that I was pretty sure that Krause had told him to try and steal my journal because it had become obvious to me that Krause in particular was really curious what I was writing down every day, and why I had stopped writing on our deck and was only doing it in the library now. His response all but confirmed it to me when he said, "I don't want anyone knowing what we got in there, or what's going on in there, you understand? You talk to the C.O.s, they start poking around." He eyes the folder I am holding with my journal and notes and says, "What are you doin'? You're on some bullshit."

"Can you define the bullshit?" I said like a smart-ass. Krause seethes and then barks, "Bro, I think it's time you get the fuck off this deck." He eyes my folder again. "You're takin' your life into your own hands with whatever bullshit you are on. You need to go request a move—like now—before things start happening to you that you don't want."

Start happening?

I walked away and went to Tremaine's cell. He was there reading. I told him about what happened and what he thought I should do. Tremaine said, "Man, tell them [the Administration] *everything*. Protect yourself, and don't let them fuck up your sentence, because they will. Their main goal right now is probably to fuck up your out date. Get out of here. And make sure that if they do jump you, it's on record *way* ahead of time, so they know they were out for you. That's your only hope of not losing your good time or gettin' shipped."

So, inadvisably, I went to the C.O. and asked him what was the best way to get moved to another housing unit. The C.O. asked, "Why do you need a move?" But he knew exactly why. Then he said, "If you're fearing for your safety, you need to 'drop a slip' [fill out a request form] and tell them that you need immediate assistance." The response time was unknown, and he provided no further information. I got the sneaking suspicion he was intentionally giving me the wrong information.

As he's saying this, Krause and Cockeyed Bob appear, looking enraged. They see me filling out the slip, and they start freaking out. At this point I'm totally confused, but I complete the slip and drop it into the box. They basically pull me back to the cell and begin grilling me on what I was doing. I told them I did exactly what they wanted, I requested to be moved. They asked what reason I gave, and I told them, my safety. Then they really freaked out, and it was contagious, 'cause I caught it next.

"You're getting us all dragged into Internal Affairs, you know that, you stupid fuck!" Krause spat. Then he and Cockeyed Bob say a few things to each other quickly in some form of shorthand I didn't catch, and suddenly I realize . . . *they're scared. They're actually scared.* They bolt back to our cell and start hiding things, what I really don't know, and then they leave to go out and wait in the lunch line and presumably inform the rest of the White Power bloc what had happened. Tremaine comes walking up shaking his head and looking grave.

"Man, you better watch your back. Those boys are gonna get you long before you ever get to talk to any Administration." Then he laughed and patted me on the back. "Just make sure you ain't talkin' to me when they come atcha."

I don't know what to do. I'm really freaking out now. But I do know one thing, I don't owe these guys *anything*, and I'm going home on my out day come hell or high water. I'm not staying locked up the whole year because of these assholes. I can't believe that all this has come about because I refuse to be a racist. This fucking place is insane!

AUGUST 5, 2005

I locked my notes in my lockbox yesterday afternoon and stayed outside until I was forced to come back for dinner count. The minute I stepped in the unit, they were all there, glaring at me with seething hatred. Thankfully, I didn't have to interact with them, and there was a new C.O. on duty, a fairly cool brother who didn't much care for the White Power bloc. After dinner yesterday I went to the library, totally stressed and shaken, hoping to have a few hours of peace and quiet before I would be forced to go back to the unit and into the cell with them. At this point, I could think of very little else in the world that would be worse.

I had already created—or, more appropriately, responded to—a situation that had set into motion an inevitable series of events. I had to decide whether or not to ask for immediate intervention, or wait patiently and quietly for them to respond to my request. If I act now, there will invariably be a "situation," and I will need to go into protective custody, which means segregation and, eventually, shipment to another facility. If I wait, every moment I continue to live in that cell will put me in the way of immediate and direct harm.

These guys may have been dysfunctional sociopaths out in the world, but they are master inmates and know the system inside and out. I was told they would sacrifice at least one of them to jump me, which would get both of us shipped out with another year tacked on our sentence. At the very least, I was told, they would plant something on me or accuse me of stealing or some other offense, to get me shipped.

Most of this was imparted to me by Tommy, this middle-aged white guy from the Mid-State Region who got locked up for burglarizing his own home while in the midst of a messy divorce. He related to me a similar experience he had had with a former cellmate where he had to seek protective custody.

"You have to prepare yourself mentally for the consequences," he said. "But you haven't done anything wrong, so you have the potential to come out relatively unscathed. Even if you get those guys shipped, and the White Power bloc jumps you somewhere on the yard, you'll just take a beating and be quiet about it and you'll get to go home on your parole date. It's a shitty choice to make, but it's prison. You gotta live with it if you want to live."

When Tommy and his cellmate threw down, Tommy spent a week in seg "for his own protection" while they segged his cellie for 60 days. But here's the messed-up part of it. They couldn't ship his cellie out because the guy had turned State's evidence in a murder case and there was a hit out on him in every joint in the system. Ironic as it is, he was at East Moline for *protective custody*. They offered to ship Tommy, but he refused. He told me that if they offer it to me I should refuse too.

"Stand on your principles like you have been. They will see you through this. They're the sick ones, not you," he said.

Just then another inmate passed by the table, and Tommy waved him over. His name was Darryl, a brother about my age who is the "chief law clerk" at Sweet Moline, which basically means that he taught himself how to do legal research and now assists other inmates with legal issues related to their cases. He had already done 15 of a 20-year sentence, had a perfect conduct record and a shit ton of good time accrued, and claimed to have seen all that there is to see inside IDOC. When I told him my story, he immediately said, "You need to talk to a White Shirt immediately, do not pass go, do not collect two hundred dollars. Trust me, you don't need that bullshit."

Darryl then went and downloaded my story to the librarian, a tall and kind middle-aged woman with long dark hair and thick glasses that all the inmates call "Miss Pat." She had been at The Sweet Moline for decades and had engendered tremendous respect from the small cadre of inmates who worked for her and used the library. She was also much respected by the Administration. Pat got on the phone in her office, behind a closed door, and called around to see which White Shirts were on duty. She told me you had to be very careful who you trust, because not all of them were "friendlies," meaning, sympathetic to inmate plight. Apparently she found one she considered sympathetic. She disappeared from the library for a few moments, and when she returned she went into the back room where all the books were stored and very discreetly gestured for me to follow her, slowly.

Quickly she whispered, "Go to the medical wing and ask for Lieutenant Q. He'll be there waiting for you. Don't ask for him if other inmates are around. Wait until you are alone. Walk slowly

when you cross the yard and be inconspicuous." Then she winked
and gestured for me to leave, while she remained behind.

After making sure no one was watching me go into the Main
building, I went up to Medical and was quietly ushered by a nurse
into an isolated room in a part of the building they weren't using.
No one saw me or knew I was there. After a moment, Lt. Q, a
large Filipino man, entered the room and I told him the whole
saga. Much to my surprise, he understood.

"You are rare in here," he said, shaking his head in what appeared to be disbelief, but also a kind of resignation to the pervasive racism and bigotry, which he seemed to lament. "Lines are
drawn and they are not to be crossed. They don't understand who
or what you are, so they respond like they do. Here at East Moline
we have some racial mixing because of the open movement policy,
but in any other facility, oh boy, you'd be in for a time."

This was now abundantly clear to me.

Lt. Q finished by saying, "We'll move you immediately. Go
back to your unit, be very quiet, stay out of their way, and wait
for word." Then he was gone.

One hour later, back in my unit, sitting out in the day room,
the C.O. on duty appeared, told me to pack my shit and head
over to C Wing, which was one of the four cellblocks located in
the newer building behind this one. Krause, Cockeyed Bob, and
The Klansman were in the cell when I came in to grab my shit.
The minute I began to strip my bed they knew what was up, and
the three of them leapt up and began hiding contraband again. As
I walked out with my lockbox in my arms, they glared me down,
and I understood that this was far from over. I was just being re-
called from the trenches, as it were, but the war would continue.

On C Wing I ran into a number of brothers who had shipped out
from Stateville with me, and they were all happy to see me again.
It was a fun little reunion of sorts, me bobbing in a sea of brothers.

Big Mo' said, "Shit, when you left-out of B Wing we all said
that they should have just talked to you for a minute before

puttin' you in with those Klan motherfuckers, joe. You just a light-skinned nigger, and they warn't never gonna turn yo ass. But iz all right now, you home baby. Let them mufuckas say shit to you now and it's on!" He gave me a big hug, and about three other cats came through to offer pounds and love.

It didn't even hit me how utterly stressed out I was over this whole situation until after I took a shower and sat down in my cell with my new cellie, an 18-year-old kid named Ronnie who they called "Ron-Ron." He had a TV, so we flipped to TBS and started watching *Blade Runner*. It was heaven.

All at once I felt as if I had been awake and running for two weeks straight. Word traveled fast across the deck, and all night long brothers stopped by my cell to welcome me and hear my story. Very quickly, in a very strange and weird way, I had become something part hero, part sideshow, because I was the first white guy they knew who had stood up to the White Power bloc, and who preferred to be with them. They thought it was the funniest fuckin' thing they had ever heard, and they laughed their asses off. It was pretty surreal, but it felt good and right and for the first time since I arrived, I actually felt comfortable. Once again, I counted my voluminous blessings.

As we sat watching the movie Ron-Ron caught me staring off into space and smiling, and I guess he knew what I was thinking 'cause he said, "That's right, Chuckie, you *decent* [meaning: "everything's cool and you can relax"]. You wit your *own* now." We both laughed pretty hard at that, given that I had told them the whole "stick with your own" bit that the White Power bloc had foisted on me. Very soon after that I passed out. Thanks to my new digs and a cool breeze that was sifting through the window, I slept like I hadn't slept in over a month.

The next morning I ran into Smitty and David on the chow line and told them everything. They were both happy I did what I did. Smitty vowed to get Smokey one day, then paused a second and said, "Ah forget him, he's not even worth the thought it takes to dismiss him." We went to lunch together and we were happy. It would be all right. The crisis, for the moment, had been averted.

Later, at the library, Miss Pat says to me, "if you have *any* more problems at all with anyone else, you come straight to me."

I always knew reading would pay off someday.

AUGUST 7, 2005

The weekend was peaceful and quiet. I slept, read, worked out, and watched lots of movies on TV. I had a long discussion about Chicago economics, the Mayor's race, and immigration with this new brother named Jerry, who they call "Cameo." We also talked about "divide and rule" strategies foisted on the Blacks, Mexicans, and Puerto Ricans by the police and the politicians.

Jerry is on an eight-year bit and hasn't even talked to his wife yet. He wanted to know who my old cellies were so he followed me out onto the yard and was surprised to learn that The Klansman was one of them.

"Man, I was in Logan with that cat last year, and then we were on B Wing together here just two weeks ago. I didn't know he was like that. Man . . . it make it worse 'cause he was always talkin' to black folk. But now . . . shit, it ain't happenin'. That cracker is seriously frontin'."

We spotted The Klansman and a bunch of the White Power bloc in the lunch line. They were all staring me down. Then Big Mo' and his crew came up and stood next to me staring back at them. The honkies gave up.

It felt good not to be alone.

▼

Ron-Ron is a good kid and a great cellie. It's a trip that he's half my age. It's sad, but not hopeless, because he's smart, and he has a big family that appears to love him but not coddle him. He showed me photos of his extended family, read me letters, proudly told me of his plans for his release, which will be about two weeks before mine. Ron-Ron is kind and generous and has a good sense of humor. He doesn't seem to be spoiled by the streets like so many of the young men I have met. There is still gentleness in him. It can—and should—be his eventual salvation.

Earlier in the morning I sat with Carlton, who is 18 months into a six-year bit for breaking into a mechanic's shop to steel industrial power tools. This is his sixth time in prison.

"I'm 48. Ain't nobody gonna hire me. Every time I get out I try to find a job, but no one will hire me. I'm *fit*, I can work like a twenty-eight-year-old. No one will give me a chance. So I gotta do what I gotta do to survive."

You can see how the frustration has worn him down. I don't sense the hustle in him like I do in most of the others. He seems to be genuine, but he's downplaying his drug use. He's certainly not violent, but definitely proud. He's not wrong for wanting a roof and work and food, and I try to put myself in his shoes knowing I can never really understand. I have education, youth, and whiteitude. While I will still be excluded and disenfranchised to a certain degree as an ex-convict, I have the tools to survive, and even overcome. Carlton is staring down the barrel of his declining years, and maybe I was just lucky to catch him in a reflective and contemplative space, but you gotta imagine six bits will eventually knock loose some wisdom, or at the very least, some common damn sense.

We sat at the concrete table in the common area of our tier and talked all about the drug war and what it had done to his neighborhood. It made him sad to talk about it.

"I don't really have any more friends there, they *all* dead . . . *dead*! Drugs played a part in it all. And I have to wonder why I was spared. What does it mean? What am I supposed to do? What is the message here? As crazy as it sounds, I think jail actually saved me. I am here for a reason, because jail kept breaking my cycle and getting me off the streets while everyone else was dying out there. I am not here by chance, neither are you. You're in here to talk to me right now to tell me things I need to know, and you're in here to listen to me and write down what I am saying so that other people can learn. We right where we supposed to be."

He stares across convenience store reading glasses and locks his gaze into mine. There is a deep suffering in his eyes, a certain folding of the skin that resembles the leaves of a tree dying of thirst.

"People need people, Charles."

▼

After nearly three weeks here at The Sweet Moline I finally got my work assignment, in the Dietary unit, on the breakfast shift, which means I have to be up at 3:00 am every morning. I was also approved for the Work Camp. Work Camp inmates live separately in a brand-new housing unit and get to leave the prison every day to work out in the community (part of the package deal given to small prison towns, free municipal labor). I was approved for Work Camp because I had a nonviolent record and was considered a "low escape risk," but if my parole date holds I will be released before a space opens up there.

Monday morning also began a week-long program called Pre-Start, which is IDOC's ostensible "re-entry" program. If you'll pardon a moment of rather stinky cynicism, I wonder what kind of "preparedness" they offer. Job training for jobs that aren't waiting for us when we get out? Social skills for operating in a society that shuns us? Literacy for an increasingly illiterate nation? Morality for a culture in decline? Honor for a Machiavellian system built on hypocrisy and exploitation? Family values for shattered communities? Is it more likely this program is just another line item in the budget which translates to more money for the prison?

Inmates will all agree, when it comes to the Administration, that we should believe none of what we hear from them and only half of what we see. So it all remains to be seen what IDOC will do to help us adjust to living as ex-convicts.

▼

I started reading Gore Vidal's *The Second American Revolution and Other Essays*, and I came across some material that really surprised me, although it really shouldn't have. It is certainly causing me to rethink my politics.

In a series of three essays—"The State of the Union Revisited" (1980), "The Real Two-Party System" (1980), and "The Second American Revolution" (1981)—Vidal outlines, with what today would certainly be viewed as refreshing candor, the problems besetting America 25 years ago. Is it any surprise that they are more or less the same problems facing America today? But now, those same problems are worse on a greater order of magnitude. He points to an out-of-control Defense and Intelligence establishment, the illusion of "democracy," and the constraints of the one-Capitalist-party-masquerading-as-a-two-party-system which he calls "the two halves of the banking party." He also takes a few shots at the Trilateral Commission, the "crime issue," taxation, and the bloated federal government. All fair targets for sure.

It was on the issues of drugs and crime that Vidal began to resonate with my own particular vibrato:

In 1975, I said that "roughly 80 percent of police work in the United States has to do with the regulation of our *private* morals. By that I mean controlling what we drink, eat, smoke, put into our veins—not to mention trying to regulate with whom and how we have sex, with whom and how we gamble. As a result, our police are among the most corrupt in the Western world . . .

Therefore, let us remove from the statute books all laws that have to do with private morals—what are called victimless crimes. If a man or a woman wants to be a prostitute, that is his or her affair. It is no business of the state what we do with our bodies sexually. Obviously, laws will remain on the books for the prevention of rape and the abuse of children, while the virtue of our animal friends will continue to be protected by the SPCA . . . All drugs should be legalized and sold at *cost* to anyone with a prescription. Gasps! Cries! Save our children! I pointed out that our children would be saved from the playground pusher because there would be no profit for the pusher—a brand new thought! Legalization will also remove the Mafia and other big-time drug dispensers from the scene, just as the repeal of Prohibition eliminated the bootleggers of whisky forty years ago.

I didn't add that the absolute political corruption of the United States can be traced to that "noble experiment" when the Christers managed to outlaw whisky—an unconstitutional act if there ever was one. As a result, practically everyone broke the law, and gradually lawlessness became a habit, while organized crime became a huge business of bank-like proportions (and connections). . . . Obviously, drug addiction is a bad thing. But in the interests of good law and order, the police must be removed from the temptation that the current system offers them, and the Bureau of Narcotics (DEA) should be abolished. That would be the trick of the week! If the Bureau were ever to eliminate all drugs, the Bureau would itself be eliminated. Therefore . . . the logic is clear.

Of course, today the "playground pusher" is your child's classmate, and the "big-time drug dispensers" are organized crime networks from a dozen different countries, narco-traffickers, pharmaceutical companies and the doctors in their pockets, and the covert intelligence services of a few influential nations, most notably ours, and those of Israel and Britain.

When that essay was published in 1980 there were 307,000 prisoners in the US. Today (2005) there are more than 2 million,

with another million in county jails and another 7 million monitored on "correctional supervision," which means probation and
parole. In 1980, prison expenses were $4 billion; today they are
$64 billion. And in 1980, there was no "War on Drugs" in the
form there is today, which is to say highly militarized and integral
to economic stability (jobs, jobs, jobs), which tacks on another
$30 to $40 billion.

In 1980 Congress and the Senate (led by Ted Kennedy and
Robert Drinan) tried fervently to pass the Omnibus Crime Bill
(OCB). Although defeated, it would eventually be passed years
later in a much more severe form as the Patriot Act. With chilling
prescience, Vidal mentions a provision in the OCB that allows for
the imprisonment of journalists who refuse to reveal their sources,
something we just witnessed with the Valerie Plame case.

Twenty-five years of activism and organizing by special interest groups and not-for-profits have accomplished virtually
nothing when you look at the big picture. The laws are more
restrictive now than ever, the problems are bigger than ever,
and both continue to grow, mostly fed by the Draconian nature
of the legal system. Much like how marching in the street and
chanting corny, archaic slogans does little to end war or otherwise influence government policy these days. For a *real* solution,
Vidal calls for a new Constitutional Convention, exchanging the
Executive-heavy form of government for a more democratic par-
liamentary system, abolishing the secret agencies and bureaucra-
cies like the CIA, NSA, DIA, ATF, and DEA, cutting the Defense
budget down to where it should logically be to provide for the
common defense instead of maintaining a global empire, and
end not-for-profit status for churches and organized religions.
This alone would redirect *trillions* into the building of a more
sustainable society.

Vidal also says that the most important and revolutionary act
would be for Americans *not* to vote, to show their discontent in
the "two-party system" and its lack of any real choice:

When two-thirds—instead of the present half—refuse to acknowledge any of the Presidential candidates, the election will lack all legitimacy. Then we shall be in a position to invoke Article Five of the Constitution and call for a new Constitutional Convention where, together, we can devise new political arrangements suitable for a people who have never, in 193 years, been truly represented.

Today, of course, in our increasingly multicultural, quasi-illiterate consumer narrowcast reality, this would be a daunting task. Vidal and company's efforts to call for a Constitutional Convention failed by one state, and any rally efforts were quickly put on the kybosh after Reagan won the presidency. As Vidal so poignantly concludes, "The Government has been from the beginning the *Cosa Nostra* of the few, and the people at large have always been excluded from the exercise of power."

What will it take to begin to change things?

AUGUST 8, 2005

Peter Jennings died today of lung cancer at age 67. He was diagnosed five months ago, right about the time I returned from San Francisco for the assault case with the Chicago PD, and now he is gone. I will always have a special place for him in my heart for exposing the government's lies about MDMA in *Ecstasy Rising*, the 2004 special that featured Rick Doblin of MAPS, the Multidisciplinary Association for Psychedelic Studies. He was definitely one of the good guys. We'll miss you, Peter.

I just got back from the first Pre-Start class. It was taught by another inmate, a big . . . *big* brother calling himself Yashua Ben-Israel. His birth name is William Wilson, but he adopted the new

moniker after converting to the Ben-Israel sect. These folks believe they are Black Hebrews, the lost tribe of the Israelites. He
kept it pretty real. He told us candidly that the reason he, and not
a state employee, was teaching the class was because the "Pre-
Start" program existed in name only since there was no longer
any budget to continue the program.

"IDOC's primary concern is your recidivism," he said, candidly. "What I mean by that, gentlemen, is that IDOC *wants* you
to come back. It is more profitable for them to incarcerate you
than to rehabilitate you."

Yashua explained that back when the Pre-Start re-entry program was introduced in the late '80s and early '90s, it used to be a
30- to 90-day process where you underwent counseling, vocational
training, social service counseling, transitional housing placement,
and parole education, in order to ease the transition back into the
world. That program no longer exists. The program we're taking
is a week long, but could easily be condensed into one day.

We watched an hour-long video made in 1991. Yashua told us
that most of the time we were just gonna sit around and bullshit.
He explained that there used to be 19 transitional centers across
the state that provided services for the newly released. They have
all been closed down. The recidivism rate has never been higher.
Neither have the budgets and profits for the corrections-based
economy. You do the math.

▼

Carlton came by my cell this afternoon to ask my help in reading
a letter, since his literacy skills are not the greatest. He seemed
very distant and dismayed and mumbled something about getting
some very bad news. As we went through his letter, written by a
friend of his very ill 79-year-old mother, the news slowly revealed
itself. His sisters had told his mother that they were no longer
going to give his letters to her because they no longer wished to
upset her. "Since she's not going to be with us much longer," the

letter read, "she's told us she's sick of living and just wishes that she could die now. We don't think her last days should be filled with the painful memories of her failed son."

Carlton stopped mid-sentence and tears began to fall on the notebook paper. "Man, I don't think I'm ever going to see my mother again, and my sisters won't let me talk to her . . ."

He trailed off, unable to continue. Here was a 48-year-old man who had been down *six times* losing it right in front of me. It was the first time I had seen anyone cry in this joint, and I felt so bad for him. He may have been an addict, but he wasn't a bad guy. It's so hard to try and explain the difference to people who don't know this world. There is honor and dignity in desperation, as much as there can be evil, hatred, and malevolence.

I put my hand on his shoulder—briefly enough to communicate support, but not long enough to draw attention to it (and how sad and pathetic was that?)—and I muttered, "Hold on, Carlton. Be strong. Recognize." He quickly grasped my meaning, wiped off his face, and got ahold of himself before anyone else saw what was going on. He nodded his head as if to say, *Thanks for checking me.*

Perhaps the most inhumane and unnatural feature of prison is the way emotions become a serious, *serious* liability. Grieving is *verboten*. Inmates are forced to swallow their feelings, which leads to a pervading culture of passive-aggressive sadism as well as outright aggression and violence, and after long enough, a form of prison psychosis. Inmates snap over nothing, and they lose it in such a disproportionate manner to the actual incident that provoked it that it invariably has negative, often disastrous consequences. They don't just take your freedom in here, they take your dignity, and your humanity. You are expected to be tough and cold.

It's been really hard for me. I'm emotional enough as it is, but being in here amplifies *everything*. In order to keep it together, I have to find ways to not think about the things that will make me emotional—my friends, my family, my dog—so I read incessantly or otherwise distract my mind to avoid thinking about them. Pain has to be subsumed, and anger and disgust have to be controlled, as my recent problem has shown, lest it lead to loose lips, smart mouths, and stupid confrontations. All you can do is try to laugh, or stay quiet. These are the origins of those thousand-yard stares you see on the faces of ex-convicts.

I feel so bad for Carlton. Just thinking about losing my mother rattles me hard. I can't imagine it happening while I was locked up. The guilt alone might kill me.

AUGUST 9, 2005

Further applications of the metaphor of prison being "Hell." As of today, there have been thirty-one 90+ degree days this summer. It is fucking *hot*! These cellblocks are uninhabitable brick ovens most of the time as it's too hot to be in here, but most of the time we don't have a choice. I can squeeze a few hours in at the library, which has AC, but that's about it. It's been so hot they have canceled all outside movement a few times. Trying to sleep at night is futile. There is no airflow through the cells, and worse, the bricks radiate the heat they soaked up all day. *And* I'm on the top bunk. Most times you can't even move, and you sweat and stick to the mattress and the hot itchy fake wool blankets they give you. They have all these huge fans blowing air around, which helps a bit if you wet yourself down and stand in front of them, you can cool down a bit . . . for a minute. You get so dehydrated at night you get these miserable headaches and cramps. This suh-huh-hucks! I wanna talk to the manager!

AUGUST 10, 2005

Last night at the li-berry I helped a brother named Earnest type a letter to the Department of Child and Family Services in the hopes of helping the mother of his four children retain parental custody. After I wrote it out, ran it by him, and then typed it out for him, he asked me what I wanted in payment. I told him nothing, it was my pleasure, and that I felt that no family should ever have to be split up when they don't want to be, particularly when there are as many clearly mitigating factors as Earnest described. I mean, sure, he could have played me and made the whole thing up, but it sounded a lot more like a typical DCFS screw job than the fact that his kids were in danger.

Yes, Earnest got caught selling drugs and admitted he sold them, which was why he was at The Sweet Moline. What people outside those communities don't realize is that sometimes it's one of the only choices people have. It's very easy for some white middle-class person far removed from that level of hardship to judge what Earnest did and say, "He could have gotten a job and earned the money honestly." Well, actually, no, he couldn't. Earnest had a good job as a security guard, but he got laid off, and couldn't find other work. He had four kids to feed. He had no college education. He decided to sell some drugs, he got caught, he went to prison, even though it was his first offense. Now, the state was trying to take his kids away from him. Yet he was always calm and composed, carried around a bible, and talked about the Lord more than anything else. Ladies and gentlemen, I submit to you, where is the hardened criminal here? He was no thug, he was just somebody's Pops, makin' ends.

I complained to Earnest and Tommy and Darryl, who had come around later, that I had been waiting for weeks for a package to arrive that had a money order Edie put together for me so I could buy the few basic amenities you need to survive on the inside. I had been there more than a month, and I still didn't have soap, toothpaste, toothbrush, much less more than one change of underwear or some basic commodities like instant coffee and commissary food. They don't give you these things, everything you need to live is for sale, and until you get money, you get nothing. Earnest said he'd pray for the safe arrival of my package.

Lo and behold the package showed up today full of great stuff. Letters and cards, photos of my dog, stationery for letter writing (which you can't use because you have to buy and use officially sanctioned IDOC letter stock, what they call "write-outs") but . . . *not the money*. Someone had taken the money order out.

I was simultaneously enraged and heartbroken, and it wasn't as if I could go ask someone about it. There was no one to talk to about it, nothing I could do. I *knew* someone in the mailroom opened my package and lifted my money order, but I could never prove it. You are so helpless in here, and it's so easy for them to exploit you; what are you going to do about it? So they trample your dignity that way, then they expect you to just sit there silent and take it. The grievance process is long and ultimately fruitless. It's part of the other oppressive theme of prison, *patience*. Nothing happens quickly for the inmate, and no one is lining up eager to help you.

The rage was totally fucking with my head. I wanted to snap. I forced myself to go back to my cell and shut the door until I calmed down. It was *very* hard. It took every ounce of self-restraint I had in me. There was so much pounding down on me. It dawned on me while I paced back and forth across my doorway that I kept being brought back to the same message: *Slow down. Be quiet. Think.* I've been plagued my whole life with a reckless and profound sense of impatience and impetuousness. It has always been one of my most glaring character flaws, and the source of immeasurable suffering. And now, I couldn't help but wonder if this prison was some kind of Divine test, immersion-therapy for the chronically impatient. I just wish I didn't have to come here to learn, but I suppose that since I was unable to learn out there in the world, life found a way to school me, in here.

I told Earnest and Tommy about it later that night at the

li-berry. Both seemed hopeful that it was a "clerical mishap" but I think we all knew better. You don't just "mishap" money in a prison mailroom. Gimme a break.

Earnest told me to "have faith" and said that the rage I was feeling was "the Devil gettin' all up in me during a moment of weakness." I silently granted him the metaphor if not the whole shebang.

"I prayed for you to get your package, and I have no doubt that the good lord has your money taken care of as well."

Although I had always been taught that God was not particularly enamored of banking, oh what with sending his kid to ghetto stomp the money changers in the Temple and all, I also couldn't help but wonder if this was also to see how much of my resolve I had retained since those few weeks in the cooler at Stateville when I vowed to reexamine my life. The whole "god" thing was still to me like the experience of putting on a wool sweater when I was a kid: it's hot and itchy and uncomfortable, but it comes in real handy during those few moments when you are really exposed to the elements.

It remains to be seen what happens to the money. I have a feeling that in the coming days this experience will prove to be much more valuable than I see now. The insanity of impatience is the proverbial mental prison you hear about all the time, but unlike the joint, you are both the inmate and the jailer of your own mind.

When I got back to C Wing for night count I received word that my six months of good time had been approved, making my official release date September 9th. Only a month away! I need to stay out of trouble. But man, trouble has no problem finding me. It's like my neurochemical system is ionically charged to actively conduct trouble out of the atmosphere, like a big naughty lightning rod. I mean if I could find an engineer who could help me transduce it I could probably power my neighborhood. I'm going to have to take a serious look at that too.

AUGUST 11, 2005

The American people are as dedicated to the idea of sin and its punishment as they are to making money. And fighting drugs is nearly as big a business as pushing them. Since the combination of sin and money is irresistible (particularly to the professional politician) the situation will only grow worse. The media constantly deplore the drug culture and, variously, blame foreign countries like Colombia for obeying the iron law of supply and demand to which we have, as a notion and as a nation, sworn eternal allegiance. In 1989, the former drug czar, William Bennett, declared, "I find no merit in the drug legalizers' case. The simple fact is that drug use is wrong. And the moral argument, in the end, is the most compelling argument." Of course, what this dangerous comedian thinks is moral James Madison and Virginia statesman and Rights-man George Mason would have thought dangerous nonsense, particularly when his "morality" abolishes their gift to us all, the Bill of Rights.

—Gore Vidal, "Shredding the Bill of Rights" (1998)

Yashua "gets it." Today in "Pre-Start" he broke it down.

He starts with, "Gentlemen, you may all have heard that our nation is waging a 'War on Drugs.' Do not be fooled, gentlemen. There is no . . . such . . . thing . . . happening. Our government is not at all interested in stopping the flow of drugs into this country. It is dedicated to arresting and incarcerating as many poor people . . . which usually means *black* people . . . as they can get their hands on. Trust me, gentlemen, police are not stopping and searching white people on the street in the suburbs, and those people consume five times the drugs that black folk do. You need first and foremost to understand this, and if you fail to understand this, you will continue to be a guest of the State of Illinois. Twenty years ago there were virtually no black men in federal prison. Now, the Fed joints are overflowing. And you must also understand that federal prisons exist for those caught *obtaining illegal money.*"

He repeated that last part a couple more times: *obtaining illegal money.* It was clear most of the inmates didn't get it. Yashua explained that virtually everyone in a federal prison is there on a charge that relates to obtaining money by illegal means, which, more importantly, was also never taxed. Whether it was by manipulating the stock market, trafficking guns or drugs, or robbing pensions, if you got your money by illicit means and didn't cut the government in, you're S.O.L. (Shit Out of Luck). You don't find junkies and prostitutes and burglars in federal prison.

"You can make money any way you want, so long as you pay your tax," Yashua said. "Sometimes you just need to be clever about how you pay them, know what I'm sayin'?"

He was on a roll, and he kept hittin' 'em with stuff, and they were really starting to pay attention now.

"Manuel Noriega . . . you remember who that was? He was the leader of Panama. And back while George Bush's daddy was president, one of the first things he did was to invade Panama and snatch up Noriega and bring him back to the US and put him on trial as a drug dealer. He's in a federal prison now *for life.* What you got to understand is that Noriega was the middleman in the cocaine trade. Panama's banks held drug money. But who was moving the cocaine? And mind you, this is the cocaine that ended up in our neighborhoods and gave so many of us our, uh, *new professions.* This is where the crack came from! It was the crew Bush's daddy put together to get guns to the Contras in Nicaragua. Panama was where all this merch connected, guns heading south, cocaine heading north, money staying in the middle.

"Does anyone here remember the Iran-Contra scandal? Noriega had the goods on Bush, and he started talkin' 'bout how he was gonna tell, so they had to snatch him. Whatever you have been told about the drug trade, you haven't been told the whole story, and most of what you know is wrong. And if you continue to have the wrong information, you will continue to be a victim of the system, and you will come back. Empower yourself with information, gentlemen."

Although drug possession is a victimless crime, robbing someone because you need a fix is not, and there is a substantial chasm of difference between recreational and even heavy drug users, and chronic addicts who are so desperate that they are willing to break other laws to feed their habits, or are so sick or irrational that they are a danger to others.

I've been on both sides of the fence with this one. In the 1990s I was bingeing out of control on cocaine and I would steal to feed my habit. It was awful, and it hurt people emotionally and financially. Those were crimes that deserved punishment, and I accept that. I feel great shame about doing the things I did. And even though part of me could argue that at the time I was beyond my ability to intervene and stop myself, I did on a few occasions cross the line away from a victimless crime, and so some form of justice was necessary.

So if these inmates here do feel shame about the victims they have created, and they have an addiction to blame it on (which is what I interpret them to mean when they embrace being addicts), then they can plausibly deny to themselves any real responsibility for their behavior. It may be the only thing left that permits them to continue living with themselves.

Most of the black inmates view dealing as a means to an end, a replacement economy. They have no illusions about the levels of corruption in the system, nor how high up the food chain it goes. They know the drugs they sell—cocaine and heroin—are bad for you, they've seen their families and neighborhoods decimated by them. They also *know* the cops are dirty, they see that every day too. In talking to many of them, there is a common understanding that drugs are actively and knowingly trafficked into this country and their neighborhoods are openly targeted. What is less understandable is why so many consent to and participate in the destruction of their communities. There is not a lot of civic pride going around, if you feel me.

I have such unrealistic hopes and expectations for the black community. You'd think it would be easy to explain "divide and rule" but it's not. And in hearing their immediate concerns— fearing who, over their shoulder, is trying to take them out—you learn new depths to the "divide" part. The biggest problem is the generational gap. These young boys are so divorced from their history and any awareness of the system they live in that they can't feasibly be anything but operational cogs in an entrenched system. Without any knowledge of who or what they are, they can't become something else. The older brothers have a much firmer grasp of what's really going on, but they don't have a real good relationship with the younger generation. A huge chunk of them have been in and out of prison all their children's lives, and another huge chunk never made it to middle age.

If the young boys could be educated to understand what the older men understand, there might be hope for them. They are so much smarter and more creative than people will ever give them credit for being.

Sometimes I fear that I am just another clueless bourgeois reformer.

▼

Fallout from the cell move has been minimal so far. I am getting the obligatory stink eye from the White Power bloc, and now white guys I don't even know are giving me the same look, which shows you how fast word spreads inside. I can see them whispering to each other. My only question is, how concerned do I need to be about what they are saying?

▼

When I was struggling to finally kick my cocaine problems, around the time I was 30 or 31, I decided to study martial arts because I thought it would be the sort of discipline that would be strong enough to withstand the onslaught of the cocaine craving. I was right, to some degree. It certainly was strong enough in the sense that it substituted one adrenal purge for another.

I quickly became a fairly competent fighter, and instead of craving cocaine, I craved sparring. But no sooner had I begun amateur competition when I effectively destroyed my right shoulder fighting someone significantly larger than me.

Malcolm X tells the story of how he started boxing when he was young, and found that he was pretty good at it until he fought "this big White boy" who whupped his ass. He wrote, "That was the beginning of the end of my fight career. A lot of times in these later years I've thought back to that fight and reflected that it was Allah's work to stop me. I might have ended up punchy."

As he had for Malcolm X, "Allah" stepped in to change the course of my fighting life. As I mentioned, I was in the first year of my recovery from cocaine, and one night I got drunk and got that intense, overwhelming craving that any former coke addict can tell you about. It's one of the wildest phenomena of the addiction, the actual measurable biochemical process the body begins when it wants the drug. Adrenaline courses through the system, acid bubbles in the stomach, and the bowels turn to mush. At that moment you feel you'll go out of your mind if you don't feed that need.

I couldn't take it anymore so I hopped in my car and drove to the spot in the projects that I had been hitting for years. A few gang kids, who I owed money to and had been ducking for months before I got clean, spotted me as I was going into the complex. They found me inside one of the apartments and dragged me outside, beating and kicking me the entire way.

What happened next is etched so crystal clear in my memory that I will carry each second of it with me for the rest of my life. I was being restrained by one of the four, who had one hand on my left arm, and one on my neck, pushing my head down against the driver's side roof. The other three were in front of my car, one smashing it with a mop handle, the other two behind him laughing. It was clear they were either going to put me in the hospital, or kill me, but either way, I was in some serious, serious shit. I was most definitely in fear for my life.

Time then slowed to a crawl, and all sound seemed to fade.

In those days while studying martial arts, we learned what was called a "blended street style," and I—more out of machismo than pragmatism—always carried a knife, which I clipped on the inside of my right front pants pocket. I remember looking down and seeing it there, then looking up and seeing that the dude who was holding me was not paying much attention to me as he watched his friend demolish my headlights. I looked down again, then over at his exposed belly, then down at my knife. I slowly grabbed my knife with my free right hand, flipped it open, and before the dude had any clue what was happening, I had buried it into his abdomen and ripped it back out again.

I had always loathed violence, having been the recipient of it at home, in school, and on the street. As a consequence, the very thought of hurting another person made me physically sick, filled me with pity, and has had a permanent pacifying effect.

So you'll understand when I tell you I can never and will never forget the scream that boy let out when I gutted him like I did. I saw him go bounding away hollering and all of his friends turned and watched him, stunned and unsure what had happened. In that instant of distraction, with crystal clear thinking and what felt like complete control, I jumped in my car, turned on the ignition, threw the car into reverse, and began backing out. The dude with the mop handle came at me and cracked my windshield and smashed the driver's side window. Another got in front of me, and I clipped him with the car as I drove away.

To this day, even as I write this, the screams of that boy haunt my soul. I intellectually understand it was self-defense, and I know had I not been feverishly studying how to fight, and cultivating the awareness that permitted me to take advantage of that massive adrenaline surge that literally bent time, I might not have walked away in one piece.

It took years for me to begin to process the emotions properly, but the physical effects were immediate, and absolute. God, the Universe, whatever, did *not* want me to have this power, because mere weeks later I tore my shoulder socket in that match with *my* "big White boy."

I had no health insurance, so over time the damage grew more and more severe with each successive separation and dislocation. By the time I entered prison, some years later, my arm was useless above the elbow, and I was in chronic pain. I had gone from having the confidence that I could defend myself in any situation to the real terror of *any* sort of confrontation, because I would be fighting as if I had one arm behind my back, and I would invariably lose.

The sudden realization that I was physically handicapped forced me into a *prima facie* understanding that I must seek peaceful resolutions to any and all conflict if I had any hope of guaranteeing my own safety and well-being. And because I effectively took violence off the table as even a possible response, almost all my social and political thinking centered on nonviolence as a *de facto* component to any change strategy.

I know now in my heart that force can never be met with force if what you seek is a situation without violence. Yes, the White Power bloc already jumped me once, and yes they may try and jump me again. But since I chose not to respond in kind, so far I've made out OK. I have to believe that holding fast to this will get me through whatever they throw at me.

AUGUST 12, 2005

Rules and regs for parole were explained to us today in Pre-Start. Of the very long list of things we are no longer legally allowed to do or have, of particular note was the Illinois Gang Omnibus

Prevention Bill that prohibits ex-felons from associating with other ex-felons and anyone known to be a gang member. This may seem on its surface to be a no-brainer—a law to keep criminals away from other criminals—but the underlying complexities make it a very interesting piece of legislation.

Yashua believes this law was enacted in order to lock up gang members in federal prison under the auspices of "domestic terrorism." With deep gravitas he told the young gang members in my group to be prepared for "what's coming." It may be just around the corner. The recent media and government propaganda campaigns against increasing gang activity—centered on a purported "supergang" from El Salvador called M13—seems to be laying the public relations groundwork for legally classifying street gang violence as "domestic terrorism." This would mean the end of any form of legal protections for gang members—no lawyers, warrants, courts, due process, *habeas corpus*, probable cause, appeals, or possibly even release. It would open the doors to mass arrests.

Critics will invariably claim this interpretation is shrill, paranoid, and reactive, but we should remember that prior to 9/11 and the passage of the Patriot Act, foreign nationals, even if they were accused of terrorism, were entitled to due process. Not any longer in the era of "enemy combatants," torture and rendition, and secret prisons.

The M13 argument bridges the gap between the foreign national or "enemy combatant" and the "domestic terrorist," as many purported M13 members are also illegal aliens. As soon as the American public capitulates to treating M13, a street gang, like al-Qaeda it's only a legalistic hop, skip, and jump away from extending the definition to indigenous black and Latino street gangs, or any domestic organized crime group or political entity that has an antiauthoritarian or antiestablishment philosophy, like the various ethnic Mafias or the Hells Angels, or the Black Bloc, or the International Socialist Organization, or the Animal

Liberation Front.[13] This would, in essence, bring the 1996 Comprehensive Antiterrorism Act and the Patriot Act into full collusion.[14] It would also go a long way towards wiping out groups who survive on a cash economy.

What the Illinois parolee legislation—and similar legislation in states across the nation—means is that, since ex-convicts tend to cluster in large numbers in impoverished communities, whole communities of people are legally prevented from associating with one another, even amongst members of the same family. Looked at under the rubric of "terrorism," it seems utterly ridiculous. Most gang violence is self-contained in that it targets only those in its milieu, not institutions of authority. Tragic victims of crossfire notwithstanding, street gangs tend to avoid antistate violence unless provoked by the police.

However, if social and economic conditions continue to deteriorate, or the police continue to summarily lock up or gun down innocent people, a critical mass may be reached and these communities may begin to organize themselves for change, like they did in the 1960s and '70s. Most of the major riots of that era were triggered by the violence white police visited on black folk. When viewed within this context, suddenly the potential applications of this parolee legislation become crystal clear: an organized force of millions of disenfranchised ex-felons, unable to find a decent living or redress their government, is something that must give the ruling class nightmares. Thus, managing this unruly criminal underclass is an integral part of our entire social architecture in what Christian Parenti calls the "Age of Crisis."[15]

In many ways, we can see that the momentum of awareness and change is building, destroying—for better or worse—the mythology surrounding "the criminal." It is this they fear, because we are not nearly as dangerous as they need us to be to maintain the status quo, but just dangerous enough to know how to fight back if pushed too far. I no longer fear what street gangs can do to me, but I do fear what the government can do.

This afternoon I had to give my DNA to the State of Illinois as part of a new law passed in 2004 requiring all convicts to provide samples. Although we were informed by the head of East Moline BCI[16] that compliance is "voluntary," when I asked what would happen if we refused he said, unequivocally, that failure to comply would result in us being sent to segregation, where they would forcibly draw blood from us, and then we would be shipped to a max facility, where another charge would be placed on us, and we would get more time. Would someone please show me the "voluntary" part?

I gave my sample. I thought for just a moment about refusing, on principle, but I knew I would lose any moral battle. Right now, the public wants this, or at least they think they do, because they don't think it will ever apply to them. Yet so many mass-applied social policies start out in the penal system—constant surveillance, restricted movement, forced identity recording, riot control. If the public became aware of that, they'd start seeing themselves as prisoners in their own purportedly free society, and then maybe they'd get around to changing things. But right now, just like with their acceptance of the police state rising all around them, they see having our DNA as a necessary and even desirable security measure.

I'm deeply distressed by this. I am now, truly, a marked man. They had files on me already. After two years with the Green Party and last summer's festivities in Boston and New York, I'm sure every branch of federal law enforcement has made space for me somewhere on their hard drives. I have a number—R45067—that's bad enough. But now they have *me*. How easy would it be for me to be framed now? How much is what I say and do in the future going to be tempered by the knowledge that the State will, in one regard, always have me under their thumb? I'm not naïve, I know exactly what can and does happen to people who fly too close to the sun. I've made myself believe that I've dedicated the last few years of my life to "changing the world" (which I am beginning to see may in truth be a massive prolonged and projected psychological crisis, but that's another story for another day) knowing full well that anyone who really gets close to shaking up the power structure gets it, usually two in the head, or two life sentences locked far away from the rest of humanity, or two IRS audits that wipe you out and land you on a work farm. How bad it gets depends on how big you are, and how much shaking you can cause.

What really drives my fear about being framed is that people would probably believe it. The Chicago police could have gotten away with framing me last year had they not gone too far and tried to portray me as (the irony is *killing* me!) a white supremacist militia type. But how many people would believe that a "large cache of drugs were found in his home/on his person," enough to get me sent away for a while? I suppose I made that bed for myself, so I should just lie in it. But man, it's one seriously lumpy-ass mattress.

I have to admit to feeling that—as an activist—I betrayed my fundamental values and blew an opportunity to make a statement by refusing to give my DNA. I had to keep telling myself they *already have* my blood, it was drawn at least three times since I entered the system. Underneath it I questioned how much I really wanted to be an activist anymore. Could I have withstood a couple years in a max joint to defend my principles? I don't know. Probably. I rationalize it by reminding myself that I can be a much more effective agent of change out in the world than locked away in a box somewhere.

Knowing that the constitutionality of this law and of the forcible blood-draws was being challenged in the courts did little to assuage the pervasive feeling I had of being violated in a way that the rapes I suffered never made me feel. One thing is for sure: defiance is a lot harder than it seems sometimes when the consequences get dire.

Maybe I am weak.

AUGUST 13, 2005

The following are three quotes from *The Autobiography of Malcolm X*, all of them written about his time in prison.

"Any person who claims to have deep feeling for other human beings should think a long, long time before he votes to have another man kept behind bars—caged. I am not saying there shouldn't be prisons. But there shouldn't be bars. Behind bars, a man never reforms. He will never forget. He will never get completely over the memory of the bars."

"I remember how, reading the bible in the Norfolk Prison library, I came upon, then I read, over and over, how Paul on the road to Damascus, upon hearing the voice of Christ, was so smitten that he was knocked off his horse, in a daze. I do not now, and I did not then, liken myself to Paul. But I do understand his experience. I have since learned that the truth can be quickly received, or received at all, only by the sinner who knows and admits that he was guilty of having sinned much. Stated another way: only guilt admitted accepts truth. I was going through the hardest thing, also the greatest thing, for any human being to do: to accept that which is already within you, and around you."

When I came across that second quote about Paul on the road to Damascus, my initial response was *You have got to be kidding me! OK, God, Universe, Source, whatever you are and wherever you are, I get it! I hear you, OK? No need to continue to beat me over the head with it. I'm paying attention!*

Then, this last one . . .

In the hectic pace of the world today, there is no time for meditation or for deep thought. A prisoner has time that he can put to good use. I'd put prison second to college as the best place for a man to go if he needs to do some thinking. If he's motivated, in prison he can change his life. Once a man has been to prison, he never looks at himself or other people the same again. The 'squares' out there whose boats have been in smooth waters all the time turn up their noses at an ex-con. But an ex-con can keep his head up when the squares sink."

An ex-con can keep his head up when the squares sink.
Go convict, go.
Rise, convict, rise.

AUGUST 16, 2005

I saw Yancy, the educational director, again today. He told me that in 23 years of working for IDOC he could count on one hand the number of inmates he had met who he felt would be good advocates for ex-offenders, "and two of them are in this office right now." I was with another inmate named Carl Jones who Yancy had wanted me to meet, a brother who was probably a decade older than me, had a long ponytail, and was halfway through a 20-piece. He said Carl was "an activist" but didn't explain further, and Carl said he'd talk to me about it later.

Yancy doesn't believe those who commit victimless crimes should be in prison. "When I got here twenty-three years ago I used to think that every one of you miscreants belonged here. But years later, after I took the education director job I had the opportunity to get to know a few inmates . . . not many, but certainly more than anyone else around here. The staff simply ain't interested. They have a very negative opinion of *all* inmates as a general rule. But I came to know some of their stories and after a while I got to thinking that many of them simply didn't belong in here. You two are here because of choices you made, and you both are men of principle. Through your experience here, you have developed a certain compassion for the criminal. I hope when you leave here you make good use of it."

There's so much about Yancy that flips my wig. Who *is* this motherfucker? I mean he barely knows me but for what I have told him, unless he looked me up online. That may be why he speaks with such authority about me and who and what he thinks I am. It's not like I'm quiet about what I think or anything (note sarcasm).

Yancy's right, I do want to raise awareness about what's going on in the prisons, I do want to try and change people's attitudes about the drug war, and change their attitudes about what exactly a "crime" is, and what a "criminal" is. You can't compare my crimes to those of at least half or more of the total inmate population of this whole goddam nation, so why should we all be judged equally as "dangerous criminals." I want to end discrimination against ex-convicts and see their potential harnessed. And by saying that, all I'm really saying is that I want a break, man. I don't want to be written off or shut out! I will fight as hard as I can to still be able to have opportunities in life, because I know that mine is not a wasted life, I have my best years ahead of me, and there's no limit to what I can accomplish if someone would just *give me a chance.* I want *them* to have compassion for the criminal, I want them to care what I think. Shit, it's easy to hold compassion for something you are when you want others to see you for who you really are, not what society labels you. Or should I say, it's easy to want to be treated compassionately. But to treat *oneself* with compassion . . . well, that's a much more difficult proposition now, isn't it?

J.T., known on the deck as "Six-Nine" owing to his prodigious height, lives in the cell next to mine. He's a big, lanky, grizzled white dude with a mullet who looks totally worn down by life at times, and other times he's bouncing around like the young boys.

He seems to get along with all the brothers, which is probably why he's here on this deck; he and I are virtually the only white dudes. However, unlike anyone else I have met here, he doesn't like The Sweet Moline and has requested a transfer to a worse joint in the system. He claims he is "bored" here (well, d'uh, dude it's prison, it's supposed to be boring . . . in fact, that's the one thing about prison the general public doesn't really get is just how goddamn boring it is). He says he can't handle the "infantile gossip" of this place either, which, to be fair, is pretty severe.

This morning he said he wanted to talk to me about my situation with the White Power bloc. He knows all those guys from doing time with them in other joints; apparently, J.T. is a careerist too, since he's received 18 years of sentences spread out over a few bits.

"You think it's all racial, but it's not," he told me. "It's about your station in life. Money is the primary issue—how much you got, how much you can wield. Dude, poor is poor, and *everyone* in the joint is poor. If you had money you wouldn't be here. Those guys don't hate you because you won't talk their racist script, they hate you because you came from something and it shows . . . loud and clear. You obviously had education and shit and I'm sure after you told them a bit about yourself they realized they had nothing in common with you. You represent all this other shit to them, mostly unfavorable shit, and so they decided to play head games with you, to try and drag you down into their negative bullshit. That's all they have, and on that playing field, you'd win, 'cause you're smarter than them . . . probably all of them put together. Don't let that shit go to your head, huh, 'cause that ain't so much a compliment to you as a statement on how fuckin' retarded those guys are."

I figured as much. I figured that was part of what made Smokey decide to glom on to them, since it was clear from all the shit he said the first couple of days that he didn't exactly have the highest opinion of himself either, and he probably felt more comfortable

with those xenophobic organ sacks. It was also part of what connected me to Smitty and David, since they clearly appreciated
knowledge and education and were, I feel, more frustrated than
usual about what they saw as societal limitations placed on their
potential. Think about what Smitty could have accomplished had
he been able to go to college and work in a proper laboratory on
beneficial things rather than an ad hoc meth lab in his basement.

J.T. continued. "What those guys *really* wanted to do was
beat your ass and take all your shit, openly humiliate you on that
deck. That's what used to happen before they cracked down on
the prisons and started monitoring our every move like they do
now. Inmates used to run everything, and you *had* to pick a side.
You *had* to. And trust me, dude, you would not have been able
to chose like you did here. What those guys said was true. You
would have had to run with them, or you would have been on
your own. And then they'd have you in a dress within a week. But
now, well, now they have to be very careful, especially here, 'cause
everyone either wants to be here or knows they are getting out
soon. It's the one thing keeping those guys off you right now. So
instead, they talk a ton of shit and have already told everyone in
this joint that you ratted on your cellies, dude. The racism is just
used to help them feel like they got somethin', 'cause they ain't got
shit. None of them. But you sure got somethin' . . ."

He stared right at me and shook his head like I had really
fucked up. My stomach sank.

". . . somethin' you sure as shit don't want."

"And what's that?" I asked.

"You got a rep for bein' a rat now. And there are guys out there
who take that shit pretty fucking seriously. It don't matter what
your story is, in these guys' eyes you broke the one cardinal rule,
you talked to the Man. Eventually that shit is gonna come back
around and bite you in the ass."

I said something to the effect that I wasn't really worried about
them getting to me now because a lot of the brothers knew what

was up. He looked at me like I was pretty fuckin' stupid and shook his head.

"Don't go thinkin' these black guys got your back, 'cause they don't care about you. To your face they act like you're down with them, but behind your back . . . when you ain't around here . . . look, I'm gonna say this again since you didn't seem to hear me the first time. All these guys . . . I'm talkin', these guys here . . . your 'homies' . . . all they care about is that you tricked on your cellies to the po-lice. Now look, dude, I don't blame you for doing what you did, but you have to understand, that shit is all that matters in here. The only reason any of them might treat you decent is if they think they can get commissary from you. Mark my words. Just look at me, man, I'm the proof. No one does shit with me in here 'cause I got nothing. I'm telling you . . . it's *all* . . . *about . . . the . . . money.*"

Although a lot of what J.T. said made sense, and I have no real illusions about their loyalty to me when all is said and done, I did temper what he said against what I already knew to be true, which is that every inmate has a hustle, particularly the careerists. I also knew that I did have some measure of uniqueness and station with the brothers, and J.T. does not. If nothing else, they are curious and know I am benign to them. Anyway, I'd never ask them for shit, and J.T. is always beggin'. Always. Coffee. Tobacco. Food. Toothpaste. He comes by every day to cop something from Ron-Ron, but Ron-Ron gives it to him 'cause he likes "Six-Nine." He's always calling to him through the walls. I think Ron-Ron finds him really amusing. Not too many mullets in the area of the South Side where he's from.

It's kind of ironic, too, because that same evening at dinner I was sitting with Big Mo' (Melvin) and Floyd and Myron and a couple other cats from the deck. And Big Mo' is takin' a bite, and lookin' over at me, and then smiling like something is funny, then doin' it again. And then he finally leans over and says, "You know . . . you the only white boy we let sit with us like this."

Floyd immediately jumps in with "'cause he cool like that" and pats me on the back. It was the best feeling I had had in longer than I could remember.

AUGUST 18, 2005

You're gonna *love* this.

So, the very next day, after J.T. gives me this looooong speech, inveighed with jailhouse gravitas, about the pettiness of Sweet Moline and how he never gets himself involved in these indigenous dramas, he ends up voluntarily "walking himself" to seg.

What that means is that he requested to be put into segregation for security reasons (one of the potential outcomes to my situation with the White Power bloc, which, as we know, I successfully avoided). This results in an automatic shipment to another joint. The reason J.T. did this was because he owed people in here too much *money*, and he had nothing on the books. He conned and hustled everyone out of whatever he could get, always promising repayment. He even told me over and over he was getting money for when our commissary date comes up, but I never asked for repayment, so his hustle was a little transparent.

Now the brothers on the deck are talking a *ton* of shit about J.T. "Six-Nine on some *bullshit*!" you hear shouted across the deck, over and over. Apparently he owes quite a few neighbors their cups of sugar. These muthafuckas is salty!

Apparently, from what I hear now, J.T. couldn't help himself. He was compulsively manipulative. Floyd tells me it happens when people get "institutionalized" with repeat bits and "don't get on their particulars" to cope with it emotionally. They just get into a behavior pattern that mimics the hustling they did to feed their addictions. Floyd should know, he's done nine bits, more than J.T. has. But Floyd's response to his time is markedly different than J.T.'s. Floyd doesn't ever get down, seriously. He's got like seven kids, the youngest of whom is two, and he's got photos of them everywhere. He does the funniest impression of his two-year-old daughter. He says she likes to hang on his braids.

Although Floyd is still a high-ranking member of the Black P-Stones, he converted to (at least a moderate form of) Islam, and prays five times a day here, complete with prayer mat and the ceremonial washing beforehand and everything. I think it has served to ground him and give him hope and strength (oh my, dare I say something *positive* about Islam in George Bush's America?). Anyway, being around him certainly helps keep your own emotional shit in perspective.

In hindsight, maybe I should have seen through J.T. more clearly because I knew something was up in the way he really tried to dissuade me from believing that anyone here was real. I know how in-tune my intuition is, even when my ego blinds it. But I had no idea about his rep, nor did I really care, so I guess if anything I'm guilty of a lack of reconnaissance. He didn't owe me money, and I hoped the coffee I gave him made his days a little easier. Despite his understanding of the system, he was the same as those he was decrying. Perhaps that should be the least surprising fact.

It seems like my biggest fault here has been taking a community of hustlers at their word, and reacting to them like a journalist instead of a fellow prisoner, who needs to employ a certain measure of cynicism and self-protection.

They used to say in AA that if you hung around a barbershop long enough you were gonna get a haircut. Well, if you hang around a street corner or a cellblock long enough, you're gonna get hustled.

▼

Brave New World presents a fanciful and somewhat ribald picture of a society in which the attempt to recreate human beings in the likeness of termites has been pushed almost to the limits of the possible. That we are being propelled in the direction of *Brave New World* is obvious. . . . As Mr. William Whyte has shown in his remarkable book, *The Organization Man*, a new Social Ethic is replacing our traditional ethical system—the system in which the individual is primary . . . Its basic assumption is that the social whole has greater worth and significance than its individual parts, that inborn biological differences should be sacrificed to cultural uniformity, that the rights of the collectivity take precedence over . . . the Rights of Man. The ideal man is the man who displays 'dynamic conformity' (delicious phrase!) and an intense loyalty to the group, an unflagging desire to subordinate himself, to belong . . . The monk makes vows of poverty, obedience, and chastity. The organization man is allowed to be rich, but promises obedience ('he accepts authority without resentment, he looks up to his superiors' . . .) and he must be prepared for the greater glory of the organization that employs him, to forswear even conjugal love.

—Aldous Huxley, *Brave New World Revisited*

AUGUST 20, 2005

Kate O'Hare was sentenced to five years in prison for her political opposition to the US entering the First World War. She was convicted under the draconian "Espionage Act," "Trading with the Enemy Act," and the "Sedition Act," which made any dissent against the war a high crime. O'Hare was jailed with famed anarchist and dissident Emma Goldman, who wrote that the Espionage Act "turned the country into a lunatic asylum, with every state and federal official, as well as a large part of the civilian population running amuck" as non-combatants and conscientious objectors from all social classes began to fill the prisons and jails. O'Hare published in the *St. Louis Post-Dispatch* detailed accounts of the prison conditions she and Goldman experienced, and these articles eventually led to reforms.

O'Hare wrote after the fact:

> The results gained by placing many hundreds of political prisoners in our penitentiaries have not been quite those sought by the political administration . . . As a by-effect, the searchlight of intelligent study and keen analysis has been turned into the darkest and most noisome depths of our social system—the prisons . . . The political prisoners, in common with all sincere students, found that the prisons are the cesspools of our social system and that into them drain the most helpless, hopeless products of our body, brain, and soul-destroying struggle for existence. There is no doubt that it was a good thing for our country that a large group of well-educated, intelligent, socially-minded people should have gone to prison . . . If I were ruler of the universe, I would see to it that many more respectable folk went to prison, for the good of their souls and the welfare of the country.

In these days of martial legislation like the Patriot Act, when nonviolent demonstrators are herded into temporary prison camps and razor wire "Free Speech" zones and a million citizens are incarcerated for morality crimes of a victimless nature, it seems obvious, when contemplating O'Hare's words, what my role should be once, as one Shepherd said to the other Shepherd, I get the flock out of here. If it is only to create awareness, then that will be honoring my duty to the "general welfare."

Victimless drug crimes *are* political crimes. They are the criminalization of one's lifestyle and personal choices, as well as the direct violation of the sanctity of one's own physical and cognitive self. In this regard, we of this vein are all political prisoners.

AUGUST 21, 2005

The war altered every aspect of American life. American capitalism emerged a hero for its remarkable accomplishments in providing the sinews of war, not only for the United States Army and Navy but for the Allies as well. Its prestige was enormously enhanced, or perhaps, considering the bitter criticism to which it had been subjected since the Civil War, it might be more accurate to say that the reputation of Capitalism was not so much enhanced as created. Moreover, Capitalists, elated by their new popularity and their generally favorable press, took the offensive against those individuals and groups reckless enough to criticize them. Chambers of Commerce and the National Association of Manufacturers hired hundreds of highly paid publicists to proclaim the virtues of business, big and small, and to denounce their opponents as unpatriotic and, worst of all, as 'reds', unwitting dupes of Russia or wily agents of Bolsheviks. It was a novel notion—the idea that criticizing capitalism and capitalists constituted subversive activity. What had been, almost since the beginning of the Republic, a common exercise now fell under a ban. Criticizing capitalism could (and often did) result in the critics being clapped in jail.

—from "WWI: America Enters the War" in *A People's History of the Progressive Era* by Page Smith

Not only were publicists hired to sell capitalism, they were also hired to sell the war. Edward Bernays, the nephew of Sigmund Freud who is largely credited with inventing public relations, helped Woodrow Wilson "sell" World War I to the American public, essentially by inventing a marketing slogan: "Making the World Safe for Democracy." Bernays openly acknowledged that PR "is really just propaganda, but we couldn't use that word because the Germans already had." If you want to see something that will blow you away, see the BBC documentary *The Century*

of the Self. It basically explains how consumerism was invented
and promulgated as a means of social control. Think you're living
in a free market? Think again. The choices you think you are
freely making when you purchase consumer goods are in reality
a carefully calculated exploitation of your baser instincts, done
as a means of getting you to buy into a larger system of control
without your knowing.

Using his uncle's theories of the unconscious, particularly those
that purported to govern the sex drive, Bernays showed American
corporations how to make people buy material goods they didn't
need by connecting those products to their unconscious desires
and unmet needs. He used the tremendous influence he gained
(through making a few people incredibly rich and powerful) to
propose that the same principles be used politically to control the
masses, who were deemed volatile, unruly creatures governed by
hidden passions. Maintaining control was the primary goal of the
social engineers, and consumerism and other material indulgence
became a formidable tool.

Slowly strip away the ability for people to take care of themselves, one by one turning each necessary survival skill over to
the marketplace—growing and preparing food, building a home,
making furniture, clothing, even our faith and our pastimes—
which are then sold back to us piecemeal, to keep us helpless and
dependent, with lots of distractions and medications to help keep
things running smoothly like a machine, key word *machine*.

This social-control-through-indulgence model was what
Huxley was excoriating in *Brave New World*. It was a critique
of consumerism, conformity, collectivism, and the vapidity of a
culture based in pleasure seeking. There, freethinking and human
attachment was either outlawed or genetically modified out of
the human species. In its place was a dumbed-down class-based
society overrun by high-tech entertainment, sexual promiscuity,
and a powerful, all-purpose intoxicant/narcotic/dissociative drug
called Soma, which was used to quell any unpleasant feelings.

Golly gee whillickers, Batman, why does this scenario sound soooooooooooo familiar?

It's interesting to note that the two major future dystopia novels, *Brave New World* and *1984*, portray societies where the religious or spiritual self has been hijacked and transferred to other social-control constructs. In *1984* the oppressed citizens of Oceania, clamoring for survival in their bombed-out world of austerity, worship the State through a cult of personality built around the Stalinistic image of "Big Brother." The purportedly free citizens of *Brave New World*, unwittingly enslaved in a never-ending state of adolescent indulgence, shrouded in ignorance of one's own history, worship the market in the form of "Our Ford," the god of industrialization.

Carl Jung, Freud's student and eventual rival, thought Freud was missing the point altogether. He thought compulsive behavior addresses a spiritual loss or deficiency. Because the addictive experience is mimetic of the spiritual experience, you can have an imitation of bliss or oneness through indulgence, but it doesn't last. Jung believed only a true spiritual awakening will end this feeling of emptiness.

Likewise, only a global spiritual awakening will end the indulgence that is ravaging the planet.

AUGUST 22, 2005

Ron-Ron was released today after serving 11 months in custody. Late last night before lockdown, as he was coming back into the cell, the lights suddenly flipped on (I had gone to sleep early) and a sea of brothers—at least ten—poured into the cell yelling "Get his ass!" My first thought was total panic and confusion: I thought they were after me.

But they were after Ron-Ron to give him the time-honored, good-natured goodbye "beating" known as the "exit treatment."

They all jumped on his bed and pounded him a bit in the arms and legs where the charley horses roam. He was hollerin' his ass off, and I yelled, "Good lord, the revolution is here!" Then, as fast as they came, they were gone. Ron-Ron lay groaning and laughing on his bunk.

We went to sleep soon after that and got up early and talked for a while before the 7 am count. We cleaned up the last of his shit, they released us to movement, and then he was gone.

Stay home, son.

AUGUST 23, 2005

Before I left for prison, in the months I was languishing on house arrest, many of my friends and colleagues in the activist community had been telling me that I had before me "such a unique opportunity" to help reach out to, connect with, educate, and organize one of the nation's largest disenfranchised populations, namely, us convicts.

It stood to reason, they argued (and I would eventually internalize) that if only these men could become aware of the larger circumstances of their situation, they would endeavor to change those circumstances, and cease allowing themselves to be manipulated by the system. I thought that if only they could see the "War on Drugs" for the sham that it is, how it is used to control and disrupt their communities and fill the prison system to reap huge profits and perpetuate a "correctional economy," then maybe a spontaneous movement might emerge, and finally the proverbial "winds of change" might begin to blow.

Good luck.

Although I have been guilty of naïveté on a few occasions in my life, I never considered how utterly naïve I was in thinking that some white guy raised in the upper-middle class could foment a sea change of opinion inside one of the most dangerous and tightly controlled constructs of our society. Not only was I not from their world, but I very soon came to realize that I had terribly miscalculated the actual level of interest and receptiveness of the inmate population to these circumstances. Yes, I had a far greater familiarity with their world than most, if not all, of the white people I knew, because I spent so much time in the ghetto buying and consuming drugs or living in halfway houses, but that hardly translates to the trust needed to change a people's reality. I was dead wrong about what I now see were highly romantic and idealistic notions of how much could be accomplished in this regard.

First of all, these guys already know the game is rigged. The young ones may not know how the 1960s riots their fathers and grandfathers participated in led to the situation they and their communities are in now, but they *do* know that the cops are dirty, and they know no one in their neighborhoods owns planes, ships, trains, and cargo trucks to be moving "weight" [large amounts of drugs] into their neighborhoods. In other words, they know the drugs are intentionally funneled into their communities. They ain't stupid.

What they are, young and old alike, is beat down. For some of them, prison is the only rest they get. The minute the gate swings open for them, they gotta hit the ground running or else they starve. They don't have a lot of time to read and attend meetings. And if they ever wanted to try and go protest something while on parole, they can get sent back in a heartbeat. These guys are concerned about staying alive. They don't give a rat's ass about politics. Ultimately, they are kept in line by fear, desperation, and exhaustion. And anyway, who would they redress? Who would listen to them? They've been ignored for three generations under these policies, and there is little hope of a mass re-enfranchisement of so many forsaken souls.

Mine eyes have seen the gory coming of the overlord.

Talking to Edie on the phone one night, and she just came right out and asked me, "So, after this experience, are you more or less hopeful for humanity?" Without hesitation, and with complete candor, I said, "Far less hopeful than I ever imagined, verging on hopeless." When pressed to explain, I offered one of the axioms of *1984*: *Ignorance Is Strength*. The awareness I have now, the consciousness I have of the truth of the world, drains me.

There is a passage in *1984*, part of *The Theory and Practice of Oligarchical Collectivism* (the "book within the book") written by the "traitor to the State," Emmanuel Goldstein (a character based on Leon Trotsky; the name is homage to the anarchist Emma Goldman) that goes like this:

> Throughout recorded time there have been three kinds of people in the world, the *High*, the *Middle*, and the *Low*. The aims of these three groups are entirely irreconcilable. The aim of the *High* is to remain where they are. The aim of the *Middle* is to change places with the *High*. The aim of the *Low*, when they have an aim—*for it is an abiding characteristic of the Low that they are too crushed by drudgery to be more than intermittently conscious of anything outside their daily lives*—is to abolish all distinctions and create a society in which all men shall be equal. Thus, throughout history a struggle which is the same in its main outlines recurs over and over again. For long periods the *High* seem to be securely in power, but sooner or later there always comes a moment when they lose either their belief in themselves, or their capacity to govern efficiently, or both. They are then overthrown by the *Middle*, who enlist the *Low* on their side by pretending to them that they are fighting for liberty and justice. As soon as they have reached their objective, the *Middle* thrust the *Low* back into their old position of servitude, and themselves become the *High*. Presently, a new *Middle* group splits off from one of the other groups, or from both of them, and the struggle begins all over again.

This passage perfectly characterizes the situation I find myself in. By and large those sent into the prisons are disproportionately culled from the ranks of the *Low*. And although it is clear to at least the black segment of the *Low* that the drug war is a scam, it is not so clear to the whites. The whites have internalized the moral mandate of the *High*, by virtue of the first degree of separation imposed on the *Low*, known as "divide and rule," which is preferential separation by race. Whites who break the social contract established by the ruling order—who are also white—are derided and judged to have moral failings, which the poor whites then internalize. If you use drugs, you are a criminal, if you sell drugs, you're even worse. *Hate yourself, for you are irredeemable, but not nearly as irredeemable as those darker than you*, is the basic subtext.

Poor blacks, on the other hand, are far less likely to care what the ruling white order thinks of them, and are much more apt to view selling drugs as a legitimate economic means to an end, without nearly as much moral condemnation, although it certainly does exist, owing to the overwhelming prevalence and influence of Christianity in most of their communities. Still, the decision to sell drugs more often than not serves to divide them against their community.

In this way—uniquely American—race is substituted for class, so that claims of a "classless society" can somewhat plausibly be made in a nation whose rep was built on the marketing campaign *All men are created equal*, even though what they really meant was "all land owning white men" since they didn't actually view blacks as people. Today, if you don't own property, you aren't viewed as a person either. Conversely, the corporation that does own property is considered by the courts to be a legal person, so it is bestowed all the constitutional protections which we living people supposedly have "endowed by our Creator."

Substituting race for class keeps members of the black, white, Latino, Asian, or Muslim *Low* class from seeing affinities and common struggles and uniting to change their situation. Instead they remained Balkanized and mired in the (literally) superficial differences they see between themselves: no white inmate will ever admit that he is in the same empirical situation as a black inmate, because even if the economics are the same, there are the reinforced social and cultural differentiations and privileges their skin color gives them which they violently cling to and defend.

The subdivision of the underclass continues. The whites in prison—out of necessity borne out of being the minority—are a much more monolithic community than the blacks, who are subdivided against each other by age, and again by gang affiliation or lack thereof. The young boys who are active in gang culture prize money and material goods first and foremost, and their genuine cultural history has been replaced by the pop culture of hip hop, which serves to essentially rob them of whatever wealth they do generate by compelling them to spend it all on consumer shit. They gotta have the right clothes, music, shoes, car, hats, drinks, blunts. They don't want to hear about Martin Luther King and Malcolm X and Medgar Evers. They don't give a shit about the Civil Rights Movement, and they think people like Jesse Jackson and Al Sharpton are a joke (well . . . OK . . . sometimes they are). They don't see how they have essentially backed themselves into a social classification from which they very rarely escape. For them, life becomes a vicious cycle of hustling, prison, violence, and for some, death.

In my attempts to reach greater levels of understanding between us, I've been trying to drop this historical example on the young brothers in the hope that they see how the same energy got channeled in different directions. I talk about the cultural and generational differences between rapper Tupac Shakur and his mother, Afeni, who was a Black Panther. On the surface, they appear to be standing on opposite sides of the African American cultural spectrum. Fundamentally, one represents the struggle to empower and end the exploitation of her people and to improve their social conditions, while the other represents the divisive exploitation of those same social conditions for his own gain, namely the "I gotta gets mines" ethos of rap/gang culture, which supplants cultural unity. But underneath, both Shakurs loved and fought for the rights of their people on the larger meta-stage, and eventually both fell prey to the internecine struggles of the respective militant communities to whom they served. This does not take away from the fact that both Shakurs went on to symbolize their respective zeitgeists in Black history.

I may be guilty of mythologizing Afeni and the nobility of the Black Panthers, but it seems self-evident that the Panthers taught that the most important thing for black Americans was to be part of a united, self-supporting community. Tupac—whether by design, or as a consequence of the influences around him—represented the most devastating and divisive product of Black America, the violent and self-serving street Machiavellianism of gang culture. Tupac glamorized and gave powerful cred to being violent, self-obsessed, and materialistic; all he talked about was gettin' paid, while he gave lip service to ending gang violence in California through his much ballyhooed "truce" campaign.

Although both were embroiled in legal struggles throughout their lives, the natures of those legal struggles were entirely different. Afeni was fighting the illegal activity of the US Government, which we now know went to great lengths to eliminate the Panthers through the COINTELPRO[17] program. Tupac was in court fighting legitimate, often true, criminal charges. Although we did eventually learn that in fact the FBI was keeping close watch on the Hip Hop world, and did try to use any opportunity to divide and disrupt, on those few occasions when Tupac did speak out against gun violence and sexual assault charges, these entirely orchestrated efforts were more aimed at reducing time in prison than creating any kind of awareness or change.

Of course, Tupac's greatest crime against his own people was using his celebrity to ignite the East Coast–West Coast war. This is his legacy, which may have cost him his life, depending on who you want to believe killed him. No matter how much talk there is about Tupac being a "prophet" who rapped about the reality of life in the ghetto, who wanted to lift up his brother, history will remember him as an opportunistic pop artist and violent thug who was constantly fighting with his own people, not loving them, and that he was eventually killed by them.

Nowadays, the "thug life" persona has been so mass-adopted by black youth that it's a mainstay of Hip Hop culture, even ten years after Tupac's death. Certainly curious how the violent meme of Gangster Rap supplanted the peaceful meme of Consciousness Rap that the preceding generation of Hip Hop artists like Arrested Development, De La Soul, and A Tribe Called Quest were creating. Even though most rappers today, and the gang kids who emulate them, can only manage tired clichés, so long as black youth continue to idolize the Tupacs and 50 Cents and the literal cavalcade of copycat artists that have ridden their coattails, they won't be able to escape the consequences that come along with worshipping the dark side. If you mess around with guns and drugs, eventually you gonna either get shot or locked up.

So, the subtext to all this is to say that political concerns, particularly those that Afeni Shakur held concerning the welfare of black communities, are not even registering on the radar of these young men. Worse still, the core of the Panther's militancy—protecting their communities, even if it meant taking up arms with your brothers—has given way to taking up arms *against* your brothers. The enemy has shifted from "the Man" that oppressed them to the "nigger down the block" who might kill them. Prestige is now doled out Mafia style, based upon successful hits and how much weight you move. What the gang kids don't see is that they are doing the white establishment's job for them, which is to say, neutralizing or eliminating each other, and by proxy, the black community *writ large*, as a unified force for social and political change.

The small percentage of African Americans who were able to move up into the *Middle* got wise and distanced themselves from their *Low* brethren so that they could prosper under the dominant system, where there are places for them. There are no places for poor blacks in our culture any longer, callously dismissed as "surplus population." And so long as the "surplus" continues slangin' dope and shooting each other, they will continue to alienate themselves from decent, hard-working, law-abiding black families, perpetuating the most basic form of divide and rule. The single most powerful symbol of the disempowerment and destruction of the African American community is the image of former revolutionary Afeni Shakur sucking on a crack pipe, begging for the oppressors' poison while abandoning her child to the streets.

We've had 25 years of this kind of divide and rule. Drug and gang violence has cemented public opinion to such a degree that it is next to impossible to try and argue for ending prohibition when little kids are still getting gunned down in the crossfire and sucked into the machine of the drug trade. Our cultural views about drugs and crime are so entrenched, and so monolithic, I think, because addiction, in one form or another, touches almost everyone's life, and addiction is a deeply emotional issue.

Compounding the divide is the disillusionment held by the Civil Rights generation who largely see their leaders—those who survived, that is—as having sold out their dreams for fame, money, power, or continued relevance. It's interesting to look at the difference, after the Vietnam War and the Civil Rights Movement, between how the Weathermen were treated versus the Black Panthers. Even though the two organizations worked together as allies, most of the Panther leadership is now dead or locked up, while the Weathermen, who were avowed users of terrorism to achieve their goals, were given amnesty and their leaders now hold lofty positions at universities.

When all is said and done about the "revolution," it's pretty quickly apparent that whites pulled out their "redeemable privilege coupons" and were allowed to walk away unscathed into consumer America, so long as they stopped slumming in the slums. Black America, however, unbeknownst to them at the time, were about to have visited upon them the worst scourge yet in the form of the crack epidemic. Today, these wounds are old and scarred, and none of these men have the strength or desire to reopen them. This is made easy for them, because no one wants to hear what they have to say, least of all their children and grandchildren.

But getting back to a much more fundamental point about the malleability of the convict mentality, whether it is Malcolm X or Morpheus or Mos Def saying it, most of these minds are not yet ready to be freed. Most are hopelessly dependent upon the system, their worldview so tragically narrow, that they know nothing else and will defend it to their deaths, symbolized by Tupac gunned down in a hail of bullets ultimately by the head of his label who thought it easier to kill him than pay him the $10 million he was owed. It's almost as if the more ignorant they choose to remain, the less culpability they feel for the way things are.

In my experience, maybe one in 20 inmates are curious or receptive enough to challenge their constructed reality with a piece of alternate history. Fewer seem to want to expand their worldview. Most ridicule or resist violently.

You would think that in the "criminal" world there would be a preponderance of fierce individuality, but in prison it's the exact opposite. This place is a paradigm of conformity. There's a particularly virulent form of groupthink here that is part ignorance, part *omertà*, and part institutionalization. But when your options are so limited, and you're in a closed society, it's easy to see how that can occur.

Mumia Abu-Jamal calls prisons "repositories of rage, islands of socially accepted hatreds where worlds collide like sub-atomic particles seeking psychic release." And like the solitary spark it would take to ignite a massive prairie fire, he warns, it takes little to set the whole thing off.

But looking around here, you'd never know that.

AUGUST 24, 2005

> Remember the fairy tale about the emperor's new clothes, how a kid blurts out "He's naked!" as the emperor struts past decked out in his illusory splendor? Whatever happened to the kid who spoiled the emperor's show? Consider what has happened to black men—Martin, Malcolm, Mandela—who have shouted out "He's naked!" If the fairy tale were set in an American city today and the child cast as a black boy, we know he'd be shot or locked up or both. Nobody wants to hear the bad news, the truth exposing the empire's self-delusions, especially those who profit most from the delusions.
>
> —John Edgar Wideman[18]

What is I think most tragic and disheartening about the predicament of the young brothers caught in this cycle of gangs and drugs is that so many of them are decent, intelligent, funny, talented young men with such amazing creative potential. Again, I know I sound like the typical bourgeois reformist, but it's true. Much salvation lay in creation.

It's their complex sense of humor that is the most amazing. Despite their present surroundings (could I have handled prison at 18, 19, 21?) and the worlds they inhabit outside the razor wire (likewise, could I have handled the ghetto?) they are somehow still able to be incredibly goofy. Many of them have good hearts. I only give the "victim of circumstance" argument nominal credence, because I do believe choice and will play a significant role in our predicaments. It isn't that these young men aren't products of their environment, it's that I reject the "victim" label.

It's a psychological prison, one I know well, and one that IDOC takes full advantage of in order to regulate, in every conceivable manner, the inmate population. Be they victims of the system, or victims of the victims, it all perpetuates chronic helplessness and recidivism.

But the fact that they have so few options in life and are subjected to such an elevated risk in their daily lives is as much a crime against them as the crimes they commit against each other. It is a tragedy on such a profound level that our society must eventually hold itself accountable if we are ever to change it. Yet, we remain remarkably adept at evading the issue, choosing instead to throw more police and prisons at it.

Many are still children when they first get into the life . . . we're talking grade schoolers who, often bereft of one or both parents and positive community role models, turn to the only people they perceive as getting "respect." When "respect" is interpreted in gang culture to mean power, and power is obtained through money and through force, then naturally they will equate force with respect. Rarely does it seem that they question the validity of respect gained through fear, or forced respect. This is not a world where there is a great deal of opportunity or acknowledgment for respect gained by accomplishment or service.

These young men are screaming for healthy challenges. They're dying for someone to listen to them, to take them seriously, to acknowledge them when they say, in their own way, *Goddammit my life has value!* And they have every right to want that, because their lives are hard and have made them wiser than their years.

I mean, look at Sandy, an 18-year-old kid doing time for selling crack, but who is a kind and gentle and quiet soul. I'm willing to bet the farm that if you gave him the chance to do something creative with his life he'd jump at it and forget all about slangin' boulders. He's made it a point, on numerous occasions, to tell me how much he reads, and what he reads. He tags along when I go out on the yard, he works out with me, he runs with me, and he sometimes goes to the library. At some point during every day he comes by my cell to tell me what he's been up to.

I don't know what Sandy's condition is out in the world, whether he has any male role models in his life, whether anyone out there gives a shit about him. It's no bother to me to have him around. He's a goofy kid who laughs a lot. He talks in this thick, stuffed-up nasal tone that's part sinus allergy, part teenager, and there is this genuine innocence to him that is really endearing. Sometimes I think about him out on the streets, back in the life, and I worry about him. I worry about all these young brothers I have come to know on this deck—"Li'l Mo'" Beecham, Church, Archie, Ron-Ron, and T.C., among others.

T.C.'s situation is certainly unique. His father, Roderick, is also an inmate here at The Sweet Moline. They call him "Sinbad." He's a biiiig man, not someone you wanna sass. I work with him on my Dietary shift in the dishroom. He's the unofficial "supervisor." He and T.C. were cellies for a while until Sinbad got segged for a verbal altercation with some C.O.s. Miraculously, he wasn't shipped (the one thing you never, ever do is mouth off to a correctional officer, they will revel in the opportunity to put you in the hospital. But more than that, there is no insubordination tolerated, and dissenters are quickly shipped to another facility). That's how much juice this cat wields.

I can't imagine sharing a prison cell with my father, or son. Talk about a complex emotional predicament. On the one hand at least you are around to protect them and they you. On the other hand . . . *you're in prison*, which means that somewhere along the route of the Parental Express you fucked up and jumped the tracks. T.C. and Sinbad seem happy around each other, and they seem close. It is weird to hear T.C. call him "Daddy" though. Neither of them seem to view the other's incarceration as some kind of moral failing. For them it just is what it is.

I would like to hear what Sinbad thinks about his kid running around with guns. On one level, it's pretty clear Sinbad is no

stranger to it himself, so he'd be more apt to at least understand
T.C.'s involvement in the life. But how does he really feel about it
as T.C.'s father? If it were me, I'd be frazzled. I'd do whatever it
took to get him away from it.

Looking at situations like this, I contemplate in a new light my
own complicated relationship with my father and my desire to
someday have a kid. Case in point, I gave Sandy my contact info
for once he gets out in the event that he may ever need my help,
in whatever form that may take. Forgetting for a moment that
we would be legally prevented from associating with each other
upon our release, I don't know how much of me really believed
I would ever see any of these guys again once I got out. But my
heart wouldn't let me just ignore it. So I did what I did, even if it
only held symbolic significance, because I wanted to be someone
who cared.

The bigger drag is thinking about the millions who have
nothing and no one, two generations of black men who have
grown up with this as their reality. Mumia Abu-Jamal said this
about it in 1992:

> The children of [the Civil Rights] generation—born into sobering
> poverty amid shimmering opulence, their minds weaned on . . .
> TV excess while locked in want, watching while sinister politi-
> cians spit on their very existence—are the hip-hop/rap generation.
>
> Locked out of the legal means of material survival, looked
> down upon by predatory politicians and police, left with the least
> relevant educational opportunities, talked at with contempt and
> not talked to with love—is there any question why such youth
> are alienated? Why the surprise?
>
> They look at the lives they live and see not "civil rights prog-
> ress" but a drumbeat of civil repression by a state at war with
> their dreams. Why the surprise?
>
> This is not the Lost Generation . . . far from lost, they are
> probably the most aware generation since Nat Turner's. They are

not so much lost as they are mislaid, discarded by this increasingly racist system that undermines their inherent worth.[19]

He closes the thought by stating, optimistically, "They are *all* potential revolutionaries, with the historic power to transform our dull realities."

A lot changed in the years since he wrote those words. Like what happened to the Sixties generation before him, the market stepped in and co-opted the revolution. Socially conscious hiphop gave way to socially exploitative hip-hop, the latter seriously undermining whatever revolutionary potential might have existed in an exile nation of disenfranchised black youth, while giving the State all the pretext it needed to push for more and more infiltration, disruption, and repression.

Divorced from the awareness Mumia talks about, and mired in the vicious cycles of internecine violence and the miasma of consumer culture, the youth of today fall farther and farther afield from the necessary consciousness of their situation and the knowledge of how to change it. They are, in many respects, the front lines of change, a more potent microcosm of an American culture that seems to have lost any real meaning or knowledge of itself.

That I can escape this world upon my release, that I still have opportunities available to me, and that I still can maintain the pretense of class privilege is both my blessing and my shame. I cannot and will not lie and say I don't appreciate or at times take full advantage of my station in life. But this experience has, at the very least, shown me what that privileged state has been built upon, whose backs have been broken to shore up the few, who has gone without so that I could have more than my fair share. It has also given me a greater sense of obligation to do something about it, somehow, someway. If I make nothing of this experience, then I have no right commenting on the state of anything.

But I know myself. When I am gone from here, and it is late at night and I hear the distant crackle of gunfire, I will wonder if it is one of them, one of my homies from the joint, finally falling in this fallacious war against his brother, his people, and himself.

AUGUST 26, 2005

Li'l Mo' Beecham dropped by my cell late last night to holla'.

"You know we meant that shit we was talkin' this monin'. On the real, joe. It ain't no joke out there."

Earlier that morning (frighteningly earlier, as in 3:00 am) while we were on our work shift in the Dietary, Li'l Mo and Church and I were talking about gang life and selling drugs. Li'l Mo said something about his "enemies," so I asked him who his enemies were. In order, he explained, first were rival gang members, second the police, and third, people in his community who turned them in to the police.

I proposed to them that the system was their enemy, and that the system was enforced by the police, the politicians, and the ministers in their communities, who in turn were all controlled by the money people, the corporations, and the banks. Neither of them said much, but it was clear they were turning it over in their heads. Their worldview existed at block level—neighborhood block and cellblock. They seemed open to considering forces beyond the scope of their current level of consciousness.

I then proposed that when they killed each other—"thinned the herd" was how I put it—they were playing right into the system's agenda, and were, in essence, doing the system's dirty work for it, which was to keep their communities fractured and desperate. Then I rolled out "divide and rule," and they seemed to go with it. At the very least they admitted they spent most of their time worried about what rival gang members are up to, and the rest of it worrying about money.

Then I made what turned out to be a colossal blunder, even though I stand by what I said. I told them that they needed to "consider loving their enemies," particularly those most like themselves. Li'l Mo said I was crazy.

"When a nigga shootin' at you, joe, they yo enemy *fo' sho'*. How am I ever supposed to trust a muthafucka who shot at me?"

I couldn't argue with his logic, and the circumstances were lamentable. Still, I told him that I believed things could change, they could be *transcended*. Sure, there is a history of hatred and conflict between peoples, internally and externally, but I argued it is not our natural state and we retain the capacity to resolve conflicts. It would, however, require significant changes to the system, if not the abolition of the system altogether.

At that point, I think I lost them.

So when Li'l Mo came back later that night, it was to make sure I understood that the situation was dire for them out there, a real matter of life and death. I told him I got that part, that life didn't offer them many choices, but there still were choices, even if limited ones, and some of them were fundamental to their continued existence. They may at times be difficult, even dangerous or perilous choices, but there was a way through them, if he wanted it enough. He seemed, tacitly, to agree.

"Don't you want to get out?" I asked him.

"Sho' do, but the shit ain't easy. I been in the gang since I was *nine years old*, joe. My uncles are high-ranking chiefs . . . generals, and shit . . . I ain't got much of a choice."

"If you could do anything you wanted with your life, what would it be?"

"I'd go to college, and learn about the world beyond the South Side of Chicago."

Regular people would probably be shocked at how often these young men defy the stereotypes society tries to foist on them. This is not to say that there aren't bad people out there. Many of them are just straight-up punks and thugs, and quite a few of them belong in prison. But there is one reality that cuts right through the middle of them all: gang life is an attractive cultural and economic alternative to a life of soul-crushing, dead-end, wage-slave poverty. And once you're in, you don't get out. No pension and gold watch for these cats, they're lucky to escape with their lives.

I asked Li'l Mo what it would take for him to get out.

"Money," he said without missing a beat, then laughed as if to convey the obviousness of it.

"What do you spend your money on?" I asked him.

It was the usual list: clothes, car, jewelry, weed, night clubs. Everything promoted in *Vibe* and *Source* and on BET.

I began to explain, with an ear towards brevity, how the fundamental aim of consumer capitalism is to drain your disposable income all the while making you feel good about it. I explained how it was a measure of social control, and how brand loyalty was entirely manufactured by preying upon your deepest fears and insecurities, that corporations consciously marketed status by equating material goods with personal success. So long as he and millions of black youth like him spent their money—their hustle—on consumer goods instead of saving it or investing it in property and real wealth, they would never rise above their circumstances.

I then explained that this was in no way limited to people like him, that it was endemic across the whole culture. In fact, in many ways the so-called affluent white culture was far worse off, because they were living beyond their means on credit and inflated mortgages. In this regard, they were *de facto* debt slaves (he dug that one).

"Consumerism does not discriminate by race or class," I said. "In fact, it exploits both."

"How you see that?"

"When you buy all that gangsta shit, you make yourself a target. To the police, to other gang members. It's like you're walking around with a big sign on your chest that says, *Look at me, I'm a drug dealer!*"

"That's the point, yo. You gotta get yo respect. Can't look like you ain't got no ends, you get punked."

I asked him if he had ever seen *The Godfather*. Stupid question. He knew it almost better than me.

"Well, the reason the old mob bosses were able to hold onto power for so long was because they didn't flaunt their money. They didn't look like gangsters, they looked like little old Italian shopkeepers. You couldn't pick them out of a crowd."

He hadn't ever heard of John Gotti, so the whole "Dapper Don" thing would have been lost on him, but I tried to explain that once the mob started wanting notoriety, they got noticed, and it fucked their shit up (of course, grossly simplifying the history of the Italian Mafia in order to make a point, omitting the role of heroin and cocaine, RICO, their past collusions with the CIA, their blood feud with the Kennedys, and competition from other Mafias in their eventual downfall).

"If you keep a low profile and save your money, one day you could walk away from all that shit."

He seemed to be seriously thinking about it. But then he shook his head and mumbled, "But there are Stones everywhere," referring to his gang, the Blackstone Rangers. "Somebody will recognize me somewhere, someday. And when they do . . ." He cocked his hand like a gun and put it to the side of my head and pressed hard and went "BLAM!"

I asked him what would happen if all the gangs got together, like the five Mafia families did years ago, and decided on a truce and an equal division of territory and profits. He laughed and said, "Ain't never gonna happen."

"Why not?"

He cracked a knowing smile tinged with a certain resignation. "'Cause these niggaz too greedy, and it only takes one mufucka to ruin the whole lick."

▼

I learned today that Krause and The Klansman got split up. Apparently they had a few more dramas after I left. Big surprise.

So . . . dig this . . . Krause now has two black cellies, and The Klansman was moved to another housing unit and put into a four-man with three brothers.

Karma sure is a wonderful and silly creature.

AUGUST 27, 2005

People say they don't care about politics; they're not involved or don't want to get involved, but they are. Their involvement just masquerades as indifference or inattention. It is the silent acquiescence of the millions that supports the system. When you don't oppose a system, your silence becomes approval, for it does nothing to interrupt the system. People use all sorts of excuses for their indifference. They even appeal to God as a shorthand route for supporting the status quo. They talk about law and order. But look at the system, look at the present social "order" of society. Do you see God? Do you see law and order? There is nothing but disorder, and instead of law there is only the illusion of security. It is an illusion because it is built on a long history of injustices: racism, criminality, and the enslavement and genocide of millions. Many people say it is insane to resist the system, but actually, it is insane not to.

—Mumia Abu-Jamal, *Death Blossoms*[20]

The last two weeks have been creeping along so slowly that I've come to see how the stress and anticipation of the days ticking off have actually served to slow time down. It isn't as bad as being on ice at Stateville, but it's mental torture any way you look at it.

The days have settled into a structured tedium that never changes. With privacy at an established premium, I try to spend as much time alone as I can, and since I haven't gotten a new cell-mate yet, I am soaking up as much alone-in-my-cell time as I can get. It's just as well because every time I leave the Wing the White

Power bloc gives me relentless shit. They make pigeon calls and shout threats and say stupid shit like, "*The white man is the devil! Black power!*" They have spread around the whole joint that I'm a "stoolie" (I can't even believe they still use that term!) and told every white guy in here that I hate white people." Although it's absurd, I can live with that. What I can't live with is that they have also told everyone that I'm a snitch working for I.A. [Internal Affairs]. That kind of shit can get me killed! If I weren't a short-timer, or if I were in another joint, they would have already shipped me on to someplace else. At times, the stress is unbearable.

I know this is part of the big mind fuck. They're trying to get inside my head, get me to do something that somehow confirms their suspicions. They're also trying to make me afraid . . . at all times. The reason it angers me so much is that I can't handle ignorance. I try to be compassionate, I try to look at it objectively, but it's almost impossible. If I say something like, "Ignore them, they don't know any better," then this other voice immediately pipes in and says, "You ain't no better than them, you're all convicts." But in my heart I know I am different. And I know too that they are afraid, and that is what helps keep them ignorant. It keeps them from seeing what is *right*. And as there are so few situations where something can be seen as inherently *right*, it is here that we have to make a stand. Dr. King once said, "There comes a time when one must take a position that is neither safe, nor politic, nor popular; but one must take it because it is right." This has been the guiding principle of my life. You gotz ta keep it real.

I don't know if I will ever come to understand what is at the root of this particular sickness that pervades humanity. I can only be what I am and do what my conscience compels me to do. Is that revolutionary? I don't know. I suppose when your very existence challenges the status quo, and there are high enough stakes, then you will always be seen as revolutionary. But it is also revolutionary to speak truth in a culture awash in lies that has lost its ability to tell the difference. Schopenhauer said, "All truth passes through three stages: First it is ridiculed, next it is violently opposed, and finally it is accepted as being self-evident." What this means is that most of the time people will not agree with you, and you may not be the most popular person in the room. And usually by the time that the truth becomes self-evident to the greater body, the damage to the messenger has already been done.

Still . . . how can I be anything else but what I am? It's been getting me into trouble since the first moment I could move myself from point A to point B. The bulk of the people I have known throughout my life have never understood me, and I've rarely fit in anywhere. I've always questioned why things were the way they were rather than just accepting them as is because someone told me to. More often the response to me has been hostile, even violent. The few I have reached I have managed to affect profoundly, sometimes positively, sometimes not. I never seem to do anything in moderation.

Yet each awakened mind I encounter as I stumble through life helps me see that much more that there is hope out there, and that I'm not condemned to a miserable lonely life so long as I offer a penance of peace and compassion, patience and understanding. I know I have years of karma to rebalance, years of misguided selfishness to atone for. My biggest struggle will be learning how to be at peace with myself. If I can right a wrong, my existence is not in vain. If I can learn to accept myself, there is no telling what I can do. Prison puts a cloud around you, but there is a way to blow it off. I guess I'll have to figure out how.

For so many years all I sought was validation for my ideas, and nearly all the time I got the blank stare, or was told to talk to the hand. Nearly all the limited success I have experienced was because people were attracted to my energy, but rarely did they understand my point of view. I always took it as a sign of rejection that the established order tried to label me "extreme" or "radical" or "dysfunctional." I simply couldn't see how they didn't see the same paradoxes and hypocrisies that I did. I've always had the ability to see through illusions and recognize larger patterns. I knew I was right to question things, because I knew I was hearing lies. It made me a very angry, very wounded person, and I nearly killed myself over it.

Today it all makes sense, and prison is what finally made me see it clearly, in its most unadulterated form. After a lifetime of seeking approval, I realized that the clearest sign of my success was precisely in my being rejected. My validation is in my repudiation. If I am raising ire, then I am raising the right issues. Then I am speaking truth.

AUGUST 28, 2005

I finally got to sit down and talk with Carl, the "activist" that Yancy wanted me to meet. He had a hell of a story, but my first thought after hearing it, was, *What the fuck is Yancy thinking?* Allow me to explain.

Carl Jones claimed to be serving a 20-piece for a series of arson fires and bombings of Arab-owned businesses on Chicago's South Side during the mid-1990s. He tells a tale of how a frustrated citizen became a guerrilla vigilante, fueled by the anger he felt towards the Arab immigrant community, who he saw as invading his turf.

"It was after the first Gulf War, and all these Iraqis were coming here and the US Government was giving them preferential immigration status and subsidies and tax incentives to come and open businesses in American cities. This was at a time when the inner cities were all gutted. Most of the black-owned businesses had been extirpated, which left a surplus of cheap urban real estate for redevelopment. The Arabs who came followed the historical tradition of exploitation in the ghetto that had been in the hands of Jews and Asians before them. They opened delis and liquor stores and bought up residential property and became the new slumlords."

According to Carl, what enraged him most was that his government was willing to give foreigners more advantages and assistance than it would give him. He says he began organizing an awareness campaign aimed at educating those in his community about the rise of Arab-owned businesses, and the need for black-owned businesses, "to keep our money in our neighborhood, instead of sending it to the Middle East." He says there was a notable lack of interest amongst the residents.

It wasn't just the economics of the issue that riled him. Carl claimed it was also the continuation of "the stinging slap of exploitation." Despite the rhetorical flourishes, his delivery was dispassionate and soft-spoken. It was perhaps that which was turning out to be the most unsettling.

"These Arabs would gladly take our money, and then call us nigger and call the police if we stood outside their store with the merchandise we had just purchased from them. And every day, more of them would come, eliminating yet another opportunity for a black-owned business to open."

Carl claims to have appealed to his alderman and other community leaders, who told him they supported his ideas, but in the end they did nothing to address the situation. This was what pushed him over the edge. Whatever it was, he soon decided that, without any legitimate force to remove these "racist Arab exploiters" from his neighborhood, he would have to become that force, even if that meant through the use of force.

He acknowledges "six bombings for which I was eventually prosecuted." He claims to have been "captured" during a traffic stop when police discovered a large amount of ammonium nitrate fertilizer in his car and put him in a lineup, where he was ID'd. He says he accepted a plea agreement of 20 years mere weeks before the passage of the 1996 Antiterrorism and Effective Death Penalty Act [AEDPA] (a.k.a. the Comprehensive Antiterrorism/Terrorism Prevention Act), created in the wake of the Oklahoma City bombing. He says he's lucky. Had he been charged after this act became law he would have been classified a domestic terrorist instead of an arsonist, and most likely would have been in a far worse place than The Sweet Moline, for a hell of a lot longer.

After serving nine years, he says, he has come full circle in his reflections on the choices he made. "I realized at some point that I targeted the wrong people. I shouldn't have gone after the Arabs, I should have gone after the City of Chicago and the federal government. Would I have bombed government buildings then? I think so. In looking for a justification for what I was doing, I had convinced myself that it is the inherent responsibility of all citizens to rise up at times to overthrow a corrupt or tyrannical government. But this time has taught me that there are other ways to go about being effective."

He still claims to be committed to the strengthening of the black community once he is released in 2007.

"Of course," he said with a wink as a toothpick darted back and forth in his teeth, "it's a very different world out there today. Do what I did these days, you gonna disappear down a hole and never be seen again."

Klujtim Sulejmani ("Tim" for short), his cellmate, Ryan Boswell, and my new cellmate, Robert Cooper, all arrived on the most recent shipment from Stateville NRC filling the beds previously held by Ron-Ron, J.T., and J.T.'s cellie, who was released the day after I arrived on C Wing.

Tim is Armenian, maybe 22 or 25, from the Chicago suburbs. He is in on a two-piece for multiple counts of forging prescriptions for painkillers, but he looks to be out in six months. He was pretty quiet and unassuming at first, mostly because he was one of the only other white guys on our cellblock, and he was clearly not the penitentiary type. He is frat boy through and through.

Eventually we started talking and got along pretty well. He's smart, went to college, and he reads. He knows a lot about

American history, and has a particular understanding of how much the US has assisted Turkey following the formation of the Turkish republic after the defeat and collapse of the Ottoman Empire. Turkey is responsible for wiping out nearly a million and a half of his people in one of the most brutal (and brutally denied) genocides in recorded history.

It is clear Tim was comfortable and coddled out in the world. He has relatively affluent parents and doesn't seem to have too much to worry about. His family gives him a lot of commissary money, so he never leaves his cell. He eats all his meals there, and watches endless hours of TV on the small set he was able to purchase through the commissary. Yes, you can buy TVs. You can buy nearly anything you want or need, right there in the prison store. Commissary is an essential part of prison survival . . . *if* you have money.

Most inmates are limited to the $15–$30 a *month* they make from their work assignments, which amounts to a wage of $.50–$1.00 a day. This pittance permits them to barely afford the barest essentials: soap, shampoo, toothpaste, coffee, tobacco. Tim bought enough creature comforts to live like a king in the joint; his lockbox is packed to the rim with processed pre-pack-aged food, toiletries, and magazines. He also unwittingly bought himself endless harassment and hustling from the inmates around him, who are always trying to find a way to ride his gravy train a few miles down the line.

His cellmate, Boswell, was busted with a single bag of crack, and with a prior conviction on his record and no money for a lawyer, was forced to take a year. He is tall and lanky and mostly bald. He has a cartoonishly elongated oval-shaped head and eyes and wears big, thick glasses that reinforce the ovality, making him look like a cross between a grown-up Urkel and Yrtle the Turtle. He is friendly and funny and absolutely obsessed with sex. In fact, he admitted that both of his convictions came about because he was "trickin' off with hoes and forgot my common damn sense."

Robert Cooper is another story altogether. This is his third time in prison, but you'd be hard pressed to understand how or why. Cooper is, by all estimation, totally harmless and the very definition of hapless. Old boy can't get much right. He is short and thick and bald, has lost every other tooth in his mouth, and has a prominent snaggletooth which draws all of your attention. All he cares about is cutting hair. He has a kind of aw shucks naïveté and passivity about him you don't generally find in incarcerated brothers from the South Side. He is also unique in that he claimed not to use drugs, and he clearly was not involved in gang life.

He never really sufficiently explained what his first bit was for, but he claimed he was innocent of the charge. His second bit was for burglary and fraud, which he said was because of his ex-wife.

Cooper was going through a nasty divorce at the time. He said it began when his wife "caught the ambition bug" and "wanted that suburban thing."

"She didn't like being thought of as 'ghetto.' She wanted to be 'respectable people.' And she thought the way you did that was to buy a lot of shit we didn't need."

Coop said he was never down with that program. He said he was happy living in his neighborhood and cutting hair at the barbershop where he worked.

They grew apart, and Coop met someone else, and eventually got her pregnant. Enraged, his ex-wife kicked him out. When he returned to their apartment to retrieve his belongings on some later day while his ex was at work, she filed home invasion charges against him. And when he used their credit card, she filed fraud charges. Both, apparently, were in her name. Despite understanding how hurt she must have felt, her response seems exceptionally vindictive, particularly to take it all the way through to a conviction. Unless, of course, Coop isn't telling me something, which is more than likely the case. It always is. No one ever comes fully clean. To anyone.

Coop was on parole from that second conviction when he claims he was stopped on the street and searched by police, who turned up two bottles of vodka in his backpack which the cops claimed had just been stolen from a local liquor store. Cooper swore up and down he just bought them on the street from two Mexican guys from the neighborhood (likely the real thieves) after leaving the barbershop where he worked. When they ran his ID and saw his record they didn't buy his story or even bother to take him back to the store for the owner to ID him. He was hit with a retail theft charge, lost parole, and was sent back inside with another year added to his original sentence.

Now, either Coop lifted those bottles himself and got caught, which is stupid on a level I don't think I have to actually state for you to understand, or he got a royal screw-job, because he's an ex-con. The funny thing is, both scenarios are equally plausible. The record does matter. The minute anyone sees that, whether it's the police or a prospective employer or landlord, you're automatically in another category. With ex-offenders, guilt is assumed, regardless of circumstance. You disagree? Well, watch the news for a week. See how they treat suspects or "persons of interest" with a record, how they say ". . . and the suspect is a *convicted felo . . .*" In those cases, oftentimes the only concern of the police is gathering as much proof as they can get, even if it needs to be manufactured. *He's an ex-con, you know, he ain't Michael Jordan, what difference does it make?*

The real problem, though, is mandatory sentencing. That's what Judge Epstein told me, "There's nothing I can do, my hands are tied, the guidelines are clear." I have a feeling that if judges had discretion to consider each case on its individual merits, instead of being forced to follow the mandatory guidelines that constrain them, they would have found much more productive uses for inmates like me and Cooper and Boswell, or Ron-Ron, or Sandy, or David, or Smitty, or Pee-Wee, etc. etc. I'm even willing to defend Tim's right to have treatment instead of prison, since his worst crime was forging a prescription. As it was, we were wasting everyone's time and money, ours included, sitting around, taking up space, consuming resources.

The point is moot to Cooper. He took it all in stride, in a kind of shrugging, *Whatta ya gonna do?* manner. He's just happy he gets to spend his days cutting hair in the prison barbershop.

▼

Author's Note: The next day, August 29, 2005, Hurricane Katrina hit the Gulf Coast and I didn't make any entries during that week. The following essay describing those days was written over two years later.

KATRINA'S UNSCHEDULED VISIT

Like it did with most of the nation, Hurricane Katrina caught the inmates of the East Moline Correctional Center completely off-guard. At 3:00 on the morning of August 29, 2005, at the same time I was rising to go work my dishwashing shift in the Dietary unit, Katrina was just another storm warning for a far-away part of the country ticking across the bottom of television sets. None of us had any real understanding of her significance, or that in just a few hours the American landscape—both physical and po-litical—would begin to change in astonishing ways.

Our limited awareness of events in the outside world generally meant that the news and facts of day-to-day American life passed us by. Few showed any interest in keeping up with the news, and the only news source available to us was CNN, which meant that we got very little actual news.

By 6:00 am, as half-asleep inmates shuffled into the chow line for breakfast, Katrina made landfall, overwhelming the Gulf Coast with the deafening scream of a Harpy escaping the swirling overheated mass that was the Gulf of Mexico. Her storm surge rocked the Mississippi Basin, shattering the decayed levees that ostensibly protected New Orleans from the eager encroachment of the Gulf. Within a matter of days Katrina would also shatter the myths of security, competency, and order that generations of politicians had so shamelessly spun.

At the same time the storm was unfolding at the mouth of the Mississippi, a thousand miles upstream in the Quad Cities of Illinois and Iowa it was just another day at The Sweet Moline, the ironic yet affectionate nickname for our prison. That quiet August morning was the soft lull before the foul realities started seeping in like the polluted waters that flooded the streets of New Orleans.

When my shift ended around 10:00 am I was released to return to C Wing, my cellblock. It was now the morning open movement period, so I changed into shorts and a T-shirt and went outside to run about four miles around the yard. I came back, showered, and read a bit while I waited for lunchtime to come around. After lunch, I slept in my cell for an hour or so before the afternoon movement period began, and then went to the library until two-thirty.

It wasn't until much later in the afternoon, when I returned from the library, that I began to get a clue as to what was going down in the Bayou. The one general-use television in our housing unit was usually blaring daytime talk shows like *Springer* and *Maury*, or reruns of *COPS*. That day it was tuned to a CNN "Special Report." A few guys were gathered around the set, silent. When I got to my cell, Tim emerged from his cell next door and said, "You gotta see this." I ducked into his cell to watch coverage on his small private TV, and I didn't leave again until dinner.

I had never been in a hurricane, but my mother and grandparents went through it regularly where they lived in Southwest Florida. Only the year before the area suffered through one of the worst hurricane seasons ever, the only time in recorded history that five hurricanes hit one state in a single season. Bonnie,

Charley, Frances, Ivan, and Jeanne collectively killed 3,132 people and caused over $50 billion worth of damage. Little did we know we were just about to have the phrase "a bad hurricane" completely redefined.

I was increasingly concerned about my mother's and grandparents' safety after hearing that Katrina passed over Southwest Florida on its way north to Louisiana, but I had no way of reaching them. Before I went into prison, my mother and I made a relatively mutual decision that we would not communicate by phone while I was locked up for fear of my grandparents finding out I was in prison.

"They are old and tired and wouldn't understand," she said. Because of that, her telephone number was not among the prescreened and approved numbers I was allowed to call. Now I was regretting everything about that decision.

On the first night of the storm "The Sweet Moline" went about its usual business according to the ossified routine we followed day in and day out. After dinner and the early-evening count, I went to the library, as I always did, to write in my journal. When movement closed and I returned to C Wing the whole place was buzzing. Not, as you might think, about Hurricane Katrina, but instead about the premier of a new Fox TV series called *Prison Break*.

Prison Break was filmed on location at the infamous and now-decommissioned Joliet Penitentiary, which served as the intake facility for anyone incarcerated in the Illinois Department of Corrections before 2004. It was your first taste of what lay ahead, where you were processed into the system to await shipment to the main prison facility where you would serve out your sentence. By the summer of 2005, however, a new state-of-the-art processing center the size of an airplane hangar had opened only a few miles away. Because of that, nearly all the repeat offenders around me had done some time in old Joliet, and there were a lot of them. Rumors were already flying around the deck. Inmates were telling whoever would listen that "guys they knew" had served as the models for various characters and events in the series. It was preposterous jailhouse bullshit, but no one seemed to mind.

I had never seen this many inmates this excited about anything. They choked the two-man cells, agglomerating around every available television screen, and the collective noise of two dozen sets tuned to the same channel echoed throughout the concrete and tile cellblock lending every line a creepy *übervox* quality. The whole thing was bizarre and unsettling and smacked of a certain pointed masochism. This surreal image of men in prison blues, watching a dramatic television program about their fictional doppelgängers in a prison in which they themselves had done time, was a bit on the nose, don't you think?

I had no interest in watching, but Tim and his cellie, Boswell, and my cellie, Cooper, talked me into it. There was nothing else to do anyway; you might say it was clear you couldn't escape *Prison Break*. The four of us crammed into Tim and Boswell's cell to watch. It felt like it was a few hundred degrees inside: we were, after all, still embroiled in one of the hottest summers on record, and there was no ventilation in our cellblock. It was a virtual brick oven.

Prison Break was completely ridiculous, a sensationalistic piece of pernicious penal agitprop riddled with every tired prison cliché you could imagine: cartoonishly fiendish villains and C.O.s, prison bitches and snitches galore. Within half an hour I was dying for it to be over.

I stayed and watched until the end because it was the only way I could hear about Katrina, which updated with every commercial break. It was looking pretty grim, but there was no mention of any serious damage to Florida. I went to sleep at lockdown assuming my mother and grandparents were OK. I would not know for sure until after I was released in a week.

The next day, after another half-asleep breakfast shift, I got myself in front of a TV at 8:30 am when the C Wing television could officially be turned on. Virtually no one was on the Wing at that time of day—most were at their work assignments—so I sat alone and stared gape-mouthed at the footage of New Orleans under eight feet of murky brown water.

I had never seen anything like this. Water streaming into the city from gashes in the levees, people stranded on rooftops waving for rescue, others wading neck deep in the filthy water. There was bedlam at the Superdome and the Convention Center, and widespread reports of violence and looting (by police as well as the citizenry). Smoke rose from the skyline, and aerial shots of the city looked like we were witnessing the collapse of civilization.

By late afternoon word of the severity of the storm had spread and inmates began to crowd around the unit set to watch the ongoing coverage. This scene would not change for days, and in that time the tone on C Wing would shift noticeably. The place was usually deafeningly loud, but now all you could hear, once again, was the combined sound of every set tuned to CNN, and the same creepy *übervox*. Only now it brimmed with the fear and gravitas of bewildered CNN anchors and reporters.

We learned the governor of Louisiana had ordered the mandatory evacuation of New Orleans, but few got out before the storm hit. She asked Bush to send in federal troops to restore law and order; later I learned he sent Blackwater mercenaries instead. Buses lined the sides of the highways as teaming masses of people vied for escape. Nearly all the desperate faces in the television shots were black, a fact not unnoticed by those around me.

Then, spontaneously, someone said, "You know . . . people was locked up down there."

We silently acknowledged the helpless lockdown situation we ourselves were in and tried to contain the deep terror rising within each of us. Would we be left to die in the event of a catastrophe here? And the more important, and painful, question: Would anyone care?

The anxiety amongst the inmates lasted for days, until, almost like an answer from heaven, CNN broadcast an aerial shot of prisoners in orange jumpsuits sitting on a highway off-ramp, surrounded by guards who were leveling shotguns at them. We had no further information on who these particular inmates were or what prison or jail they were from. Yet many of the "Sweet Moline" inmates embraced the image as a palliative and let go of their fears of being abandoned to drown or starve and eventually die in prison.

I don't blame them for doing so, but I wasn't eased at all by what I saw. I knew Louisiana was home to a fairly extensive prison system, and the Orleans Parish Prison itself was right in the heart of the city. I knew that if they couldn't get regular citizens out in time, they sure as hell didn't waste any time thinking about criminals. Although I said nothing about it at the time, some of our darkest unspoken fears would be confirmed in late September when news broke that the 7,000 inmates at Orleans Parish Prison—one third of whom were pre-trial defendants who had not been convicted of any crime—were indeed left to die.

As the prison flooded with storm water befouled by raw sewage the prisoners were herded into cells with mace, locked down, and abandoned. The men completely panicked.

"They left us like dogs," one prisoner would later recount in the BBC documentary, *Prisoners of Katrina*. "Eight men in a two-man cell with no food and no water, covered with mace you couldn't wash off. It was an experience I wouldn't wish on nobody."[21]

In some cases men broke out of their cells and rioted, viciously attacking each other. The official story from the Sheriff of Orleans Parish was that there was "no loss of life." Those who were there claim to have seen dead bodies and furiously challenged the Sheriff's account. Who do you believe when you later learn that 517 prisoners would eventually go "unaccounted for"?[22]

The floodwaters also ruined the court records of thousands of criminal cases. After the OPP was finally evacuated, its prisoners were sent to facilities all over the state. Most arrived without identification or court documents, and were promptly forgotten. To make matters worse, the courthouse was closed for nine months, and the Parish lost 80% of their public defenders—who represent 85% of the defendants—because the funds to pay them had dried up faster than the floodwaters. Soon a backlog of thousands of cases choked the dockets of the few remaining advocates. Because so much evidence and documentation had been destroyed, many inmates—some innocent of any crime, others mere days or weeks from release—stayed locked away, becoming ghosts in the machine. It was everyone's greatest nightmare: The system had completely collapsed.

The black inmates of East Moline were tormented by the rapidly deteriorating plight of the largely poor and black residents of New Orleans, some of whom were relatives. Over the next few days these men would move from denial into shock into anger then into despair.

For the rest of the week the normal routine of East Moline shifted around Katrina's unscheduled visit. Inmates continued to gather around the television to argue with each other about what was or was not happening and why. It was difficult enough to be just another American, or just another human being, witnessing these historical events. But it was particularly hard watching the brothers around me go through every conceivable emotion watching their people endure blow after blow after blow while no one came to help.

They had always known, they would say, that the government hated them. But none of them would ever have thought that a whole city of their brothers and sisters, mothers and babies and grandmothers too, would be abandoned, left to suffer and die like animals.

We saw right through how the media was trying to spin it and were incensed that black people were being cast as "looters" while white people were simply "trying to survive." Eventually we would stop yelling at the TV screens and arguing with each other, and we would retreat into a somber and seething state of acceptance. There was nothing any of us could do, about any of it.

On September 6 I finally scribbled down the only words I would write that whole week:

My final week in prison was framed by the largest natural catastrophe in American history, Hurricane Katrina and the loss of New Orleans. The world as we know it changed so much in the last seven days. An entire American city has disappeared sending shockwaves racing across the country. While this is going on, in the background, the highest court of this nation is being transformed in a manner that will change the ideological face of America for a generation.

Of paramount concern to the inmates this week: What happened to all the prisoners in New Orleans? Were they evacuated? Or were they left to drown and rot? Our value as human beings in this society hinges on the answer we receive.

The Federal government has shown the deepest shades of its true colors as poor folk are left to suffer and die in filth and disease while the troops that have been deployed have orders to protect McMansions and high-end retail stores. The men around me clearly see that, in the eyes of the government, Brooks Brothers is worth more than their brothers. All this venal greed may be in vain, as we don't know whether the city can or will be rebuilt.

Everything that could go wrong did; meanwhile our government is still on vacation. Were this the plight of a white, brain-dead Christian woman on life-support about to have the plug pulled on her, they would have beat a hasty retreat to Washington to excoriate the Liberals for being cruel and inhuman and utterly without compassion. As it stands, their only priority appears to be ramming an inexperienced and ideological nominee for Chief Justice down the collective gullet of a nation already choking on the physical and political detritus of Katrina.

Just when you think you've witnessed the most craven and inept our government has to offer, just when you think you've seen all the illegal invasions, all the Guantánamos and Abu

Ghraibs, all the "free speech zones" and prison camps for protestors, politically opportunistic terror alerts, shameless corporate handouts, and merciless campaign demagoguery, along comes Michael "Heck of a Job, Brownie" Brown, the former director of an equestrian society who was appointed by Bush to be the head of the Federal Emergency Management Agency. A man so obscenely oblivious and incompetent he makes Bush look like Franklin Delano Roosevelt.

The phenomenal bungling of the emergency response and the appalling lack of concern shown by the politicians revealed that the jig is up. We know you're not really prepared for any terrorist attack or mass disaster, except perhaps to save yourselves. We know you don't care about us, and we know that anything you say and do from this time forward will be empty and meaningless pandering.

We need to see Katrina for what she is, a harbinger of things to come.

The wrath of God is upon us.

In ancient Greek mythology the Harpies were the daughters of Typhon, the last Titan born of Gaia, from which we get *typhoon*, or "violent storm." The Harpies are considered personifications of the destructive nature of wind. But with Katrina, the mythic identification goes much deeper.

The Harpies were used by Zeus to punish the Thracian king Phineas for revealing the secrets of the gods to his people. Phineas was imprisoned on an island with a giant feast laid before him that he could never eat because the Harpies would steal food from his hands, and befoul the rest with their droppings. He was left to starve, for all eternity.

The screeching Harpy named Katrina was a changeling. She first appeared as the winds of the storm driven by an angry and overheated planet, and later she morphed into the screaming contempt and incompetence of the federal government, which, after snatching food from our mouths for years, befouled both New Orleans and our faith in the federal government's ability to govern.

Hurricane Katrina washed away so much more than the Gulf Coast. She washed away the collective illusions of a nation that believed their government would always be ready to help them. She washed away the hopes of poor Americans that they too mattered in the big picture of the American Dream, and she washed away the faith that those who own and run this country are concerned with something other than their own agendas.

SEPTEMBER 7, 2005—FINAL ENTRY

My days in prison are ending up pretty much like they began, with a mixed quartet of guys in the corner of a cellblock. Coop, Boswell, Tim, and I spend most of our time together, watching TV and playing practical jokes on each other. Coop and I—as incredulous a character as he is—have had more to talk about than I ever would have guessed. We argue all the time because I keep trying to get him to care about something other than cutting hair, but I've come to recognize that I'm giving him a hard time to avoid giving myself one.

Tim's interest in politics has finally given me someone to talk to, particularly as we watch all of this shit unfold in New Orleans. It's nice to have someone laugh when you make Illuminati jokes. And Boswell . . . well . . . he's just goofy. I sometimes wonder if he realizes he's locked up. I never see the guy unhappy, but unlike Floyd or Smitty or Big Chuckie (a brother so big and ripped his nickname is "Schwarzenigger") or even Pee-Wee, who are generally happy, but also get deep, Boswell is always clowning around, and never utters a serious word. I have never, ever met anyone more obsessed with sex than him. The guy's motto should be *E Pluribus Gluteus Maximus:* "The Many Thick Behinds."

I read and sleep, watch CNN until their bullshit gets to be

too much, then I slip outside quietly and run a few miles or, if it's quiet, do a round of lifting. I only go out during the morning movement period, since I have it free while most inmates are working. In the afternoon and evening it's too big a risk. The White Power bloc haven't let up. In fact, they've become a near unified voice against me.

Irrespective of the facts, I am seen as a rat. They call me "Malcolm X." I can't go anywhere without getting harassed. Because of their constant pigeon calls, and relentless gossip that I am a narc working for Internal Affairs, which they say is the reason I'm always writing things down, most of the brothers have backed away from me as well. I think my journal, my questions, and my worldview began to get to them too. All at once they started asking me about it, and they all asked me the same question: "Are you writin' down what we're sayin' to you?" Any answer other than "no" proved unacceptable.

Old "Six-Nine" was right about one thing: Once most of the brothers on my deck realized I wasn't a free commissary ride, and that I wasn't easily duped, they stopped paying attention to me. Many of them flipped the script on me and suddenly I was to be regarded with suspicion. It's totally schizophrenic. All of this came about because a) I'm not racist and b) I'm a writer, two things that do not go well with prison blues.

Every few hours I find myself looking up at the clock and then at the makeshift calendar I made next to a picture of my dog. It's time to *go* . . . but time goes *slow*. So very slow.

Yet, as the great iron gate rises into view, all the petty nonsense and grief of prison is beginning to wash away. I am stronger now, cautious, patient, and restrained. I fear little anymore because, after this, what else is there to fear but illness and death? I am still compassionate, but appropriately guarded. Whatever naïveté I came in with is long gone. In its place is a new understanding, and a certain acceptance of this humanity-in-the-fog, lost souls seeking landfall.

There has been a settling of accounts. Life will continue to present opportunities, and I need to remember that labels are only self-applied. I am as I do, from this moment forward, so I must do what is right and give thanks every day that I am still able to rise to these challenges, make something of every day, change something in the world. I am still healthy, of sound mind. My family is safe. I haven't been silenced. I still have work to do.

By all accounts, I'm doing OK.

Bertrand Russell once said that the secret to happiness is facing the fact that the world is a horrible place. But happiness is overrated. "If only we'd stop trying to be happy," wrote Edith Wharton, "we'd have a pretty good time."

Here's to Life 2.0.

PART II
Perdition

I could not see,
for the fog in my eyes.
I could not feel,
for the fear in my life

—Daniel Lanois, "The Maker"

Perdition

CHAPTER 4
The Obligatory
Autobiographical Section

"Don't smoke crack. It's a ghetto drug."
—Tim Robbins in the title role in his film *Bob Roberts*

Something jars me awake. I open my eyes with a start to the rich saturation of sunlight in the front room, where I'm sleeping on the couch. It's a brilliant morning, and silent. From down in the lobby I hear the vestibule doors slam shut, then the pounding of feet on the stairs, and then a key hits the deadbolt on the front door and the *clack clack clack* of the lock opening resounds across the hardwood floors and bare walls. Edie bursts through the door, bewilderment and purpose plastered across her face. She looks down and sees me on the couch.

"My God. You're still *asleep?*" she says, her voice strained.

She moves straight for the small 23" television set on the bottom of her book shelf. Slowly the tube warms up and a picture comes into view. It's CNN. I can't make out what I am seeing. It looks like a giant cloud of smoke. Reporters are talking and clamor haunts the background. I look to the crawl at the bottom of the screen.

. . . both towers have collapsed . . .

I look at Edie.

"They're saying it's Bin Laden," she says, her gaze affixed to the screen.

"What the hell happened?" I say, hauling myself up off the couch.

"We're under attack," she says, in a daze. "The World Trade Center and the Pentagon are gone! I think we're at war now."

I look to the TV screen. A voice says, *In case you're just joining us . . . I don't know how that can be by now . . . but in case you're just tuning in . . . America is under attack.*

Video roll. A plane hits the top of the World Trade Center, a cameraman working with a group of NYC firemen catches it just in time. Cut to a plane flying across the Manhattan skyline and plowing into the middle of the second tower. A massive fireball erupts out the other side. Cut to people on the street in Manhattan looking skyward, crying, wailing. V*oiceover: Oh my God they're jumping, they're jumping (wail)*. Cut to the Pentagon, a gaping smoking hole along one side, no footage of planes impacting. Cut to the World Trade Center, suddenly one tower collapses at free-fall speed inside a huge pyroclastic cloud that spreads through the city streets like octopus ink through a coral reef. People run, screaming, the cloud envelops them. Cut to the second tower collapsing at free-fall speed, cross-shaped explosions blowing out left and right ahead of the falling debris *bam bam bam bam bam bam bam*! Cut to a field in Pennsylvania, and a small strip of burnt soil, and a few scattered pieces of wreckage. Cut to people on the street in Manhattan looking skyward, crying, wailing, running, covered in grey dust. Cut to firefighters and police running in slow motion. Cut to the American flag, dissolve in CNN logo and theme. Cue James Earl Jones. *This is CNN.* Cut to commercial.

Repeat.

Repeat.

Repeat.

Repeat.

Repeat.

Repeat.

Repeat.

I look at Edie. *Make sense of this. What? Why?* She's looking at me for the same. I have nothing for her. My head reels and I flush and feel like I'm going to faint. I know at that point I screamed. Then that's it.

9/11 shattered my already crumbling psyche. As it was I was barely hanging on as it was in that late summer of 2001. I had only been back in Chicago for little more than three months, having crawled back with my tail between my legs after moving out to Los Angeles on my birthday in March. My whole life collapsed by June. The summer had been spent in a haze of crack and heroin and alcohol as I was unable to face my spectacular implosion: I had left with a book contract, a writing job on a nationally syndicated radio show, and a gig editing another book manuscript, and I returned broke, jobless, homeless, and strung out, with a mountain of drama in between.

Despite the insanity of my life, and the fact that I had left her months earlier, Edie was still willing to take me in and care for me. Over the years I would pass through a dozen different states of mind about how I felt about that, examining and reexamining our relationship within the context of crisis and codependency, projection and fantasy. But in the end it was an astounding act of compassion and selflessness that became the rock upon which I would build my recovery. I would say a saner woman would never have done so, except Edie is the most sane person I know. What she did came directly from a love I was categorically incapable of comprehending at the time, but that later would become the template for how I would learn to give love myself. Edie and I began as best friends, and even though they say romance destroys the friendship, in our case it never did. She is now, as she was then, my best friend. On September 11, 2001, she was my only friend.

I have only vague memories of what I did that day. I know I drove around crying for hours, I went to the projects and smoked crack, then I drank a bottle of vodka, and screamed a lot. Edie refused to let me go by myself, so she ended up getting dragged to all these horrible places just so she could try to keep me from getting killed, which must have terrified her beyond belief. She eventually called my mother and stepfather, and they came to our apartment at some point while I was in a blackout and had locked myself inside my room and was smashing things. I was having a complete and total breakdown, and my mother and girlfriend had front row seats.

By that point in my life I had done many things that I was ashamed of, but none of them affected me like what happened on that day. When I finally sobered up a day later and came out of my room, the looks on their faces said it all. For my mother, this was the greatest indignity she had faced. At this point, the only thing that could be worse would be if I were sent off to prison.

With Edie, I felt overwhelming guilt for dragging this extremely sweet and beautiful and very very straight woman into the moral quicksand of life amongst the narcotics. I had turned my sister on to cocaine as well, and, for her own reasons, she had gone in one year from marathon runner to party girl. My brother and father no longer talked to me. I was unemployable, half insane, indigent, and volatile. And when my mother finally looked up at me, I understood for the first time that I was 31 years old and a complete and total failure.

The pain of this realization slammed into me like an iron spear shot from the ramparts of a medieval castle. If they could have shut off their love for me like a switch and walked away forever, they would have, but they couldn't, they were stuck. They loved me, and they wouldn't let go, even though I gave them nothing but pain and grief. It was the lowest I had ever been. It was rock bottom, fo realz, yo.

I had seen a lot of madness in my time, but 9/11 was the most insane thing that I had ever seen. Whatever security or mythology of America I had wrapped myself in was stripped from me in an instant and a voice inside me told me that this new world would have no patience for a person with a weakness like mine. I would either reform myself and rise to these new circumstances, or I would be pulverized like the 780,000 metric tons of concrete in the Twin Towers.

Although 9/11 broke me, it was like medically rebreaking a limb to ensure it heals properly. I broke on that day so that I could begin the long haul out. The fires in those towers ignited something within me, and rather than giving up and jumping like those whose images still haunt us today, I vowed to hang on, and survive. I was going to climb out of this even if it killed me, or at least I'd die trying.

My father once told me through a bleary vodka haze that he suspected I was conceived the night man first landed on the Moon, July 20, 1969. Even though the numbers work out almost to the day, I suspect he was aggrandizing at the time for the sake of his own mythology, which is not at all surprising if you knew my father then. Lots of babies were conceived during that one giant leap for mankind.

Regardless of whatever event inspired my conception, I entered the world on St. Patrick's Day, 1970, in St. Joseph's Hospital on the North Side of Chicago. My mother, a Sicilian Catholic who grew up a few blocks away off North Avenue in Old Town, was badgered by an Irish Catholic delivery nurse to name me Patrick, "lest he be cursed." Pre–Vatican II Catholics believe that if your child is born on a day honoring a particular saint, you have to name the child after that saint or else face the sins of pride and blasphemy. My mother was never one to take shit from anyone so she had the nurse replaced with a more demure personality and went on to name me Charles Bradford Shaw, after my father's father, Charles Nolan Shaw, who had died young, nine years before I was born.

My mother, Carol, came from a poor family that had been in the country for two generations. Her mother's family, the Giancolas, were peasants from the tiny central mountain village of Gebillina. The village and much of the surrounding area was destroyed in the 1968 Belice earthquake, but the family got out long before that. The Giancolas emigrated to the US during the great European migration of the Turn of the Century. They made port in New Orleans and survived by working with the families of freed slaves as field hands for cotton sharecroppers in the post-Reconstruction South. They lived in tents as migrant laborers until they made enough money to buy a train ticket to Chicago. They would eventually settle on the North Side in Old Town, a formerly German neighborhood that was being overrun by Italians whose tenement district south of North Avenue was slowly being demolished, eventually to make way for the infamous Cabrini Green housing project. It was in this neighborhood that my grandmother Francesca Giancola, met my grandfather Salvatore Lombardo.

My grandfather's people, the Lombardos, were fallen nobility from centuries back who had been exiled from Lombardy in the north of Italy to Sicily back when it was a penal colony. The Lombardo clan were much more prosperous. They owned farms and olive plantations in Altavilla Milicia, about 15 miles southeast of Palermo and in some cases had gravitated into *Cosa Nostra*. My grandparents both tell stories of growing up in Prohibition-era Chicago, how they would find bodies in the stairwells of their neighbors' homes, and gangsters would roll through their neighborhood shooting at each other.

My grandparents were laborers, each of them holding many jobs over the years driving delivery trucks, operating street cars, making pottery. My grandfather served in the infantry during World War II. He fought in the European theater and became a decorated veteran, winning the Bronze Star for valor. My mother came into the world in 1946 during the first year of the postwar baby boom and grew up with her older brother and younger sister across the street from St. Michael's Cathedral surrounded by her extended family, who lived in a series of houses on the same block. My mother's whole world existed within a few-blocks' radius.

My father, Robert, four years older than she and born just as the war was beginning, was from the South and West Sides of Chicago. My father was a Fortunate Son. He was adopted at birth into a powerful family of Norwegians who owned successful businesses and were deep into Chicago politics. My great-grandfather "Pops" was a fixture in the Illinois Republican Party, having served as Chicago Alderman, Committeeman, and Commissioner of the Park District. My father says that his earliest memory is that of him sitting in Pops's smoky basement on Cottage Grove Avenue helping him stuff fake ballots into the precinct boxes on election night (in Chicago, we vote early, and often).

Because of Pops's connections, my father had few responsibilities or expectations. Although a mediocre student, he was given a five-year scholarship to the University of Illinois only to flunk out after spending most of his time hustling pool. His lack of focus, though, was also largely influenced by the tragic death of his father, Charles, my grandfather. Despite Pops's affluence, his daughter, June, my grandmother, married a simple man who worked in a metal shop. One day "Chuck" went to work and had a heart attack and died. For the rest of my father's life he would not only mourn the loss of his father at age nineteen, but suffer the agony of never having said goodbye.

To avoid the draft during the Vietnam War, my father, through Pops' political connections, was given "deferred" status as the "sole provider" for my grandmother June, even though she was plenty comfortable. In many ways, Pops was more a father to my dad than Charles Shaw ever was.

When my parents got married they were very young. My mother was 19, my father, 24. They were deeply insecure people, my father because of his looks (he was a chubby kid who had acne scars), my mother because of her working-class ethnic background and her lack of a formal education. My mother was fiercely intelligent, and an A student who won a scholarship to college on her own merit but couldn't attend because her father

Salvatore, the prototypical Sicilian male, refused to let her go, claiming that a woman's place was in the home (this was 1960, mind you, not 1910, which makes it all the more astounding).

In many ways, my mother, who was well-stocked with fierce ambition and drive, got married so young to escape this world and become somebody. She also married young to escape the violence that pervaded her home. My father, a far more reserved and simple personality, thought that he was in paradise. My mother's beauty was breathtaking, and for my father it was love at first sight.

I spent most of my childhood in the Chicago suburbs. Three years after I was born my parents adopted my sister, Suraya, who is Native American. Four years after that they had my brother, Zachary.

My father spent most of his eventual 20-year career as an executive with what we now know as the Time-Warner Corporation. During the 1970s and early 1980s he was also a partner in Celebration Flip Side, Chicago's largest event booking and promotion agency at the time. Flip Side booked major rock acts in stadiums like Soldier Field and the old Chicago Amphitheater. Because of this, I spent much of the first 12 years of my life running around backstage with my own personal security guard at rock shows that an older version of me would have killed to see.

My father was very good at what he did because he was an affable personality who could sell anything, and, more importantly, he knew instinctively from growing up around Pops that if you wanted something from someone, you had to make sure they were having a good time, and their needs were met. My father was exceptional at pleasing others.

We were a tight family when I was young. We did the usual things other suburban families do, augmented by weekly stadium shows and bootleg copies of first-run movies like *Jaws* and *Star Wars* on Betamax that my father was able to obtain years before they were commercially available. Yet, we were not without our troubles.

I was an exceptionally hyperactive kid with an explosive temper who was almost terminally bored in school (figure that, a Sicilian with a temper) and thus very quickly became a "problem child" in the eyes of the school district. In their attempts to discover what was "wrong" with me, my parents learned about a new diagnosis called Hyperactivity Disorder, later called ADHD. I became one of the first generation of Ritalin kids, having begun treatment in the mid-1970s with one of the pioneers in the field, a neurologist named Millichap. I remember many trips into the city to have test after test, and the grave and anxious moods my mother would be in whenever we would have to do so. I spent a number of years drugged on Ritalin and Dilantin, an antiepileptic tranquilizer that was in vogue as a treatment in those days. My mother said that I turned into a zombie overnight, and after a couple of years she took me off meds permanently.

I am convinced that it was this early introduction to powerful stimulant drugs that hardwired my brain to respond so dramatically to that reward mechanism, and as a consequence of this hardwiring, I became an extremely high-risk candidate for stimulant addiction in my later years. This diagnosis also began my childhood pattern of changing schools every two years, "for a fresh start," until I went to college, which kept me alienated from other children by not permitting me to form any long-term bonds. My life was mostly a living hell because I was a social outcast with few friends who was constantly terrorized by other kids in school and in our neighborhood.

Living in a mixed-race family, even in the progressive feel-good 1970s, was difficult in white suburban America. Most of white America was in the suburbs in the first place because they wanted to get away from Black folk. My sister was probably the darkest face in town until Walter Payton, the Hall of Fame running back for the Chicago Bears, and his family moved in. To their credit, my parents took the time to teach my sister and brother and me about my sister's Native American heritage, and to be proud of it.

Things changed for us drastically in the early 1980s. A brutal recession, intentionally engineered by the Federal Reserve, rocked the entire nation, pushing unemployment to its highest levels since the Great Depression. Celebration Flip Side suddenly went under

after my father's partners were indicted for tax fraud, and the
financial hit was tremendous to our lifestyle, which had grown
dependent upon the big wad of cash my father would bring home
after each show.

My father was also sent out on the road by Warners for nearly
two years while they were opening up the nation's first home video
market. The strain of my father's travel schedule which led to a
series of infidelities he committed along the way, and the burden
of having to raise three kids essentially by herself (one of whom—
me—was more than four parents could handle) beat the hell out
of my mom. And so, knowing no other means of coping, she beat
the hell out of me. It was during that period that she became
violent and abusive in a way that would have a permanent effect
on me. That was also the time that a family moved in next door
whose eldest son would go on to molest me for nearly three years.

When it was time for me to go to high school, my parents decided to send me to Northwestern Military and Naval Academy
in Lake Geneva, Wisconsin. My grandfather Charles and my great
uncle Don attended the school in the 1930s when it was respectable, but by the time I arrived, Northwestern had become little
more than a state repository for incorrigible urban youth sentenced by juvenile courts, with only a smattering of full-paying
families, like ours, who were kept in the dark about the academy's
dealings with the criminal justice system, while at the same time
flattered into holding onto the ridiculous pretense of prestige.
While at the Academy I spent two endless years brutalized by
older cadets, hazed, beaten, tortured, and terrorized, night and
day. At one point I was jammed in the mouth with a flagpole and
had four teeth shattered. During my second year a fellow classmate named Asturizagga began raping me at least once a week.

Asturizagga was a member of the Latin King gang in Chicago.
Although only 17, he was universally feared by everyone. "Astro,"
as they called him, was the first person I ever smoked pot with. I
considered us friends, until I woke up one night with him on top

of me. Between the fear of his reprisal, and the fear of anyone else finding out, I kept my mouth shut about it. I learned years later that I was not his only victim. I also heard he had been shot and killed sometime in the 1990s.

My parents didn't believe me when I told them about the hazing and the beatings and the night treatments. I couldn't even fathom how to begin to tell them about the rapes. I was so ashamed and terrified that I wouldn't tell anyone.

I began smoking cigarettes and pot and drinking heavily, every weekend, whether at school or at home, and often during the week while at school. My intention was to get myself kicked out, but even though I got busted at least three times, they refused to kick me out because my parents kept giving them money. I don't know how I eventually did it, but by the end of the year they finally kicked me out . . . after the last check had been cashed.

I found out years later that the school had finally been shut down after a class-action lawsuit revealed the kinds of torture and abuse that had been going on for years.

My last two years were spent at Lake Forest Academy, another repository for spoiled rich kids, however this one had girls, and was closer to home. My senior year I took a film class and, for my senior thesis, I had to write a short screenplay. With bone-chilling prescience I penned a film about a high school student who got mixed up with crack cocaine and died at the end. It was called *Life's Been Good*, and I received the highest grade in my class. This early validation in many ways laid the foundation for my whole writing career, as well as the chaos that would envelop me in just a few years as my life began to imitate my art.

On October 19, 1987, on a day known to history as Black Monday, the stock market lost almost a quarter of its value. On the day before the market crash I had a crash of my own when I went to a Bears game with friends and was in a nasty car accident that scarred a friend's face for life. My parents were in New York celebrating yet another promotion for my father and an award for his 20 years at Warner Brothers, and they had to rush home early to retrieve me from the ER. The next morning as I lay in bed with a busted wrist and a minor concussion, the market crashed, and in a sickening coincidence, my father was fired after it was discovered that he had been embezzling from the company for years.

This was a total shock to my mother; she trusted my father, and was never one to ask where the money came from so long as it showed up on time. My parents were in New York celebrating yet another promotion for my father and an award for his 20 years of loyal service at Warner Brothers, and they had to rush home early to retireve me from the ER. The next afternoon as I lay in bed at home with a busted wrist and a minor concussion, the stock market crashed. That was hardly the worst of it. Arriving for his first day in his new position, my father is confronted by his superior about a series of luxury car payments that were charged to his company expense account. Almost inconceivably, my father immediately caves and confesses that he had been embezzling from the company for years, to the tune of hundreds of thousands of dollars. He was not-so-politely shown the door, and prominently added to the industry blacklist, *persona non grata*, never to work in his field again. Tragically, it was not the last time he would steal, or be fired for it. What my father had been stealing from his employer was almost equal to what he had been making, so overnight our very, very expensive consumer lifestyle lost its entire source of income. The only reason he didn't go to prison was because he would have dragged too many other people down with him. So they quietly swept him under the rug and out of history. He was 41, the age I am now.

COLLEGE BOY GETS SCHOOLED

I had been accepted at Boston University, and even though my father had lost his job, my parents enrolled me in the fall of 1988 and off I went as if nothing had changed. My mother went into the workforce, ostensibly to pay for my education, and took an entry-level position in philanthropy at a small private PR firm in Chicago.

Before the spring semester of my freshman year, the hardest drug I had ever done was marijuana. My roommate at the time, Brian, a journalism student from New York City who was obsessed with the Beat writers, turned me on in short order to LSD and mushrooms. For money I worked in night clubs as a bartender and doorman and had a work-study job at the university.

The first time I did coke was in the beer cooler of a live music club called The Cage. It was little more than the dingy basement of another club called Molly's, but it was owned by three seniors at BU who would become my best friends and my first community of people. Cocaine was everywhere in the 1980s, both literally and perceptually. I had just turned 19, and had read a dozen books that glorified cocaine use like *Bright Lights, Big City* and *Less Than Zero*. These books were not only marketed to young adults but also taught in high schools. It was in so many movies of the day that, if the idea was to dissuade us, they sure as hell did a piss-poor job. A bar-back named Larry got a gram for me and took me into the beer cooler to do it. Instantly, it was the best feeling I had ever had in my life. It was as if it had been specifically designed for me. I fell in love with it and was soon obsessed. I could think of little else.

Three or four months of subsequent heavy cocaine use and an overdose on alcohol landed me in rehab the summer after my freshman year. My mother had to fly to Boston to retrieve me from an ER. My housemates had found me unconscious on our front porch, sandwiched between the screen door and the front door, trying to get in. And so I was introduced to Alcoholics Anonymous, and I continued to go to meetings for a couple months after I returned for my sophomore year.

My first sponsor was a mustachioed gay man named Frank, who called himself "an old leather fag." Frank was a true mother hen and had half a dozen young sponsees of both genders and orientations. He was very sweet, and generous, and compassionate, and he was exceptionally patient with me. He was used to mentoring working-class street kids, so he thought I was a rich spoiled brat, which I was. He wanted to humble me, so he began taking me to his weekly AA meeting for gay men who had AIDS.

You have to remember, this was 1989. There was no cocktail, no protease inhibitors, no nothin'. If you got AIDS, you withered and died, quickly. I was the only person in that room who was not under a death sentence, and the enormity of it silenced me into submission. Over the course of that year some 30 men from that group would die, and they mostly died alone, in agony, as social pariahs, mocked and derided as non-persons. The experience, this witnessing, forever radicalized me.

In the end, the problem with abstinence at 19 is that you're not even remotely done experimenting.

▼

In October of 1989 my grandmother June, my father's mother, passed away. She had been very sick with emphysema and spent her last years mostly alone in a nursing home. Because she had never revealed to my father any information about his birth family, he was highly suspicious of his origins. For reasons I don't remember my parents chose not to fly me home for her funeral, so I never got to say goodbye to her. The next summer, however, while I was living in a roach-infested apartment near Fenway Park with my girlfriend and two others, my grandmother came to me in a prophetic dream that rocked me to my core.

In the dream, I am walking through a wasteland shrouded in fog. Everything is dead, the trees are bare sticks, the ground is burnt soil. I come upon the ruins of my home, and hear screaming in the distance. I look into one of the rooms and see my parents. The room is empty but for some rusted bedsprings, on which my mother sits rocking back and forth, screaming. My father is holding his hands over his ears. They are both completely insane and do not recognize me. I run from them, but my lungs feel hot, and when I try to breathe, smoke pours out of them. I trip on the earth and my right arm goes plunging into our pool, which is filled with a thick black liquid like tar. My right arm immediately seizes up in pain, and I can't make it work. I roll over on the ground, and in the distance, I see my grandmother appear seated on a windowsill. Light radiates from behind her.

They're in pain, she says. *And you're going to hurt them more.*

I woke up crying uncontrollably for nearly half an hour, terrifying my girlfriend. I couldn't help but shake the feeling that she was trying to warn me, prepare me for what was coming. I could never have understood at the time that I had just seen my future.

▼

In 1992 things began to come unglued in a way that would never be repaired. I rang in the New Year at home in Chicago with my family. Moments before we left our home to go to our party, my father, already a few vodkas down, surreptitiously told me that my mother had cancer. He then informed me that he had been sworn to secrecy, and I was not allowed to share that information with anyone, least of all my sick mother.

I had started using coke again my senior year after my girlfriend at the time got into it heavily. My friends and I would talk about what it took to become a great artist and, invariably, someone would always say: *Suffering . . . you have to suffer for your art.* We would talk a whole ton of shit about how we wanted "suffering" thrust upon us so that we could become great artists.

One night in the early spring of '92 a group of us stood on the roof of a brownstone in the Back Bay as a strong Atlantic wind off the Charles River pounded down upon us. The moon shone steady and clouds raced across its face. With an Absolut bottle dangling from my hand, drunk, high, and acting like a pompous ass, I screamed out to the heavens, "Hit me with everything you got . . . Show me what suffering is!" I was "tough" and I could take it and I wanted to "be real."

Be careful what you ask for.

The next day my car was stolen from in front of my building. My father soon informed me that the insurance company would not cover the claim, and he could not afford to replace it. To add insult to injury, as if to hammer the point home, I had applied to some of the top graduate creative writing programs in the country, certain they would be fighting over me, and within a week had been rejected by every one. My graduation was only a few months away, and I had not planned for anything except more school. I had no job and was acting like college would never end.

I graduated in May 1992 with a BA in English and a B average, but learned the day of my graduation ceremony that my diploma and transcripts were being withheld due to an "outstanding balance." Imagine the feeling of walking onstage with your whole family watching, the day they've dreamed about their whole lives, seeing me handed the cardboard roll, expecting, finally at last, to watch my ornate diploma, symbol of all their sacrifice and perseverance, slip effortlessly into my hand, and instead, a bill flutters out. At first it was total confusion, then—less acknowledged, denied, and ultimately suppressed—total devastation. My father explained that it was an "accounting error."

By the summer of 1992 another brutal recession had a hold of our economy. Even though I was competing with PhDs for restaurant jobs, I decided to stay in Boston instead of going back to Chicago. My sister, Suraya, was in her second year at Emerson College and we rented an overpriced place in the Auditorium district right off Massachusetts Avenue. The minute we moved in, things went to hell.

I was lucky to score a job as a bartender at the Cactus Club, which made me decent money, but between the alcohol and the hours, it was hell on the system. One night in early June I was walking home around 3:30am after working all evening. I was cutting through a residential side street when I heard footsteps in the darkness behind me. I turned around to see three men following me. I kept walking, and they began making catcalls and kissing sounds. One of them shouts, "Hey, faggot! Nice tights!"

I stopped at the corner and turned around, and they stopped a few feet away from me. They looked to me like drunken Northeastern University frat boys. I asked them what they wanted. They kept calling me faggot and taunting me, so I told them all to fuck off and I turned and began to cross the street. The next thing I knew a white hot burst of pain exploded behind my left ear and I lost my vision and balance and fell to the ground. Then everything went black.

I came to on the sidewalk in a pool of blood. My pockets were turned out, my wallet was missing, and my wad of nearly $300 in cash that I had just earned that night was gone as well. Next to me was a softball-sized chunk of asphalt covered in blood, and behind one ear were flaps of skin. I stumbled home.

The next morning I horrified Suraya when she saw me passed out on the couch, my head haloed by a seeping bloodstain. I dragged myself to Boston City Hospital to learn I had a concussion and a laceration that required stitches. The police told me, when I reported it, that I had been the victim of gay bashing, which was a big problem in Boston in those days. I told them that wasn't possible, because I wasn't gay, and they just laughed at me. They never did investigate who might have done it.

Less than a month later, having been fired from the Cactus Club for excessive drinking on the job, and now working down the block at another bar where my sister also worked, I left after work one night to walk home at around 2 am. As I headed west on Boylston Street a car pulled over and a man called from the window, "Charles?" I turned to see a car with four men, and hanging out the window was a man named Billy I used to work with four years earlier at another bar.

"I thought that was you!" he said. "What are you doing walking home by yourself at this hour when you could be an inch deep in coke with me and my friends! We're going to a party in Brookline, come with us."

He had me at "coke."

I got into the car and zipped off to the party. Once there, I realized I was the only straight male in the entire room, and they were all acting very strange, as if they were all in on some kind of inside joke. They grudgingly gave me some coke, and then someone came and gave me a drink. That's the last thing I remember.

I woke up the next day to a flood of sunlight coming in from a skylight. I was in a dormer room on the top story of a house, lying naked on an exercise mat on the floor. As soon as I moved I knew that I had been raped, repeatedly. My clothes were strewn about me, so I quickly gathered them up and crept out of the room. The house was empty, so I walked right out the front door, on to the street, and four miles back to Boston in a total daze, holding half my clothing. I told no one . . . for years, silently living with unfathomable shame and violation and the omnipresent terror that I might have been infected with HIV. All because I couldn't say no to cocaine.

To cope, naturally I sank deeper into more cocaine, in ever increasing amounts, to the point that I began looking for it on the street, something that nice college boys don't do because they have dealers who will deliver to them. Twice I was lucky enough through some desperate homeless guys to score powder on the street down in the South End. The third time I tried, the guy brought back crack rock. That was all it took. I spent the next two days with this homeless man smoking incessantly on the street and in some housing projects in the Roxbury neighborhood, until I ran out of money and had to walk home a number of miles, crashing, dehydrated, and fiending for more.

A week later I was walking home from work and as I turned the corner onto our street I saw this little guy about my age sitting cross-legged on top of a US Postal Service mailbox. He was dressed all in black and was sporting a beret. He asked me if I wanted to buy some hash, and I told him yes and invited him to my place down the block to check it out. He told me his name was Moishe and that he was from New York. As we were smoking the hash, something told me to ask this guy about crack, and when I did, he almost leaped through the wall, telling me he can get the "best shit there is . . . right now!"

We took a cab to the same projects in Roxbury I had just been in with the homeless guy. He hopped out, ran inside, returned a few moments later, and we went back to my place. He went into the bathroom, and a second later I heard him puking violently. He came back out with a handful of bags and proceeded to show me how to build a pipe out of a small one ounce plastic liquor bottle like you get on airplanes, a section of a Bic pen, some aluminum foil, a rubber band, and cigarette ash. We sat down to smoke, and that was it, we were off to the races.

Moishe existed in an entirely different dimension of crackdom than I did. He had been using for years, and the drug cops in Roxbury knew him by name. He was so totally paranoid about getting ripped off or busted that he would swallow the bags after he copped and then puke them up later. Sometimes it would take an hour of heaving before they would come up. It was miserable, and when he and I would go on three-day binges we might go back and cop eight, nine times, and go through this every time. We would smoke until there was no more money, and no other means to obtain it, and then we would sleep for a day or two. Then, one day, Moishe disappeared. Just like that he never came around again. I figured he got popped and was in the joint.

Within a few months, I had seen and experienced everything that I had imagined at 18 when I wrote my high school screenplay. Except for my own death, it had all come true.

On Thanksgiving of 1992 the bottom fell out. I was in my apartment alone. Suraya was with her boyfriend and his family. I received a call from my mother who told me to sit down. She then told me that we were totally bankrupt, that the bank was foreclosing on our home, that our cars had been repossessed, our credit cards canceled, that everything was gone. She told me that she had just that day discovered that my father had been unemployed for a year and a half without telling anyone. He had been pretending to go to work every day, going so far as to shower and dress in a suit and have my mother drop him off at a fictional place of employment every morning. I could tell that my mother was in shock.

Soon I would discover that my father had not paid for most of the four years I had attended BU, and I was suddenly being handed the bill. He had borrowed somewhere around $50,000 in student loans and had taken out credit cards in my name that had been canceled and sent into collections. Since my sophomore year he had been sending me into the university registration office to sign promissory notes every semester, which I was led to believe were my "registration papers." This left me solely responsible for a $100,000 college bill, without a diploma or formal transcripts that would have permitted me to get a decent job to pay them back. It was insane.

Then, my phone began ringing off the hook with collectors badgering me about debts I knew nothing about. Men in suits started showing up at my apartment in Boston demanding I give them my American Express card (this was in the days of carbons, when purchase transactions were not made instantly as they are today over the interwebs).

I freaked out, went to a public detox for five days to hide out, and tried to stay clean. I hooked back up with my sponsor and began to go to meetings again, but it didn't last long. Within two months I was using again, and slowly everything I owned was disappearing out the door, into pawn shops and the waiting hands of eager dealers.

I was generally paralyzed in those days. My parents had raised me to live an affluent life, and because of that, and because my mother was so hyper-controlling and rarely let me do anything on my own, I was effectively useless except to consume, and since I was broke and could not find steady work, I wasn't much of a consumer either. I did not know how to build or fix or make or run anything. I did not know how to accomplish any kind of administrative task like paying bills or balancing a checkbook. I never dealt with school "paperwork"; my parents always did. I did not know the first thing about taking care of myself, because I had been preparing for a life in which others would be paid to take care of all of those things for me.

It never once occurred to me that to be rich was to be more or less helpless.

A week later a thick letter arrived in the mail. In ten typed pages my father outlined for me the history of my parents' marriage, explaining that he had "never really wanted kids," that he was "forced to have them" by my mother's family, and that he would have been much happier had it just been him and my mom. He concluded the letter with an itemized bill for how much I cost him over the course of my life, from birth until that moment. It was some astronomical number into the hundreds of thousands.

I didn't know at the time my father was having a total breakdown. I hadn't been around him in a long time, and he was such a pathological liar by that point that he made it sound like everything was fine in our day-to-day life. Now he was collapsing under the weight of the deception and the enormous lifestyle he built around mostly illicit money, and he couldn't cope. Had I known he was losing it, and was not just a bastard, I might not have gone out and gotten blind drunk and ended up in the projects wheeling a shopping cart filled with my stereo equipment, sobbing, when the police picked me up for drunken-disorderly, knowing exactly what I was trying to do.

They threw me in the drunk tank and were going to release me in the morning, but I was so wasted I thought I was being busted for drugs. I sat there on the ground in that police lockup feeling like my world had collapsed and I had been spit out for the wolves. How was I going to tell my mother about this? I wanted to die.

I inadvertently came across the deadbolt key to my apartment inside the breast pocket of my shirt, which the cops had apparently failed to find in the pat-down. It was one of those big Schlage

keys with a sharp tooth at the end. I took the key and slashed both
my wrists lengthwise down the vein (the right way) until the skin
and muscle ripped open and I began to bleed. Then I passed out.

I woke up in the psych ward of Boston City Hospital heavily
sedated, strapped to a mattress on the floor outside the nurses'
station. I would remain in that state for days. When my mother finally tracked me down and I spoke to her on the phone, she asked
me why I had done it. I had never heard her sound so afraid in
all my life, and it was at that moment that I first truly understood
how much my mother loved me. I told her I couldn't stop smoking
crack, and I'd never be able to pay back all the money that was in
my name, and that pretty soon she was going to be gone too and
no one would be left to help me. I felt so utterly helpless.

I couldn't bring myself to tell her about the gay bashing and the
rape. I'm not sure it was even in my conscious mind at the time,
I had pushed it down so deep. When she asked me what I meant
when I said she would be "gone" I told her that my father had
revealed to me that she was dying. My mother calmly told me that
yes, she had had cancer, but they had managed to get all of it and
she was fine, she wasn't dying.

"And Dad's letter!" I wailed into the phone.

"What letter?" she asked, and so I told her.

For a moment there was nothing but silence on the other end of
the line. My blood ran cold. Very low and soft, my mother said,
"I need to find your father. I will call you back later. Do not go
anywhere until you talk to me again," and she hung up.

It was in her voice. If she could have killed him, she would have.
I believe that was the moment my mother decided to finally divorce
my father, and come rescue me in Boston, for the second time.

I was released after five days of observation once they determined I was "not a harm to myself or anyone else." I came home
to find that my sister and I had received an eviction notice since we
had not paid our rent in six months. Within days my mother arrived and we had to pack up in secret and move out in the middle

of the night. Between the three of us we had enough money to rent a truck and drive home (gas was $1.00/gallon in those days). I drove most of the way, and my mother stared silently at the bandages on my wrists.

Back at home, things got steadily worse. My father didn't just owe creditors unbelievable sums of money, he also owed friends and family, people we had known our whole lives. He was still living with my mother in our house, but he had moved into my room, so I was couch surfing in my own home.

My father had rapidly become something of an outcast in our town, and as if anyone should be surprised, in his desperation to find value and meaning and acceptance, he wandered into the local Evangelical Christian church and went and got himself saved. From that point on, our anger and disapproval no longer mattered to him. He told us, "Jesus has forgiven me, and since Jesus was big enough to forgive me, do you all think you are more important than Jesus?"

Looking back, it was obvious my father had gone round the bend and had a complete breakdown. He was clinging to anything that got him out of bed in the morning. Everyone in his life hated him except his church friends, so I don't blame him for wanting to be with them. But at the time, it came off as the most selfish thing we could think of. At this point I very well may have hated my father. At the very least I had lost any semblance of respect for him. At worst, I wondered where my real Dad had gone, and who this awful stranger was who had taken his place.

One evening, two or so months after I returned home, four Cook County Sheriff's deputies rang our doorbell. One was holding a shotgun. We answered the door, and they informed us that we had 30 days to vacate. As if trapped in a container of unshakeable denial, my father refused to help us pack, and left for a weekend retreat with his church. The rest of us packed an entire home into a truck and headed off to the city, where my mother had rented a three-bedroom apartment for the four of us. It was the last time I would see my father for a while.

CHAPTER 5
Cheating Death (and Other Things) in Chicago and LA

I'm sure Tolkien was only playing with metaphors when he described the relationship between Gollum and the Ring of Power, but I've found few portraits of addiction more profound. Living on the Gold Coast of Chicago mere blocks from the Cabrini Green projects was something like living in the Shire next to Mordor. The Ring constantly called out to me, and it was not long before I was out on the prowl, looking to cop, feeling my true self slowly continue to warp and distort into someone (or something) I was no longer able to recognize clearly.

Throughout late 1993 and into 1994, thanks to my mother's burgeoning network of connections, I worked in a series of law offices as a paralegal. The workload was exhausting, and the pay was miserable, but it beat waiting tables, so I bit my tongue, lowered my pride, and fought the Tie and Cubicle War every day at 8am. A lawyer I worked with had a crooked doctor who would prescribe whatever he wanted, so I got a stockpile of painkillers, tranks, and benzos. We would get weed and coke delivered to the office. I began getting dangerously drunk after work and wandering into Cabrini, fully dressed in a business suit and trench coat, disappearing for hours, smoking crack in a mental fog, only to pop out of it and realize, with horror, that I was completely vulnerable. It's a literal miracle I made it out alive and never got popped by the Po-Pos.

One night I was jumped by two guys who wanted to rob me. One kicked me in the head with an iron-toed boot and my forehead split right open, requiring 11 stitches. Less than two weeks later, in the middle of a deep freeze when the temps were hitting 15 below zero, I went back again, totally wasted, to cop powder cocaine and was given China White heroin instead. Too wasted and jonesing to listen to what the people who sold it to me were trying to tell me, I opened two of the bags, dumped them on the table, and, thinking they were coke, blew both of them up my nose.

The last thing I heard, or remember, was someone saying, "Aw man . . . you shouldntadun that . . ."

I woke up in the Northwestern Memorial ER with a blinding pain in my chest and along the side of my face to find two doctors and a nurse's aid standing over me looking like they'd rather be treating Joseph Goebbels. They informed me that I had been discovered by a patrol car in Cabrini Green face down in the street frozen to the pavement. I had collapsed inside the row house where I had snorted the dope, and the people I had bought the drugs from could not revive me, even after dousing me with cold water, so they opened the door and rolled me onto the street. The paramedics had to pour warm saline on the pavement to be able to pull me up off it without ripping my skin. The extreme cold, they told me, was the only reason I was alive. Hypothermia had slowed down my metabolism enough to turn me into a Chucksicle, ironically saving my life.

At the hospital they thawed me out and hit me with Narcan and adrenaline, jump-starting my heart—hence the awful pain in my chest. They explained in great detail all the time and energy and expense they had put into saving my life, and then one of them said, "And you're not even worth it . . . because you did this to yourself."

▼

I was never a superstitious person and I never believed in things like omens until I moved to New York City in the summer of 1996. I had been in regular contact with a close friend from BU who was becoming a well-known actor. We were talking about making a short film together from a script I had written called "Lost in My Own Backyard," a Beckett-esque tale about a man trapped in a studio apartment, slowly going insane.

I was engaged at the time to a woman who had just graduated college and whose father was a drama teacher at my brother's high school. She and I had been together for nine months. Foreshadowing the dynamic I would eventually have with Edie, Alison and I were best friends, but it wasn't much of a romance, it was more of a codependency. I moved in with her at Purdue to escape Chicago, because I couldn't stop smoking crack there. I had a good clean year with her in Indiana, most of which I spent incessantly writing screenplays.

On the day that we arrived in New York, my fiancée's cousin met us at 23rd Street and Ninth Avenue in Chelsea and we three decided to walk to the Village and grab dinner to celebrate. As we made our way down 20th Street, headed east towards Eighth Avenue, a short figure approached. It was a man roughly my age wearing a hat and a baggy shirt. As he came into view, I immediately recognized him as Moishe the Jewish crackhead from Boston I had met four years earlier.

He shuffled right up to the three of us, just like how I remembered him shuffling before. He looked like he'd been in the streets the entire time. He was hairy and dirty and his skin was ruddy red. His fingers were black, and he smelled like smoke and car exhaust. He asked if any of us had a cigarette.

My fiancée's cousin had one and as she dug through her purse Moishe stared at me. Something way down in there jarred loose a bit, and he cocked his head and stared more intently. I was sure he had recognized me when he said, "You really look familiar," but he followed that up with, "Did you grow up in this neighborhood?"

"Nope. Just moved here."

She gave him the cigarette and lit it for him. He took one more look at me, and then shuffled away.

I walked away feeling as if I were going to faint. Two million people live on Manhattan Island and he was the first person I met on the street. I knew, somewhere inside me, that I had made a huge mistake in coming here, and that this city was going to swallow me whole.

My fiancée, Alison, was a restaurant management trainee who spent 60 to 70 hours a week at work. I bartended at night in the West Village, so we never saw each other. She was also rapidly losing interest in men, so when we were together, we were rarely "together." As a consequence, I began sleeping with her cousin, Leah.

To make matters worse, just as I was finding myself back to some semblance of steady physical and mental health, after abstaining from cocaine for nearly a year, I learned that my friend the actor was deep into blow, and before I was there a week, my clean time evaporated. Henceforth we spent most of our time together railing lines and talking about how we were going to make a movie.

Eventually I cobbled together a script and we found two more actors to cast who were also college friends from the same circle. We found a local DP, and began readings and rehearsals. Then my friend got cast in this abysmal film called *Starship Troopers* and he left on a three-month shoot, and our project was dead in the water. I had no other prospects and sank into depression.

The area around Washington Square Park where I worked was crawling with crack, and within two months I had lost my job and blown all my money. Alison, who hated New York to begin with, used my crisis as an excuse to move us back to Chicago. But our neighborhood in Chicago was teeming with crack as well, and within two months she had thrown me out.

I went to stay with Leah's ex-boyfriend and his roommate, who all belonged to the same theater company. I had been helping them with their new production, so they let me couch surf, but eventually they began to see that there was something off about me, and I think word got to them through Leah, so they asked me to leave and I was forced to go live with my mother again, at age 26.

Less than a week later I disappeared on a week-long binge. I stole money and jewelry from my mother and sister that I pawned, and I broke into the basement of the place where I had been staying and repaid the guys who had so kindly let me stay with them by stealing a guitar and a bike and pawning both, with every intention of "paying them back later."

Afraid to go home, I met this junkie chick and her boyfriend who had this nasty place in Uptown where they were gonna let me crash if I scored for them because they were both getting dope-sick. Dude was going to drive us to the West Side and we were going to cop there. Worse, he had convinced me to try heroin (consciously) for the first time.

I had this feeling like I was skirting the edge of my own mortality, that once I turned down the dope path I would be entering a whole new world of pain and suffering, one from which I quite likely would not escape.

You may choose to interpret the following sequence of events any way you like, but after 14 years of contemplation, I can come to no other conclusion than divine intervention.

It began when dude couldn't get his car started, so he sent me and his girlfriend down the block to an auto supply store to get a new distributor cap. As we were returning with the part we cut across a parking lot in front of a pawn shop and were almost run over by my mother and sister, who were pulling into the parking lot at that very moment.

I took off running, and my mother took off after me on foot. My sister threw the car in reverse and began chasing me backwards down a one-way street. I cut through an alley and an empty lot and slipped away from both of them. I ran back to the apartment building, past the dude who was still under the roof of his car watching me go, and just as I ducked into the vestibule of their building to disappear, perhaps forever, I reached inside my jacket pocket to check on my wad of cash meant for our drugs, and could not find it.

I frantically searched my pocket, turning it inside out, but the money did not materialize. So what did I do? I turned around and ran back down to the sidewalk and began looking for it. Within a moment my mother and sister came around the corner and confronted me. I ignored them in a panic, looking for the money. Then a patrol car came racing up to the scene, and my mother yelled, *"That's my son and he's on drugs . . . stop him!!"*

Something about that snapped me out of the trance I was in and I just froze. I suddenly realized I was in a shitload of trouble. The cops grabbed me, smashed me into the brick wall of an apartment building, cuffed my hands behind my back, and began searching me. When one of them reached inside my jacket pocket, he pulled out my wad of bills.

I stared at them dumbfounded, and somewhere in the distance, I could have sworn I heard God laughing.

YOU HAVE THE RIGHT TO REMAIN SILENT FOR A REASON

When I first disappeared my mother went to the police to ask for help. She told them her son was on drugs and might be in danger and asked if they could do anything. They said, "not unless he has committed a crime," and then asked if I ever stole anything from her. Her expression said it all, so they told her the only way they could help me was if she filed charges, which would generate a warrant, which would permit the police to pick me up. If she didn't do that, there was nothing they could do for her.

So she had complied, and while I was missing, a warrant for my arrest had been issued by the Evanston police. When the Chicago Police grabbed me that day in uptown, after my mother and sister had so frantically chased me through the ghetto, they ran my ID through the system, it came back with the warrant, and they initially took me into custody on those grounds.

While I was in custody, the detectives assigned to my case sat down with my mother and me and told us that since I was a first-time offender I was "automatically" going to get treatment instead of a felony charge. All I had to do was outline what I had done, admit I was a drug addict, and ask for treatment. They assured us that the system "was packed with real bad guys" and that they were not interested in locking up a "nice kid who obviously just got a little screwed up."

My mother told me to cooperate, and I, delirious from lack of food and sleep and crashing off a week-long binge on high-grade crack cocaine, did whatever they told me. No sooner had I signed my name to the documents than they told me to stand up and then they handcuffed me and began to haul me away. When my mother asked what they were doing they told us, "He's being booked for residential burglary, lady, what do you think?"

"But you told us he'd get treatment!"

"Right. And you believed us."

That wasn't the end of it. So the Chicago police had me for burglarizing my friend's home, and the Evanston police had me for felony theft of my mother's and sister's jewelry. I was in an epic shitstorm, one that looked like it was going to rip me apart like a F-class tornado.

The Chicago police had an air-tight burglary charge. Because I was so cracked out and trusted the cops, and even though everything I took was recovered and returned to the rightful owners, I still gave them a signed confession, everything they needed to get a Class X conviction for home invasion, which means big promotion points for them and a mandatory four years for me. They had a written confession that they had tricked me into giving them, and I was such a naïve fool I didn't know that they give you the right to remain silent for a *reason*, and you don't sign *nothin'*, not now not never, whether you are guilty or innocent. They had photocopies of my ID at the pawn shops, and they had witnesses who saw me sell the stuff, yet the best they could have charged me with without my confession was "possession of stolen property," which was a misdemeanor.

The Evanston police would not allow my mother to drop her charges no matter what she tried to do, so when I went to appear before the bond judge I was looking at being sent down to County with a hefty bail. Aside from that brief terrible night in the precinct lockup in Boston, I had never been in jail before, and I was terrified.

Somehow, while I was in a holding cell awaiting my hearing, my mother tracked down a public defender and pleaded my case to him. The PD somehow believed her and argued to the judge that I was OK to be sent home because I was a *college-educated* first-time offender "from a good home" and that my mother was there in court. Moreover, he argued, I knew the victims personally and had lived in the house; I had been using drugs but was now headed to rehab. I was released on an I-Bond—meaning I was released to my own recognizance until my future court appearance—with the stipulation that I had 72 hours to get myself into a treatment center somewhere.

It was here that my mother and I, together, came face to face with the reality of money in the criminal justice system. The divorce and bankruptcy devastated my mother, and she was left to

shoulder the bulk of the debt because my father was basically indigent. She was also under the thumbscrews of the IRS, who had
her on the hook for back taxes she knew nothing about, taxes my
father had ducked out on. She was determined to pay back every
cent, restore her credit, and get back on her feet.

Despite her lack of a college education, my mother worked
very hard, was very smart, and steadily advanced in her field. In
late 1996 she was working as the executive director of the Chicago chapter of the American Cancer Society raising millions
every year. She had a modest salary while at the same time putting
my brother through college and paying back this landfill of debt.
The government and other creditors took a huge chunk of every
paycheck, so even though she was stable, she didn't have anything
saved. I of course had nothing. My arrest was going to completely
wipe her out. Rehab and lawyers cost money. Lots and lots of
money.

My future stepfather, who had been dating my mother for only
a few months at that point, floated the $6,000 bill for a stint
in treatment, a 90-day program at the Gateway Foundation. He
also paid my defense lawyer's $10,000 fee (whose services I con-
tracted after he came to the rehab and made a presentation to the
inpatients in an entirely new form of ambulance chasing that was
more like shooting fish in a barrel). A total of $16,000 bought
my freedom. If I hadn't had that, if I hadn't been white, if my
professionally dressed white mother had not been in court with
me, and if I hadn't had a treatment center to run off and hide in, I
would have been in prison. The State had everything they needed
to send me away.

I received a felony conviction for "attempted residential burglary" and, thanks to the lawyer, received five years of probation
since he successfully argued that I had broken into the basement,
not the house, through an already broken window, when no one
was home at the time, and after the theft the merchandise was
returned. But mostly he got my charges knocked down because I

could afford to have them knocked down, and because I appeared to be a sympathetic defendant who had just "lost his way." That last part may have been true, but there is no denying that I got off because of race and class privilege.

I didn't believe in things like karma back then, and I laughed at people who did, but it's so clear to see now that somehow I eluded fate, slipped a tackle long enough to avoid going to prison that time. I asked myself why, why, in the face of the worst thing I had ever done, was I spared the fate that almost everyone would agree I deserved? When I search my soul, what I believe is that I was spared prison because the police were trying to make it a Class X case, a dangerous violent felony, which it wasn't. If I had been convicted of a Class X, I would have spent years in a maximum-security facility, and my life would have been very, very different from what it is today. I believe I was spared only because there was an equally nefarious motive trying to screw me. But karma never forgets, and eventually, I would have to answer for this.

I left treatment in January of 1997, moved into a halfway house in the Humboldt Park neighborhood, and took a job at the Anti-Cruelty Society. I had stayed clean for barely two months before I was getting high again, and each time I would binge, I would get kicked out of another halfway house, and lose another job. Somehow I managed to score a temp-to-perm position at *Playboy*, and fucked it all up within three months. By the fall of 1997, I was homeless, no longer able to make job interviews or assignments, and almost out of options. In desperation I went to an AA meeting at a club in the Lincoln Park neighborhood and met some guys who were living in the Salvation Army shelter on Clybourn Avenue. They took me there after the meeting, and it became my home for the next several months.

In the shelter, of almost 200 men, I was one of about ten whites, and the only one of the ten under 50. We lived in a barracks-like setting, worked six days a week picking up, moving, or selling donated goods, and went to religious services all day Sunday. We ate three good meals a day, and were treated with dignity. We had health care, addiction treatment, and even a few dollars in spending money each week.

But there was no escape unless you left and became homeless again. There was no way to earn your way out, you couldn't make enough money. There was no way to go look for work, because you were always working for them. And if you did leave the shelter, you couldn't even get public aid to help you transition, because when you first arrived at the shelter the Salvation Army made you get on public aid to help defray their costs. They made you sign a proxy contract giving them total control over your benefits, and the center where I stayed kept taking from your state account for months after you had left. The one time in my life I took public aid I never even saw a dime of it.

It sounds Dickensian, but it really wasn't that bad. I was used to living in this kind of setting since I had been to both military school and rehab, both highly structured, generally same-sex experiences. Sure I missed women and freedom, but the hardest part to bear was the shame and psychodramas you played on yourself when you were reminded that you were fucking *homeless*. It was humbling to have to pick out your clothes from the resale shop, and never have much more money in your pocket than for a few packs of cigarettes.

Still, if for no other reason, the experience was totally worth it because I got to play keyboards in the Salvation Army gospel band and spent a number of Sundays playing to black churches on the far South Side where I was the only white face for miles. These were Southern Baptists and Evangelicals, good church folk, who danced down the aisles, sang from their toes, and looked at me with an endless mix of amusement and suspicion. *Dat young white boy got to be in dat shelter 'cause a drugs*, their expressions said. When I would have my one trademark solo in this song called "Oh Happy Day," they would howl with laughter, not to tease me, but because I had rhythm, could play, and never let it get to me. It was some of the most fun I ever had in my life, and the purest form of spiritual expression I had ever experienced. I wasn't even a Christian, and I hated church, but these people knew how to throw down for the Lord.

When I eventually left the shelter, it was to move in with a woman I had just met in AA. I managed to stay clean for almost nine months. This was the middle of the tech bubble and there was so much temp and contract work available for copywriters that for the first time in my professional career I started to get steady work as a writer. I also wrote creatively for the first time in nearly two years. I pulled out an old manuscript of a novel I had begun that was based on my family history called "Unfinished Portraits." I outlined the rest of the story, and then wrote it all out as a screenplay.

I had begun "Unfinished Portraits" in 1992 in an attempt to make sense of my Byzantine family history and its epic collapse. It was inspired by a conversation I had had with my father while I was still in college in which he speculated that the reason he knew nothing about his birth family, and there were no records, was because he might be the child of his grandfather, Eden "Pops" Brekke, by another woman, a mistress, who was then given to Pops's daughter June and her husband, Charles, to raise as their own.

I took my family's true story and interwove it with a gothic mystery about the origins of the fictional Montgomery family and their fallen fortunate son, Nolan, based upon my father. The main character was Evan Montgomery, based on myself, a promising artist who went to law school on a scholarship, and through political connections, after his family went bankrupt. The narrative is framed around Evan's two-week Christmas vacation with his mother, and flashes back to previous generations, as Evan receives notice that his estranged grandmother, who disappeared when he was just a boy under a shroud of mystery, has resurfaced in a nearby nursing home and is on the verge of death. Before she dies she wishes to see her grandson again, and tell him the truth of his family history. In discovering this truth, Evan must decide what to do with his life. It was a dark allegory, with a huge unexpected plot twist at the end, just like the industry people liked.

Chicago was awash with independent filmmakers in the late '90s all trying to make the next low-budget smash with venture capital that came from the tech boom. Through contacts I made in AA I hooked up with some indie producers who made their money in commercials. With a solid script to shop we spent months courting investors, and slowly cast the film and put together a production plan.

In the meantime I had been hired to teach screenwriting at Columbia College and, being part-time and thus paid a flat rate for each class we taught, I took on a four-class load immediately, which is a tremedous amount of work for a part-time employeee with no benefits and no job security, on top of the work required to produce and direct "Unfinished Portraits." I began to moonlight as a production assistant on commercial shoots, which, if you've ever been on one, you know are extremely long and exceedingly boring and repetitive. Despite working 70 hours a week, I still barely had enough money to survive.

In hindsight, I took on way too much, far too soon. And these things unravel in the strangest, and quickest, manner, quite literally leaving you stunned as if Tased, fumbling around trying to figure out what the fuck just happened.

In August of 1998, at the height of my sobriety and productivity, I took a trip with an AA friend to New York to be her date at a family wedding. The minute we stepped out onto the Manhattan pavement, the unique smell of the city bore straight into the buried repository of traumatic memories I held of my life crumbling in Manhattan only two years earlier. Something just snapped. A week from being nine months sober, and two days away from a massive Jewish wedding of a few hundred people, I simply disappeared into the projects off 134th and Amsterdam in Harlem to smoke crack with a naked Rastafarian painter and his prostitute girlfriend until two hours before the ceremony. I was stone cold sober when I made the decision to get into a cab and go looking for fucking crack. It was literally as if someone else had hijacked my brain and taken over complete control of me.

That may have been the moment that I first began to seriously question if escape was even possible.

YOU'RE TOO JUNG FOR THIS

Shortly after the epic relapse I suffered in New York City I left the Twelve-Step program, again, and began using regularly, trying to hide it, not knowing if I was at all successful, but convincing myself of it anyway. Somehow, I still managed to hold onto my teaching job, but after a binge in which I missed a commercial shoot, my partners in the film project began to seriously consider jumping ship. I was already on double secret probation with them, and they were waiting for the first opportunity to bail.

I moved to a new apartment in Humboldt Park, and within days had managed to find two regular hookup spots off California Avenue. One was a town house that had been taken over by crack dealers, the other was a garden apartment that was a shooting gallery for local junkies. In those days the area was swimming in both high-grade Mexican Brown tar and China White dope. Before long I had begun shooting speedballs as a means of coping with the brutal cocaine crashes.

In November, about a month after I had moved in, my new roommates caught me stealing money and kicked me out, so I asked one of my students if I could stay with her. Her name was Tiffany, and she was a relatively sheltered kid who had just moved to Chicago to study film after spending a year with a touring company of *Up with People* performing in a kind of perky, puerile corporate-sponsored right-wing propaganda musical that used corny American iconography to program kids with a more or less neoconservative worldview. After a year of this Pollyanna Puritanism, Tiffany seemed rather inclined to go slumming with the bad boys.

Fascinated by my dark side, and wielding a huge crush, she let me stay in her huge two-floor apartment on Belmont Avenue in Lakeview that she shared with a smarmy guy in his twenties named Peter and another woman Tiffany's age. And of course, with my luck, how surprised do you think I was to learn that Peter had developed a crack habit, which he managed to more or less hide until my arrival? Once I was there, I spotted it rather quickly; there's something about a crackhead's eyes that are all-telling, fixed in a constant state of craving, a perpetual irritability and anxiety, and an ant-like busyness.

Before long the place was full of people getting high, as every night Peter would bring home new drug-addled strangers. In exchange for free drugs, I in turn taught them all how to cook and shoot up. It got to the point that every night I was taking orders and running off to the ghetto to do everyone's shopping.

Maintaining a habit is *exhausting*. It takes massive inputs of energy, and eventually your mind and body will deplete itself, and you will get tired, and lazy, and sloppy, and impatient; all that leads to *stupid*. Once you get into the stupid, you start getting busted, or killed.

Normally, whenever I would hit a spot to cop, if it wasn't a street transaction, I would go in one door and out the other. I would case the spot beforehand to make sure there were no cops or gang ambushes lying in wait, and I always checked outside through the windows and the peephole before I left. If I got a ride from someone, I made sure they parked around the block.

A few days before Christmas 1998, on a cold and snowy evening, I was having dinner with Tiffany and two of her friends who were visiting from out of town. We had planned, for once, to go to the movies and have a simple, drug-free, low-key evening. Peter came home just as we were finishing dinner and flashed a wad of cash and begged me to cop for him. I told him no, so he offered me $50 and said he'd drive me. Before I could even mount resistance, I felt myself surrender to the craving.

Tiffany looked at me: *No, please!* Although she was down with experimenting, and had already gone in for her fair share, she had grown tired of Peter's bullshit and the steady stream of creepy drug addicts who were in and out of her place. I distinctly remember hearing a voice tell me to *stay!* even as my feet were flying down the stairs.

When we arrived at the spot in Humboldt Park, I told Peter to park around the corner and I would meet him there. I ducked down an alley and went up into the town house through the back porch. I got an eight-ball of crack and ten dime bags of heroin, which I stuffed deep down into the fingers of my big winter glove. At the last second, I took out one tiny tinfoil bag of dope and stuck it in the small change pocket of my jeans, intending to snort it in the car once we were away. Then I left, but instead of going out the front door as I should have, for some reason I went out the back.

I opened the door to see a car idling in the alley. I should have jumped into the gangway and run, but I didn't. I stumbled down the stairs, and out of nowhere a TAC cop pops out from behind a garage and grabs me. In front of the unmarked TAC car is Peter, sitting in his car. He either didn't trust me or was jonesing so bad he couldn't wait for me where I told him to, so he pulled behind the house to wait, with the lights on and the engine running. Unbeknownst to all of us, the house was under surveillance. This drew their attention, and they rolled up on him to check him out. When I came out of the house, they were waiting for me.

The cop grabbed my big winter gloves but didn't find the drugs stuffed way into the fingertips. He handed them back to me and grumbled, "Hold these" and started patting me down. I looked over at Peter and smiled because I thought we were in the clear, and that's when I felt the cop's finger slip into my change pocket, like a snake slithering down a rabbit hole. He extracted the dime-sized foil package out of my pocket and yelled, "Bingo!" I felt like I was going to vomit or pass out.

I was already on felony probation, and I'd just been popped for another felony possession charge. My first thought was, *I am definitely going to prison.* The enormity of it was too much to handle. I flushed into a sweat, which began to freeze once it hit the cold winter air.

It was bad enough I got busted, but then Peter said, "I don't know nothing about that, he just asked me to give him a ride to his sister's. Can I go?" They pulled him aside, whereupon he begged to be let go, claiming total innocence, and they *let* him. He took off like the Road Runner, hanging cloud of dust and all.

At my bond hearing the next day the judge saw I was on probation. He read aloud with heavy sarcasm that I had listed my profession as "Instructor, Columbia College."

"What do you teach at Columbia?" he asked.

"Screenwriting, sir. And narrative development." I felt like a complete idiot saying it.

The judge laughed. "Well, now you've got plenty to write about. $50,000 D bond. Enjoy County, Professor."

This was the first time I was sent on to Cook County Jail. I would end up staying for almost three weeks without any contact with the outside world. In that time, I convinced myself I was headed to prison. My court date was scheduled for late March, three months away, and there was no way I was going to be able to come up with the $5,000 (10%) necessary for me to bond out. I very quickly had to resign myself to my fate and begin making plans to drop out of society after my release.

Two weeks later I received notice that I had a visitor. When I walked into the visitation area, I saw Tiffany on the other side of the glass. She was near tears, and she sat down and told me everything that had happened.

When Peter returned to the apartment that night he told everyone that I had run off with their money. She refused to believe it, but when I didn't return myself that night, she wondered if Peter might have been telling the truth. It was after a few days, when I failed to show up for class or come home, that she knew something was wrong. She confronted Peter, and he eventually capitulated and told her what had really happened.

Eventually she tracked me down at the jail, and told me that she had given her consent for me to stay with her on EMU (Electronic Monitoring Unit), otherwise known as house arrest. Peter would of course still be there, and I went deep into a rage thinking about how I was going to make that punk-ass bitch pay. Two days later I was transferred to EMU and ended up back at the apartment on Belmont, this time with a band around my ankle and a monitoring box plugged into the phone.

Peter was waiting for me when I returned. He put on a total show. He hugged me and begged my forgiveness and said that he "had just been scared and freaked out" and that letting me stay with them was his way of making it up to me. He then proposed that we "celebrate" my return and he reached inside his pockets and pulled out some rocks and dope.

"See, dude. I made my own connect," he said. "Yer all good, man. You just chill here."

When I informed Columbia that I had been arrested and was on house arrest, they fired me. By the end of the first week, Peter had ripped me off twice, claiming he had been "burnt" by his connection, and I was left with no more money. Facing a cold-turkey detox and a few years in prison, I decided it was time for a break.

I stayed clean in spite of the circumstances. I fought through it, and one Friday evening, three weeks after I arrived on house arrest, my monitoring box rang. When I answered it in terror, a voice told me I was being transferred to "Day Report" and to be at the jail complex at 32nd and California at 6 am with my monitoring box.

The Cook County Jail Day Report Center is probably the one thing that saves County from complete blanket condemnation. Amidst a level of corruption and brutality that would make Nero blush, Day Report is a progressive anomaly. It was launched in 1993 as a kind of diversion program to combat overcrowding, which had overwhelmed both the jail and the EMU. Nonviolent offenders, mostly drug offenders, are transferred into Day Report as spaces open up.

There they spend their days attending basic drug treatment classes, eventually moving into individually crafted educational plans. At night they are free to go home. If they remain clean (via daily and then weekly tox screens) and do not incur further charges or commit infractions while attending the program, slowly the amount of hours the inmate has to spend in the program decreases.

The program is rather brilliant, all things considered. It gives nonviolent offenders a structured environment with accountability, but it also gives them flexibility and the chance to improve their situation if they are willing to apply themselves. It also costs a fraction of what it would cost to continue housing, feeding, and monitoring them inside the jail complex, thereby releasing the jail from the lion's share of liability, since inmates are ROR (released to own recognizance) each night.

Every morning at daybreak along California Avenue a hundred-odd men line up outside a doorway that is adjacent to the gate at 31st and California and wait, sometimes hours, until they are admitted to the jail complex. They wait whether it's raining, snowing, sub-zero, or 105 degrees. Over the course of an hour or more, one by one they enter the facility, passing through metal detectors and pat downs.

Once inside, they line up again and are given plastic specimen cups and sent into the washroom to provide samples, under super vision. The men then congregate in the main room of the Day Report center, which resembles the average school cafeteria. Arrayed amongst picnic tables, the collection of mostly young, mostly black men banter with each other or sleep with their heads down, awaiting the start of the day's program.

Although the overall aim is to avoid holding these offenders in the jail, the center is not at all shy about sending people back into custody. On the day I arrived, as a kind of cruel introduction to Day Report, we were awaiting the start of the day when the doors on the far side of the main room crashed open and three Cook County sheriff's investigators in plain clothes, badges clipped to their belts, strode into the room. The inmates immediately fell silent and settled into their seats. The lead investigator pointed into the crowd of seated inmates.

"That one, there."

All heads turned at once to the locus of attention, a black male who looked to be in his thirties.

"Stand up," the lead investigator said.

The inmate complied, and quickly the two other Investigators surrounded him and cuffed his hands behind his back.

"You dropped dirty again, your vacation is over," the lead investigator told him before he was marched off the floor. He would now spend the next day and a half reprocessing back into County. Everyone else in the room slowly lowered their gaze to the floor and silently breathed relief.

Freedom is a powerful motivator. Most of the inmates admitted to Day Report stay in the program until their cases are resolved if only to be able to sleep in their own beds. But the periodic scene of a violator being hauled off to the jail is an essential part of maintaining order. All day long these men—most of whom did not have the patience to sit through high school—are confined to classrooms. Those who remain clean, show up every day, and do not commit infractions will slowly move up through the program. Higher levels mean more free time and less hours spent at Day Report, or, if you choose to take advantage of it, more in-depth educational programs like GED certification. After a while, you can completely earn your freedom, like I did.

Within a week of entering Day Report I left Tiffany's apartment on Belmont and moved exactly two miles west to the Beacon House, a halfway house run by a doctor friend where I had stayed on a few occasions throughout my time on the streets. I was committed to staying clean this time. I was already on probation, and by any interpretation of the law, I was bound for prison, but I wasn't ready to give up, so I cleaned up and showed up, every day.

Very soon the chief who ran the program, a very kind older black man named Junius Jones, recognized that I was different from most of the other men in Day Report, and he quickly saw that there wasn't really a place for me in the program. I was well beyond the educational range the program had been designed for, since the vast majority never finished high school. But it wasn't just my education. Chief Jones saw something in me—what I can't say—that moved him enough to bend the rules. Instead of going through the program, or going back to the jail, I would help him out by taking over the GED certification class.

Every day for three months I showed up, taught class until noon, and then was permitted to leave. I received weekly drug tests and stayed clean the entire time. I soon began to feel healthy again. I went back to AA meetings at night (a requirement of living in the Beacon House) and began to socialize with people again. When my court date came up, a friend from AA who was a defense attorney represented me for next to nothing, and Chief Jones came to court and asked the judge to give me a break because I had worked hard to stay clean and help others and I had "so much going for me."

Even though I had violated felony probation with another felony, the judge let me off with what amounted to a slap on the wrist. I would get another felony conviction on my record but would only receive one more year of probation as a consequence. This meant I was bound to the state until March 21, 2001.

I couldn't believe it. I was actually free to go. I walked out of the courtroom, hopped the bus back north to the Beacon House, and smiled like a hippie hittin' a nitrous tank, happier than a pig in shit. How did I keep dodging these bullets? However I did it, though, I knew my luck was going to run out eventually.

There are those moments when events converge and we are forced to ask ourselves if we are perhaps dammed, that regardless of our intention, or action, there is already a predetermined outcome to our future we simply cannot avoid. I had one of those moments in New York the day I arrived and saw Moishe the Crackhead on the street in my neighborhood. That omen unleashed the madness that would consume the next three years of my life. Now, just as I was escaping those three brutal years barely intact, I found myself being forcibly dragged into the next three.

I was clean and living at the Beacon House when I began seeing Red. She was from Downstate Illinois, and was finishing up a master's in social work at the University of Illinois at Chicago. She had been clean and sober for a number of years. We met in AA about a year before we started seeing each other and had been attending the same weekly meeting in Wicker Park for a few months. After only a month of seeing her she invited me to move in with her. Everyone I knew . . . and I mean *everyone* . . . told me I was making a colossal mistake moving in with her this early in the relationship, this early in sobriety. But of course I knew better, and would be fine, I said.

Within a week of moving in we learned our neighbors were Latin King coke dealers who also bred pit bulls for fighting. We also found out our landlord, who lived above us with his wife and daughter, was strung out on their coke, and was prone to some bizarre and perverted shit without warning; on a few occasions he tried to have sex with Red, and one time exposed himself to her.

Then, on a trip downstate to Bloomington to see Red's family, I learn that her younger brother and virtually everyone he knew were deep into blow. Less than a month after we moved in together, I was right back where I had started, except I was consuming more than ever, because now my girlfriend was in on the act, and it was all around me in ways it had never been before.

Things of course got much worse. Red had Asperger's Syndrome, and her symptoms were growing worse the older she got. Although she was high-functioning and in grad school, as soon as she graduated she began to go downhill fast. Combine that with all the cocaine we were using, and she began to literally devolve before my eyes.

The time we spent together was very dark. Although I managed to stay employed as a freelance copywriter, which paid enough to fuel my drug use, my life fell into total chaos. Red's inability to understand social cues or ulterior motives got her into a lot of trouble, like with the landlord, and especially the Latin Kings, who were quite interested in getting her strung out and then whoring her ass. We needed to GTFO of that neighborhood quick, so we moved to the Ravenswood area on the North Side and rented studio apartments in the same building, you know, "to have space." The day we moved in, a group of young Latin Kings were retailing crack in the vestibule of our building.

Overnight Red and I became regulars with the Kings, and they extended us credit, which is a bad, *bad* idea under any circumstances (my theory was that they too were trying gain control over Red to pimp her out). We got in deep with them, and at one point had to hide out for months inside our apartments, ducking in and out through the back gate to avoid detection, then cowering inside with doors bolted and shades drawn. They would crawl over the fences and climb up the back stairs and pound on our doors and generally scare the shit out of us.

Early one morning just as the sun was about to break the horizon I sat inside my third-floor apartment staring out my balcony at the King boys on the corner doing their thing. I had just paid up my bill with them and was standing up to go down and ask them for more when a white van drove past and opened fire on them. I witnessed the entire event from my window. One of them, a kid named Gizmo, was shot up pretty bad. The others were forced to disappear for a while.

I never thought I'd ever hear myself say, "Thank God for that drive-by," but there it was.

Red got pregnant twice, and had two abortions, which only served to push her deeper into herself. She moved to another building farther north to get away from the Latin Kings, and very soon thereafter was raped when two men forced their way into her apartment. She became unable to hold down a job or keep her apartment, and eventually she was forced to go back home to Bloomington to live with her parents. My sister, Suraya, moved into Red's apartment.

By late 1999 the economy was roaring, and I was, for the first time in my adult life, not living in a recession; I was in fact able to find good steady work through creative talent agencies that were awash in contract jobs for Internet start-ups and advertising firms. In early 2000 I was placed in a copywriting job at an ad agency, and that was where I met Edie and we became best friends. Although our relationship was platonic, throughout that year we were virtually inseparable, and spent most of our time completely soused.

I was living a double life. Mere months from jail, with two felony convictions and on probation, I managed to slip into the corporate world through the loophole of contract employment in an economy that put people like me into demand for the first time in my life. I spent my days "brainstorming" corporate double-speak, and my nights drinking and doing cocaine.

I really don't know how I kept it together for as long as I did. Perhaps it was the sheer manic energy created by having enough money to eat, pay rent and bills, and still have a few hundred to blow on drugs. For the first time in years I wasn't totally desperate. Edie and I had a lot of fun together. I hid my cocaine usage from her. We drank together. And drank. And drank. I was also writing

again in a substantial manner. After reading the Irving Stone novel
Lust for Life, about Vincent van Gogh and his struggle with madness and addiction, I was inspired enough to forge ahead with
finishing the novel version of "Unfinished Portraits."

In my efforts to understand my addiction better, and the effects
of the violence and sexual abuse I had suffered in my past, I began
to study the work of Carl Jung in some depth. This provided me
with a brand-new understanding of the addictive process and
introduced me to the spiritual component of addiction. I fairly
quickly became obsessed with his work, and in late 1999 I wrote
and published "Introduction to *The Sinner's Treadmill*," a long,
somewhat rambling essay on addiction and recovery, with *The
Jung Page*, an early Internet community of Jungian scholars.

In hindsight, I see that essay as a kind of linguistic symbol of
the struggle going on within me. It cobbled together for the first
time some of the central ideas that would eventually drive my long
march out of addiction. To begin with, it was a screed against
AA, which I had stopped attending once and for all. The basis
of my denunciation was that AA was a "self-help" program that
was dominated by other non-professional recovering people who
were prone to projecting their issues onto others, and in many
instances, doing them more harm than good.

Still, I took the fundamental precepts of AA with me, and for
the first time began to really grapple with the idea of what a "soul
sickness" might be, and what a "spiritual awakening" might mean.
Jung was the first to say that transcending consciousness through
altered states is a natural and necessary part of our psychological
makeup. It is a healthy expression of our ego trying find a way to
dissolve itself. In other words, Jung was the first person to say drug
use was normal, and not a moral failing. This then was how Bill W
grasped on to the idea and used it to create AA.

Through Jung's fascination with ancient spiritual traditions I
began to think about spirituality for the first time in my life. The

language was unfamiliar to me and the experiences alien, as I had no spiritual life to speak of. I used to joke that God had kept me out of prison, but I didn't realize I was telling the truth, in a manner of speaking.

Jung discovered what he felt was the nature of the disconnect between humans and the world around them, the "soul sickness," in his time with the Pueblo Indians of Taos, New Mexico.[23]

1924 saw Jung once again in America, this time in New Mexico visiting the Pueblo Indian chief, Ochwiay Biano (Mountain Lake). His dialogues with the chief, which Jung recorded in his autobiography, *Memories, Dreams, Reflections*, gave Jung his first picture of how non-white people view the white man. The whites, Ochwiay Biano said, "are always seeking something. What are they seeking? The whites always want something; they are always uneasy and restless. We do not know what they want. We do not understand them. We think they are mad."

"Why is that?" asked Jung.

"They say they think with their heads."

Jung showed his surprise at this answer and asked Ochwiay Biano what he thinks with.

"We think here," the chief replied, indicating his heart.

Thinking with the heart? That was certainly a new concept. *Sure, I get it*, I told myself, but I didn't yet. It would be a long time before I would truly understand this, and until such a time as I did, I would remain imprisoned in my rational-mental mind trying to forge an intellectual solution to a spiritual crisis, something that by its very nature defies logic and reason.

I found myself stuck in an infinite feedback loop as this theme would continue to resurface in my life, continually returning to my orbit like a wayward comet, brought by messenger after messenger until I would heed.

Fascinated with the spiritual transformation Jung experienced in his time with the Pueblos, I began to toy with the idea of dropping out, moving to Taos, exploring what Jung explored, and writing a book about my experiences. It seemed like a good plan, and I knew I needed to get away from Chicago. But before I could realize that ambition, I received my biggest break yet.

KARL ROVE RADICALIZED ME

At the time I met him in the late '90s, Cary Harrison was a rising Chicago radio personality who had garnered some exposure for his brief stint (and legendary antics) as a huckster on the *Home Shopping Network*, which he then parlayed into a cable entertainment show called *Screen Test* that went on to win a number of CableACE awards. Since then he has hosted radio programs on stations in Florida, Chicago, New York City, and LA, including the first-ever GLBT morning drive-time talk radio show for Sirius Satellite Radio. He's currently in Los Angeles appearing regularly on stations like Pacifica/KPFK/LA Public Radio and on WABC (NY) and KABC (LA).

In the late 1990s, Harrison was producing a series of off-the-wall radio shorts he called *Reality Checks* for a Chicago AM talk-radio station. In these shorts Harrison probed the fantastical underbelly of American culture for tales of the absurd. *Reality Checks* mixed these unbelievable stories with trenchant satire and political commentary, "Did You Know?" style historical reporting, and acerbic iconoclasm that took great pleasure in tossing sacred cows on the grill. Harrison is brilliant, well-read, and possessed of a near-unparalleled vocabulary, a frighteningly funny man not at all insane despite a career in radio.

His full backstory would require a book of its own (but his website is a good place to begin). He hails from one of the oldest families in America. His ancestors emigrated in the 1600s to what is now known as Maryland with a land grant from King George. His family owned slaves and built an enormous fortune.

Eventually many of them decanted to the Chicago area, and Harrison grew up on, among many places, Chicago's North Shore, where he attended Lake Forest Academy ten years before I did. By the time Harrison and his twin sister (or, as he calls her, his "twister") had reached adulthood, the fortune had run dry, the blue hue had run out of their blood, and the politics had shifted somewhat radically.

Harrison wrapped up his family's contentious past with a beautiful spiritual coda, his award-winning NPR radio-documentary *Sledmore*, named after the family plantation, which follows Harrison as he goes back to his ancestral land and repudiates his family's slaveholding past. I helped pen the script and felt honored to contribute to such a remarkably honest and brave piece of reporting.

In 1999 Harrison relocated to Los Angeles when *Reality Checks* was picked up for national syndication by the now-defunct American View Radio Network. He asked me if I would be interested in writing for the show, and although I had no experience with radio, there was no way I was going to pass it up. Harrison was a great teacher, and I learned fast. Over the next year I would research and write scripts from my studio apartment in Chicago, and in that time I would begin to sow the seeds of my own political awakening, delving into subject matter that was entirely foreign to me at first, but would ultimately prove revelatory and life-changing.

Harrison is one of my most cherished professional mentors. He believed in me when few others did, and he always had compassion for my addictions, although I was never truly honest with him about the extent of them. He taught me about the dark under belly of the American political system and the hidden history behind some of our nation's most significant events. Most importantly, he taught me how to approach these topics with humor, an essential tactic in getting people engaged in "serious" or "depressing" or even just intellectually daunting issues that would require a rather broad understanding of history. Political satire is an art form, and when done properly, it can be one of the most powerful influencers of public opinion.

By late 2000 *Reality Checks* had penetrated 215 radio markets, and I was delivering half a dozen scripts a week. We were setting the stage for another large expansion into new markets, and preparing to diversify our content into more long-form material. Harrison encouraged me to move to Los Angeles, decrying Chicago as provincial and claiming that I, like him, would be able to find whatever it was I was looking for on the West Coast.

I wanted to make the move, but I couldn't afford it, certainly not on the meager wage American View paid me. But it was only a matter of time, and if I were able to find a way out there, things were looking so promising for us that soon the show would be making enough money to support all of us comfortably.

Then, as if the universe heard my pleas, I was approached via email by a "forensic psychologist" from Los Angeles who worked as an expert witness in court cases. He had read my essay on addiction and recovery on *The Jung Page* and was interested in co-authoring a book on addiction and spirituality. I was only too desperate for a break like this, and because of that, I wasn't thinking rationally. I became overeager to get involved in the project, for it represented the first time in my life that I felt my ideas were being recognized by others, or so it seemed. And with all the name-dropping this gentleman laid on me he made it sound like we'd move a million copies. In this project I saw everything except what I needed to see. To that, I remained willfully blind.

In January of 2001 I traveled to Los Angeles to visit Harrison and meet with this gentleman to discuss the book project. He was a rotund middle-aged gay man from the South with a Blanche DuBois accent. He lived in Hollywood at the base of Runyon Park, and he claimed to be a Marquis descended from French nobility. He also told me that he was an "officially ordained Hindu Swami," but I had no idea what that meant.

He offered to relocate me to Los Angeles and let me stay with him until I found a place of my own. After I discussed with Harrison the future plans for *Reality Checks*, it seemed like it was the right thing to do. I returned to Chicago to pack my things into a truck and wait out the last few weeks of my five years of felony probation. The day my five years expired, March 21, 2001, I hit the road for Los Angeles.

Never one *not* to complicate matters for myself, the night before my departure I stayed up all night snorting coke with my sister and a woman I had just met. I left in the middle of a snowstorm that lasted until I reached Kansas City. Completely exhausted and crashing, I got a motel room for a day to recuperate.

Eventually I made my way to Taos to visit a woman named Cedrus whom I had been corresponding with over email for almost a year. She, like the Marquis, had read my addiction essay on *The Jung Page* and felt compelled to reach out to me. Cedrus was a PhD who practiced Jungian psychology, mostly in Europe. She was peculiar, deeply intuitive, and nearly 20 years older than I, dripping with feminine wisdom.

I had told her about *The Sinner's Treadmill*, a book on addiction and spirituality that I wanted to write in Taos, but the minute the Marquis offered me the deal, I forgot all about my book, and Taos. She felt I was making a big mistake moving to LA. She said I was doing "other people's work" instead of my own, and that was cutting me off from much-needed growth and healing.

When I arrived in Taos, I am sure she sensed the chaos that was my life, even though I had hidden most of it from her in our correspondence. The eyes don't lie. I looked drained and panicked. She asked me if I was sure this was what I wanted to do, that I could stay in Taos instead and really focus on myself. She knew people and could help me get set up. I thought she was crazy for suggesting it, since I felt I already had one bird in the hand with the Marquis. In hindsight, of course I wish I had listened to her.

The moment I landed in Los Angeles, everything went wrong. After I unloaded my truck, the Marquis informed me that we were having a little celebration that evening in honor of my arrival. He had ordered an ounce of cocaine and asked a few of his friends to come join us, "and everyone is getting naked, no questions asked!" I couldn't believe my ears. *Are you fucking kidding me?*

The Marquis then went on to tell me that he used to launder money for the mob and got deeeeeeeep into blow but "rarely indulged anymore." He said that this was a "special occasion." Suddenly, all our previous conversations about drug addiction and the intimate details of my life story made much more sense in context. He knew exactly how to manipulate me, how to control me, and what my response was going to be; he knew that I would be unable to resist. And I knew exactly what kind of trouble I had landed in.

That first night in LA turned into a three-day coke binge, and the Marquis's apartment began to resemble Caligula's chambers. Although I managed to hide out for most of the time in the back bedroom, drifting in occasionally to hoover up a few lines, each time I returned I found the Marquis and his "friends"—who turned out to be a couple of gay street prostitutes the Marquis frequently patronized, and their random cohorts—involved in group sex on the living room floor. At one point, one of the street boys came into the back room and asked me if I wanted to "go get cigarettes" with him (I was a smoker at the time). I jumped at the opportunity to leave the apartment. Halfway down the block, he asks me if I smoke crack, and the next thing I know we're on Hollywood Boulevard copping from Mexican gang-bangers.

WELCOME TO LA

Within a matter of days I figured out that the Marquis was not so much interested in a co-author as he was in a combination secretary and houseboy. He had just lost his last houseboy, and figured I would fit into the role nicely. His idea of writing a book was for me to sit and take straight dictation as he lay on the bed in a silk robe. He expected me to sleep in his room with him at night.

I had to get out of there, but I didn't have any money, and other than Harrison, I didn't know anyone in Los Angeles. I was totally dependent on the Marquis for support since I didn't make enough writing for *Reality Checks* yet to afford an apartment. I was trapped, and I was scared. I knew the Marquis wouldn't force himself on me, it would be the last thing he ever did, but once he realized I was not fair game, my welcome would be suddenly withdrawn and I'd be out on my (still intact) ass.

In the meantime (as if there could even be a "meantime" to all that) Harrison and I wrote a week-long series for *Reality Checks* we called "War Crimes Week." Our format was like the game show Jeopardy, and each day we had a quiz that focused on the career of another prominent war criminal. You can probably surmise that we were not talking about Hitler and Pol Pot. We chose to write our series from a foreign perspective, and as such, we chose George H.W. Bush, Henry Kissinger, Colin Powell, Norman Schwarzkopf Jr., and Wesley Clark.

Because Harrison's politics at the time tended to skew libertarian, we were programmed on both left-wing and right-wing talk shows. It had gone over well while Clinton was in office, but these were the early days of the Bush Administration and Michael Powell's FCC, and there was a massive conservative backlash going on. With the delay caused by the outcome of the 2000 election, the Bush Administration got off to a late start but was now truly seizing power, everywhere.

The moment "War Crimes Week" hit the air, most of the right-wing talk shows revolted, led by the reprehensible Ken "The Black Avenger" Hamblin, a self-hating black man who was famous for excoriating his own race on his show and playing "Another One Bites the Dust" every time a black death row inmate was executed. Hamblin began screaming to our syndicator, American View, that either we go or he goes. Despite the squawking, the head of our network, an ex-Marine colonel named David Addington,[24] decided to keep us.

Less than a month later we ran a two-part series on attorney general nominee John Ashcroft, who was in the midst of his confirmation hearings. Largely sourcing our script from a Fairness and Accuracy in Reporting story that ran in January of 2001, we revealed that Ashcroft was a "Neoconfederate," someone who supports the return of the South to its antebellum ways, and that Ashcroft had provided the following endorsement of the Neoconfederate magazine *Southern Partisan*:[25]

> Your magazine also helps set the record straight. You've got a heritage of doing that, of defending Southern patriots like [Robert E.] Lee, [Stonewall] Jackson and [Confederate President Jefferson] Davis. Traditionalists must do more. I've got to do more. We've all got to stand up and speak in this respect, or else we'll be taught that these people were giving their lives, subscribing their sacred fortunes and their honor to some perverted agenda.
>
> —John Ashcroft,
> *Southern Partisan* magazine interview
> (Second Quarter/1998)

Now, call us crazy, but somehow we thought this would be germane to the debate on Ashcroft's qualifications to be America's Top Cop. He was so extreme and unpopular in his own home state of Missouri that he lost his 2000 senatorial bid to a dead guy (his opponent, Mel Carnahan, had died during the campaign). After explaining how Ashcroft gave former KKK Imperial Wizard David Duke his start in politics, we also reported that *Southern Partisan* was a favorite of the Oklahoma City bomber Timothy McVeigh, and asked the following question: *If McVeigh is considered a terrorist and murderer for his beliefs, what then is Ashcroft?*

When Ken Hamblin heard the segment, he refused to run it on his show, and he picked up the phone and called Karl Rove,

George W. Bush's political Svengali. Right-wing radio was one of the main conduits for distributing BushCo talking points to the public, and the administration enjoyed a cozy relationship with many of the hosts, often paying or otherwise plying them for favorable coverage.[26] Rove in turn called Addington at American View and told him that if we weren't dropped from their roster by morning he'd have the FCC ten feet up his ass before the day was out. Addington had no choice but to relent, and, overnight, we lost nearly 200 markets, and I was out of a job.

Welcome to life in the Bush years, kid. You ain't seen nothin' yet.

It pains me to think how naïve I was. I couldn't understand how we could get fined, or lose our show, for reporting the truth. I still struggle these days to understand how millions of Americans could have voted for these people. Not only were they illegitimate and craven, they cost me the best job I ever had. From that moment forth, my beef with the Bush Administration was personal.

Harrison was not picked up by another syndicator and was forced to let me go. Desperate, and under enormous pressure to get out of the Marquis's apartment, I looked for work, but it was the middle of the dot-com recession and the agencies that used to employ me were now asking me if I knew of any openings anywhere. Los Angeles is not a nice town to begin with, but it's downright cruel to those who are struggling, and fairly quickly it overwhelmed me and I began to panic. I was not prepared for or capable of handling this level of stress in a town where I knew no one.

I begged my mother to send me enough money to begin renting a room that I had found in a house in Hollywood a block away from the Capitol Records building. It was known for being Jimi Hendrix's residence while he was in LA. The moment I got that cash in my hand (money is one of the three main triggers for addict; the others are sex and stress) my addiction took over and I blew it all on a three-day binge. When I showed up to move in without the rent, they wouldn't let me in, so I was homeless. I wandered around the streets of LA for a few days before my pride was sufficiently quelled and panic took over. I called Edie and begged her to help me. She bought me a ticket home, and I was on the next plane out. I left all my belongings in LA.

So, getting back to 9/11 . . .

9/11 may have been the event that got me out of bed, but I was still very much asleep, and full of fear and insurmountable shame. For once, these negative forces conspired to push me in an entirely new and positive direction in life. I was tired of being weak, of being a liability, of not getting any respect, and not having any confidence. I was going to change that, and the first thing I was going to do was quit using cocaine and get myself into shape. I decided that I was finally going to do something I had wanted to do my whole life: learn martial arts.

I threw myself into it obsessively, channeling all my energy into training, and within four months I was in the best shape of my life. I was also a bit of a zealot. I was just waiting for the right opportunity to show off my skills, waiting for the wrong asshole to say the wrong thing to me. Then came the horrific trauma of the stabbing in the projects when I nearly killed that young gangbanger, and whatever progress I had made was annihilated.

I didn't tell Edie. I kept it secret from everyone. This was a huge mistake on a psychological level, because it compounded my (still unrecognized) PTSD tenfold, but I had no choice. I couldn't run the risk of anyone finding out or being party to knowledge so long as the possibility existed that I could be charged with a crime. I was unaware of the extent to which the stabbing affected me until Edie and I took a trip to New York City in December of 2001 to see Ground Zero. I had completely locked away the grief I felt over the harm I had caused that young man, instead opting to live in a near-permanent state of agitation, which had terrible consequences.

We were visiting an old college friend who had just recently gotten engaged. The four of us went out drinking the first night we arrived and got reeeally drunk. We were walking home through the Village, attempting to cross the street, when a car behind us rushed up and slammed on the brakes, screeching to a halt mere inches from me with the horn blaring. From inside the car a group of Puerto Rican guys began screaming out the window at me.

Something in me snapped. The next thing I know, without even thinking, as if I'm watching myself from a distance, I've pulled out my knife and thrust it at the driver's face, screaming for him to get out of the car. From behind me I hear my friend's fiancée yell, "He's gonna get himself killed!!" My friend grabs me by the back of my jacket and hauls me out of the street. When we get back to his apartment, drunk and enraged, I take off looking for those guys (in a city of 8 million people) and don't come back for hours, effectively tormenting Edie. By then, my old friend was done with me.

It wasn't until we got back to Chicago that the real effects of that chain of events hit me. Edie was terrified. She had never known me to be violent or aggressive, and I certainly was unfamiliar with it myself. But something larger was going on. Something within me had had enough. On an unconscious level, my psyche was no longer going to allow me to be victimized in any way, and so it was fighting back, any way it could. And since I could defend myself now, I wasn't afraid, and some part of me wanted to exact revenge on whoever was stupid enough to challenge me.

Although their actions originate from deep within the self-preservation instinct, PTSD sufferers are incapable of connecting that instinct to rational thought, and, as a consequence, it's often those closest to the sufferer who become the victims of abuse. Although I was never violent or abusive with Edie, what this would mean for me in the coming years would be, in its most benign form, an inability to trust or to form intimate bonds, even with her, and in its more acute form, a constant state of anger, defensiveness, and conflict with those in my life.

▼

I was pretty ignorant in those days. I was only at the very beginning of the steep learning curve that was my education in *realpolitik*. Even though I was disenfranchised from the larger culture, I still believed in the fundamental "truths" of the American mythos: that we were a democracy governed by the rule of law; that we were essentially a benevolent and free nation; if anything, we were a benign hegemon, a reluctant Superpower. I didn't really see the US as an empire or understand a shred of its imperial history. I certainly didn't see it as repressive, in spite of all the drug war reality I had been choking on for years. It was like I had a weird form of Stockholm Syndrome. Even with the proper historical and factual context, which most Americans were lacking, nothing about the official explanation of the 9/11 attacks, nor the American response to them, made any rational sense.

Moreover, the national climate felt like the Red Scare all over again, that the real enemy was not terrorism but criticism, and that these new laws were meant to control us, not combat terrorism. What made it worse, almost surreal, was the rather overt and bizarre choice of certain language that gave the entire nation an atmosphere of Orwellian doublespeak.

The USA *Patriot* Act (Uniting and Strengthening America by Providing Appropriate Tools Required to Intercept and Obstruct Terrorism Act of 2001), the Department of *Homeland* Security, or Operation *Enduring Freedom*. The No Child Left Behind Act left plenty of children behind as fodder for military recruitment. The Help America Vote Act populated the country with touch-screen technology that stole votes. The Office of Faith-Based and Community Initiatives subsidized tax-exempt churches and permitted them to engage in partisan political activity. It was pretty clear that the new emperor was a naked fool.

It was in this context that I was trying to make sense of my own life and find some measure of stability, but it seemed like the rules of the game were changing by the minute, and I didn't like where we were headed. I suppose that if I had to identify one moment when I decided to become an activist—or perhaps it's more appropriate to say the moment I decided I couldn't just sit back and let things happen, I had to get involved somehow—was during the 2002 State of the Union Address, which I covered for *3:am Magazine*, a relatively new and somewhat obscure literary site. The sheer arrogance of the "you are either with us, or you are with the terrorists" message the US was communicating to the rest of the world portended a very dark future. In less than one hour any hope for rational thought or international assistance was jettisoned out the escape pod while we collectively watched the neoconservative agenda, as well as the concept of the (ahem) Axis of Evil, emerge as national policy.

Noble as this may sound, what really drove me was not altruism. I didn't so much want to save the world as I wanted to clear my name. I did not know this consciously at the time, but deep within me my ego self had concocted a strategy that it was slowly rolling out step by critical step.

In this strategy I had identified an enemy, "The System," which was inherently unjust. "The System" was unjust because it had taken a nice boy like me and turned him into a criminal. I was a victim. Now I was setting about finding ways to bring this system down, first by exposing its lies and hypocrisies, and then by turning the people against it, by any means necessary.

If this sounds familiar to you, it's because it's a common syndrome amongst the abused, disenfranchised, and disaffected. For people who have been oppressed their entire lives by abusers, those who have been violated, those persecuted for lifestyle choices, or those who have been denied access to the finer things in life on the grounds of race and class, or even those who just don't fit into industrial society, there is a near-universally shared obsession with justice, and a drive to topple the existing order.

This is why radical politics is so attractive to these types; it attracts the wounded and the naïve, the ideological and the idealistic, the angry and the malcontented, the ostracized and the isolated, by giving them all a vision of a perfect society in which each of them is recognized for their strengths and values, and, no one goes hungry, and no one goes to war, a world where everyone can find a mate and support children and realize their greatest dreams. It is a world where money and beauty do not rule, and of course, it is a world that does not exist. Had I only known that back then, I could have stopped myself.

On a more personal level, I was desperate to prove myself to the world, which I felt had forsaken me. I wasn't so much in a place of recovery as I was in a place of insurgency. I was fighting back against the dark forces arrayed against us, both literal and metaphorical, which reflected not only the war the Bush Administration was waging on the world, and upon its own people, but also the war going on within my psyche between my ego and shadow. I was desperate to prove I had worth and value, but I hadn't the slightest idea how.

PTSD FOR YOU & ME

The fundamental reality cutting through everything I did in 2002 was that I was an addict in early recovery at the same time that the nation itself was in recovery from the devastating trauma of the 9/11 attacks. But rather than taking the time to develop some kind of recovery plan, I simply put it out of my head and stubbornly plowed headlong into the fray of social change, while the nation plunged ahead in an equally reckless manner into militarized vengeance, and domestic repression. Neither I nor the nation seemed willing to examine how we got ourselves into our respective messes in the first place.

In the year since I returned from Los Angeles I had managed to have at least one breakdown, and in the process of getting back on my feet I quit smoking, eating meat, and using cocaine. I also spent most of the year training four days a week at The Degerberg Academy of Martial Arts in my Lincoln Square neighborhood, studying a devastating blend of martial art disciplines and street fighting techniques that were collectively known as the 'Chicago style.' I was in the best shape of my life until I tore out my right shoulder Without health insurance I could not get the shoulder repaired, and after a certain number of bad dislocations it became permanently damaged and relatively useless.

I believe that while I was training I was able to channel the untempered energy welled up inside me, the energy I had been furiously tamping down with powerful chemicals my entire life. Once I lost that option, I immediately became an inordinately-high-percentage candidate for total relapse, since the long-term recovery rate on crack addiction is somewhere around 1% to 5%. As I mentioned, I was not interested in any kind of addict recovery program, and although I had been loosely engaged in therapy, I was not serious or regular about it. To compound matters, I was still drinking alcohol in amounts ill-advised by even the most liberal harm-reduction advocate.

Edie recognized all of this. She saw the turmoil going on inside of me, and had to endure my endless rants and suffer my infantile outbursts. She saw what happened when something triggered a trauma-based reaction, how I coiled back like a viper and struck out indiscriminately. She was so patient and supportive, but I don't think she believed I was going to make it without some form of intervention.

What Edie had on the rest of the people in my life, my family in particular, was that she was the only person on earth who knew everything that had happened to me, even things I do not reveal within the pages of this book. My family, on the other hand, was unaware of nearly all of it; in hindsight, it's no wonder they thought I was either evil or insane. Without the knowledge of these mitigating circumstances, or the willingness to accept their part in our collective history, they were at a loss to explain why I was the way I was.

I think it became too much for Edie one night when she collapsed in our apartment, without warning or provocation, and cracked her skull open on the iron radiator in our kitchen. I rushed her to the hospital, which thank God was just a block away, but no doctor could ever find out what had caused her collapse. Had she told them the truth, however, I am certain they would have said it was emotional strain.

It really hit home for me when Edie said she had seen the film *Pollock*, about the lives of Jackson Pollock and his wife, Lee Krasner, and that in their story she saw a mirror of our relationship. She realized, like Lee Krasner, that she was doomed to be the caretaker for an emotionally unstable artist/addict.

There is one scene that takes place during a particularly healthy and productive period in their lives when they were living alone together on Long Island away from the temptations of the city. Jackson suggests to Lee that they have a baby. She attempts to humor Jackson, but he sees right through it and pitches a fit. Enraged, he smashes a record player and breaks the chair he is seated in.

Heartbroken, and realizing that things will never really change for them, Lee points at the carnage Jackson has wrought and says, "I will not bring a child into *that*!" Watching Edie quietly shed a tear, in her graceful and dignified way, told me everything I needed to know. She may have loved me, but in many ways I was more her problem child than her partner.

I think because she didn't know what else to do, and was grasping at straws, she made a decision that nearly everyone in her life advised against, which was for us to adopt a puppy. It was a spontaneous act; one day we decided to go to the Anti-Cruelty Society to look around, and this three-month-old all-black shepherd/lab puppy was the first dog we saw. He was furiously pawing at the door to his cage. We took one look at him and knew instantly that he was ours, particularly when we saw that the adoption card posted outside his cage read:

DON'T LET THE CUTENESS FOOL YOU!

VERY BAD BOY!!

EXPERIENCED DOG TRAINER ONLY!!

Beyond the obvious parallels between myself and this incarcerated puppy dog, I knew from my time working at Anti-Cruelty that discipline cases like him never got adopted, and were quickly euthanized. If we didn't save him, it was doubtful anyone would. Even so, I practically had to threaten the adoption agent to give him to us, so reluctant were they to adopt him out to anyone, particularly to someone they had fired years ago.

Everyone thought Edie was crazy for entrenching herself deeper in a relationship with me, and I'm not sure she even knew the significance of what she was doing at the time, but bringing that puppy into our lives was the first major step in my healing path.

We named him Milhouse after a character on *The Simpsons*, who himself was named after Richard Nixon, whose middle name was Milhous. In truth, Milhouse had far more in common with Tricky Dick than he did with Bart's sidekick. For one year he was rotten to the core, and consumed his way through everything in the house. He ate every one of Edie's left shoes. He ate an entire set of deck chairs. He ate an antique high-backed stuffed dining chair, disemboweling the seat cushion and shredding the stained cherry wood. He ate my keyboard, mouse, mousepad, a dozen books, and all the brims on my baseball caps.

I realize the more effete and critical minded will pillory me for waxing sentimental about puppies, but Milhouse is a central part of my story, and in many respects, one of the most important figures in my life. For it was Milhouse, before anyone or anything else, that was the first to penetrate my myriad layers of emotional scar tissue and reach my wounded heart. From the moment I met him I was madly in love with him, and for the first time in my life I cared about someone more than myself.

There was something in the simplicity of the love between us; it was on-demand and never conditional, it was never retracted, and it was never used as a tool of manipulation. Milhouse didn't care that I had been a crackhead or that I had a criminal record or that I once stole from my friends and family or that I had been raped or any of the legion of tragedies of my life. He loved me, and his love was the first that I ever trusted.

THE PRIEST, THE RADICAL, THE HEALER

I owe many debts of gratitude in my life to those who never gave up on me and were able to see into the core of my being and recognize the person who was trying to get out, but few of these debts compare to that which I owe my mentor, Thomas Goforth.

For more than 40 years Tom has been a practicing psychotherapist, but he is so much more than that. Tom is very much a paragon of the "conscious" segment of the Baby Boomer generation that did not retreat into the vapid materialism of Yuppiedom. He went to school to become an ecumenical priest, and his first job out of seminary was as a chaplain at the Cook County Jail.

Having confronted the existential and bureaucratic misery of Cook County, he moved on to St. Leonard's House, one of Chicago's oldest and last remaining prisoner re-entry programs. In the early 1970s he helped form a radical free therapy collective and worked closely with the Black Panther organization, at times shielding them from Chicago's infamous Red Squad, which, in 1969, murdered the brilliant and charismatic young Panther leader Fred Hampton while he was asleep in his bed.

In the 1980s much of the radical counterculture that Tom belonged to was either forced underground or forced to assimilate into Ronald Reagan's America. There is no greater symbol of the

insanity of that period than the "Yippie vs. Yuppie" debate tour
of Yippie co-founders Jerry Rubin and Abbie Hoffman.

Rubin burnt out after the Vietnam War and the Chicago Seven Trial.
The constant harassment by COINTELPRO drove him to a break-
down, and he retreated into the safe, Feel-good confines of the New
Age Esalen culture to heal. When he re-emerged, he had assimilated.

Rubin became enchanted with Reaganomics and the idea of
Yuppie. Hoffman called him a "sellout," but Rubin rebuffed him,
claiming he had "joined America rather than fighting against it"
and that, "in order to be a part of the solution, rather than part
of the problem, we have to work from within." Rubin believed
activism was dead, that it had become negative and cynical and
fraught with letdowns. He charged that "abuse of drugs, sex, and
private property" had made the counterculture "a scary society in
itself." He truly believed that "wealth creation is the real American revolution" and he told people to make as much money as
they could, and then use that money for social change.[27] Many
suspected he had been brainwashed.

Throughout the 1980s the counterculture slowly transformed.
Many came to the conclusion that the revolution had failed because the movement was too young, that there were no elders to
help guide the movement in its development because a corner-
stone of the Sixties revolution had been a war against the older
generation. It was Rubin who first exhorted American youth to
"never trust anyone over 30," and those chickens eventually came
home to roost. At the end of the Vietnam War, the Boomer generation realized that it had a lot more growing up to do.

Taking the Gandhian adage that we must "be the change we
want to see in the world," the counterculture turned the revolution inward and morphed into "personal growth" or "personal
transformation," more formally known as the "Human Potential
Movement." The main premise was that the more people evolved
emotionally, psychologically, and spiritually, the quicker society
would approach a tipping point and spontaneously shift.

This was when Wilhelm Reich, Jungian psychology, Eastern and New Age Spirituality, Esalen and EST, and a dozen similar memes entered the consciousness movement. Out of this shift "came a political movement that sought to create new beings free of the psychological conformity that had been implanted in people's minds by business and politics."[28]

Tom became part of this movement, studying Reiki, yoga, meditation, holistic medicine, and archetypal psychology. He adopted this personal growth philosophy and made it the foundation of the private therapeutic practice he built over 40 years, where he still works 18 hours a day.

I was a curious mix of cynical and desperate in the summer of 1998 when I first went to see him through a friend's recommendation because of his specialization in addiction. It is a miracle that I ever set foot into his apartment for a session, let alone that we would ever become friends. After a lifetime of shrinks and therapists who did little more than collect inflated fees from me and my parents, I was convinced that their only intention was to keep us sick, and thus, keep us coming back week after week. If we ever got ourselves cured, we'd no longer need therapy, and would cease to hand over our money to them.

Tom was the first therapist who didn't react defensively when I told him this. Rather, he said, he wouldn't charge me while we were getting to know one another, and after that he'd work on a sliding scale. That way, he said, he only got what both parties agreed he was worth. In the ten years that I saw him as a therapist he probably charged me less than a quarter of the time.

Over the years Tom would grow to become my trusted friend and confidant. We shared many affinities, and I can't help but think that we played a crucial role in each other's lives. Tom had struggled with abuse as a child and overcame its lingering syndromes though his focused inner work. He was the first to teach me about concepts like wounding, projection, non-judgment, unconditional love, nonviolent communication, and other psychotherapeutic models. He was one of the only positive male role models in my life for many years, and in many ways he taught me more about being a man than my father could have ever dreamed of doing. Over the years he has worked with many of my friends and their friends, holding space as a true elder of our community.

Of all the points in this story line that I could have used to introduce him, it seems most appropriate to bring him up now, right around the time that the years of therapy he had been doling out, mostly for free, finally began to show some progress.

There I was, 18 months removed from a crack addiction, just beginning to *feel* again after being numb for a decade, and what was seeping out of me first, breaking out of the dungeon of my shadow, was the deep malevolent shame I held for all the things I had done in furtherance of my addiction. For all the reasons I had originally gone astray, I now began to clamor for acceptance from the mainstream of American society.

Tom explained that, on an unconscious level, I was both acting out an abusive syndrome related to the violence and violations I had suffered and I was desperate to be accepted back into society and have my intellect validated. He said my fear of rejection was so strong it warped my sense of reality and caused me to see affinities with those who stood in direct opposition to my core beliefs. Tom was also the first to suggest to me that I had Post-Traumatic Stress Disorder, and that it was probably at the core of most of my pathology. At last I'd been given plausible explanations for who I was and what had happened to me. I was not simply a "drug addict" like all the recovery programs had tried to tell me.

Tom helped me focus on these core issues. I had known only crisis for 20 years, and nearly every relationship I had built in that time had fallen apart as a result of crisis or conflict. I was pathologically incapable of forming healthy and lasting relationships because I had no experience of either. Everyone I worked for, everyone I attempted to collaborate with, everyone I attempted to communicate with, everyone I attempted to love, I drew into conflict with me because that was the only way I knew how to relate to others. Somehow, I was never able to see that it was I who needed fixing, and not they.

It was Tom who would help me form a new consciousness, and a renewed commitment to bring change into my own life and the world around me, somehow, someday, someway, as he had vowed to himself so many years before.

CHAPTER 6
A Bond to Survive the Universe

The Buddhists believe that enlightenment is the awareness that frees a person from the cycle of rebirth. All this really means is that you finally learn enough about how things really work to avoid making the same mistakes and, thus, going back into karmic debt. It does not necessarily mean that enlightenment is a form of deliverance, or if it is, that it is liberating in the traditional sense. In many ways, enlightenment is kind of like a spiritual camel that carries you through the vast deserts of alienation. It's a reliable animal, at times even life saving, but it's also stubborn and petulant as hell, prefers to be left alone, and won't hesitate, if given the opportunity, to spit in your face.

Enlightenment demands ritual sacrifice, and what it demanded of me, the price I paid for peering behind the curtain, the first casualty in this war of truth and consciousness, was my dear friend Edie. How different our two worlds had become, and how the clock had already started ticking on our relationship.

My relationship with Edie was bittersweet. It began as a genuine friendship, and we really had good times together. But we were somewhat forced into a relationship by my circumstances, and our mutual codependencies. This combination forced Edie to function both as partner and as parent/caretaker. Anyone can tell you that will absolutely destroy a relationship.

In the beginning stages of my recovery, I was incapable of taking care of myself. I was both unable to find steady employment and ignorant about how to manage my own affairs. Although we were as close as brother and sister—for she knew more about me than anyone on the planet did—we were never much of a romantic couple, barely intimate or affectionate with each other. I was not raised with much affection and had never really known affectionate people, so I was *extremely* uncomfortable with even the most basic verbal and physical displays. We did not think as a unit, so as our relationship wore on, we became less like partners and more like roommates.

I attribute this to some obvious factors, the first being that I had the emotional maturity of a teenager. A well-known aphorism of addiction is that you stop developing emotionally at the age you start self-medicating. This rendered me incapable of having a real, intimate adult relationship, because I had virtually no experience of being an adult.

Add to that the physical, emotional, and sexual abuse I had suffered, and you had to wonder if I had ever really experienced love. I knew one thing: I was suspicious of anyone who professed to love me, and I wondered what was wrong with them to make them think that they did. If someone did profess love for me, it was like a poker player revealing a tell. I equated it with weakness, and it would invariably taint or destroy the relationship. Even though I refused to bring this belief into my conscious mind, at my core, deep down where it mattered, I believed I was unlovable.

This did not mean I was an unfeeling person. On the contrary, if I had one true weakness it was that I felt too much and had little ability to control that feeling. This naturally led to my many varied efforts to discover a means of numbing these uncontrollable feelings. Now that I wasn't numbing them any longer, my emotions were waking up and clawing their way out.

The first stage in this emotional healing path is the Rage Stage. Rage is an easily identifiable outward expression of fear, wounding, and shame. It is an understandable first wave, since it results from years of emotional repression and is formed by the confluence of all these unparsed emotions.

Beneath the Rage is stage two, Sadness. Sadness doesn't stick around too long in the emotionally undeveloped, it's too powerful and penetrating a feeling. It either percolates into Rage, or gets sealed deep inside a pressurized cyst of unexpressed Grief, which is stage three.

Here's the thing. If you stop numbing yourself but don't strip off the rage layer, the sadness and grief welled up below it will eventually force their way up like a zit. The sadness and grief will get stuck under the outer layer, become irritated and infected, hurt like hell, and eventually rupture, all causing more rage. Rage may be the key symptom of emotional awakening—a kind of psycho-spiritual pus—but the root cause of the infection driving the rage is that much deeper-held grief. I first began to grapple with this three-headed monster as the year 2003 rapidly came to a close.

Along this serpentine, pothole-strewn path to healing, there are those milestones when we recognize that something is indeed changing within us. These are usually the times when nothing we feel makes sense, and we can't seem to identify just what the hell is "wrong" with us. Often, these realizations come in the form of metaphors, which I experienced firsthand when I went to see Sofia Coppola's *Lost in Translation* and left the theater in tears.

I would see the film again, and again, and each time I would be consumed by a deep, draining sadness. Hoping to gain some clarity, I described what was happening to Tom Goforth and expressed to him that I feared I was having another breakdown. I was relieved when he disagreed. He felt I was waking up, and that

I was probably experiencing projected or deferred grief. Something about the film connected with the ocean of unexpressed grief I had sealed within me, triggering a sympathetic identification with the plight of the characters. This deeply rooted pain I was too terrified to confront head-on was, in a manner of speaking, making a prison break, attempting to sneak out attached to the underside of other emotions.

The explanation for my melancholy response to *Lost in Translation* was quite simple, actually. It is a film about loneliness and alienation, two of the emotions I was struggling most with at the time. The story focuses on the lives of a middle-aged movie star in the twilight of his career, forced to do Japanese commercials to pay the bills, and a young newlywed fresh out of college with no idea of what she wants from life. Both are married to spouses who seem to find everyone and everything else in life more interesting than their partners. The two meet in a Tokyo hotel and form an impromptu friendship, borne not out of physical but rather spiritual longing. They briefly fill the gnawing void deep within themselves by seeing, hearing, and appreciating one another for who they really are.

In the end, the film exists as a snapshot of two lives intersecting for a brief but intense moment, and as such, its commentary on the nature of friendship is clear: one can live with someone their whole life and not know a thing about them, but a chance encounter in a foreign land can create a bond that would survive the universe.

I so desperately wanted a "bond that would survive the universe" with someone. I was running from the admission that I did not have that with Edie, that although she was the best friend I ever had, I was not in love with her, and we were not meant to be together. The time was coming when I would have to walk away from the literal saint-like love, comfort, and security she and Milhouse had so selflessly given me, and go back out into the terrifying world and start all over again.

I knew on some level, even though I wasn't entirely there yet, that in order for me to really heal my past and take control of my life, I would need to learn how to make my way in the world, to take care of myself physically, emotionally, financially, and spiritually. Being in a relationship with Edie was like being Bill Murray imprisoned in the Tokyo hotel. Outside the hotel was a hostile, foreign world that paralyzed me, a world I did not fit into. Inside the hotel it was comfortable and safe, yet I was alone, and no one spoke my language.

To be fair, I wasn't exactly giving Edie what she wanted or needed either. I knew she was unhappy. I could feel it pouring out of her, and as such, I absorbed her sadness out of guilt. From a place of love she had given everything, risked and sacrificed so much more, just to give me a second shot at life. The weight of my karmic obligation to her was staggering, and yet, I couldn't even love her properly.

At the same time, I was desperate to find meaning. The more I listened to my conscience, the more I realized that I needed to stand for something, that I had been to the frontiers of the culture for a reason and I couldn't just pretend I didn't know what I knew. I felt obligated to a higher karma than the one I had with Edie. I knew my only salvation lay in helping others, and so, I began the inevitable fourth, and fifth, stages in the recovery process, the Outrage and Indignation Stage, and the Messianic White Knight Quest for Justice Stage.

I picked Tom Goforth's brain about his radical past and asked him whether it seemed like the right thing to do to jump headlong into the fray and dedicate myself to activism full time. Tom expressed ambivalence. On the one hand, he understood the call to service, and the irresistible allure of living by one's passions. In that way his radicalism was hard-wired.

On the other hand, he had seen the downfall of the movements in which he was involved, and then those movements that followed and failed too. He considered the current state of affairs substantially worse than back in his day, and he admitted to a deep, abiding pessimism about the direction in which the country was headed.

"You can't seem to get anywhere these days doing things the way we did them in the Sixties," he said. "I'm not even sure there's a viable alternative. Yet with the way things are going, with these maniacs in charge, it's almost a crime to stand by and not get involved."

I think this was why, in retrospect, Tom conveniently chose to take me at face value while overlooking all the screaming indications that I was rapidly developing a savior complex. A more objective voice would have pointed out the rather sizable potential for burnout, heartbreak, and disillusionment that activism carries with it. It most certainly would have pointed out the overwhelming risk of relapse, much less the chronic cynicism that generally results.

Yet, it was undeniable that history was repeating itself, and on some level, it had to be that people like Tom—who had been true believers and had invested so much of themselves into the Sixties movements—still believed that another kind of world was possible. It was already apparent that the failures, missteps, and lack of closure from the Sixties and Seventies were playing themselves out in the lives of so many Boomers during this new period of national tumult.

"NOW YOU'RE GOING TO FEEL THE POWER OF THE CHICAGO POLICE"

It's the night of April 28, 2004, at approximately 10:30. I'm in my car headed west on Montrose Avenue, just about to pass under the Ravenswood viaduct. Two blocks from home the car in front of me slams on its brakes and screeches to a halt, nearly causing me to rear-end it. Before I even have time to react, from the backseat of the car in front of me two flashlights immediately train on my face, effectively blinding me. I hear all four car doors fly open, and the two flashlights split and move in opposite directions to the rear of my car. Once they pass I can see that four people have surrounded me.

To my right is a woman with a blond ponytail. Outside the driver's window is a Latino man. Although I cannot clearly identify the two behind me, I can tell peripherally that all are wearing jeans, jackets, and bulletproof vests and carrying guns. It's only then I realize that the car in front of me is a standard issue unmarked Ford police interceptor.

This is the TAC Squad.

"You like riding my back end?" the Latino TAC barks at me.

By now, my heart is racing, and I'm scared. "You almost caused an accident," I stammered.

He motions to the female TAC. "Let's check the car," he says. She steps forward and opens my passenger door. The Latino TAC continues.

"Get out of the car and show me your license, registration, and proof of insurance. We need to take a look in your vehicle. Do you have anything on you you shouldn't?"

I sit there and stare at him, frozen. It takes me a second to remember I don't have drugs on me this time, haven't done anything illegal, and have nothing to hide. When I do, I recover my senses, and realize that, for the first time, I actually have a choice whether I will comply, or protest.

This realization is both empowering and exceedingly dangerous, because it's only too easy to take advantage of it and push it too far. I had seen the Chicago police bend and break the law so much that I was unsure who was cop and who was criminal. They have such a total disregard for basic human decency that in Chicago the phrase "abusing authority" is a polite euphemism. I'm not going to take it this time. Since I know I haven't given them anything remotely resembling "probable cause" to search my car, I refuse to comply.

"I'm sorry, but I'm not getting out of the car, and I do not consent to a search. You do not have 'probable cause' to search my car, and it was you who almost caused an accident."

"Are you fucking serious?" He laughs. "Lemme explain to you now, you don't want to do that, you won't like the outcome."

He then steps forward, sticks his face in my window inches from me, and sniffs at the air.

"I detect a strong odor of alcohol," he says sarcastically. "Looks like you've been drinking. Now it looks like I have my 'probable cause.' See how that works? Outta the car."

I refuse again, so he reaches in the window and grabs me by the throat with one hand. He opens the door with the other hand, and hauls me out of the car. He handcuffs me behind my back and shoves my face against the roof in the exact same place and manner as the gang-banger who I stabbed more than two and a half years earlier. The other two male TAC officers quickly move behind me, intentionally trying to stay out of my field of vision. My blood runs cold. This is quickly getting out of hand.

The female TAC with the blond ponytail begins tossing my car while the Latino searches my pockets. He pulls out my wallet, and tosses it on the trunk, telling one of the two TACs behind me to check it out.

"You don't have consent for this search," I keep repeating, but I realize I'm shaking. "This is an illegal search. You do not have consent."

Behind me, the one with my wallet says, "Green Party! ACLU! Voting Official! A real citizen here."

"You ever been arrested?" the Latino TAC asks me. I ignore him and repeat, "This is an illegal search. You do not have consent." My teeth begin to chatter slightly, which he notices. He knows I'm afraid, and he's wondering why.

"See who he is," he tells the TAC with my wallet, who in turn heads for the squad car to pull up my record. This is what I'm afraid of. Once they see I'm a convicted felon, the entire situation is going to change for the worse.

From inside my car the female TAC emerges with a handful of fliers and other handouts that I had collected at various political meetings.

"Hey," she says, waving the fliers at the Latino. "Is this them?"

In response, the TAC standing behind me says, "We got one of 'em?"

"You think cops are 'dirty' huh?" the Latino says, sardonically.

From the squad car I hear, "We got multiple hits: Burglary, drugs, half a dozen disorderlies. He ain't no citizen, he's a fucking punk."

The Latino pulls me backwards off the car by my handcuffs, holding the back of my neck with his other hand. He begins to pull my body back and forth in front of him.

"Uh oh . . . looks like he's resisting arrest," he says, and then throws me onto the street behind my car, holding my arms behind me so I fall flat on my face. In the process he yanks my right shoulder out of the socket, which by that time, nearly two years after the initial injury, is in bad shape and dislocates easily. I scream with pain and then roll over and look up at him. He's hovering over me laughing.

I scream at him, "*I want a field sobriety test! I demand a field sobriety test! This is bullshit, you can't do this! I demand a field sobriety test!*"

"Hey," Latino says to his buddies, "did you guys know we can't do this?"

"No no . . . ," one TAC says, "we sure can't do this."

The pain in my arm is so severe I scream again, and the Latino laughs and calls back to the others, "Looks like we got a 'crazy' here, better call for a transport!"

At this point I realize I'm going to be arrested. I stop screaming and roll myself into a position where my arm hurts least, and try to breathe through it. Within two or three minutes a paddy wagon arrives with another regular patrol car, so now there are three police vehicles blocking traffic on Montrose, making a huge spectacle of me.

The uniform cops exit their vehicles and together with the four TAC cops form a tight circle a few yards away. They begin laughing at me. Then, the Latino steps up to me, rolls me over on my chest, and puts his knee into the back of my neck, smashing my face against the ground. He leans down close to my ear and says quietly:

"Now you're going to feel the power of the Chicago police."

He yanks me off the ground by my handcuffs, unwittingly popping my arm back into the socket. At this point I'm dazed and sweating and realize I cannot say anything else. I'm just so relieved to be out of pain. The two uniformed cops stick me in their paddy wagon and transport me to the Addison and Halsted Street station in Boystown, while my car is impounded. The Latino and the blonde with the ponytail are waiting when I get there. From what I can gather, the other two TACs are not present.

I refuse to answer any questions during the booking process. I remain completely silent. In my mug shot, I cross my arms in defiance, staring straight into the camera, clearly communicating *This is total bullshit and you know it.*

Later, while I sit cuffed to the wall in the TAC office on the second floor, another female officer, apparently at random, says to me, "You people think it's fun to hurl bags of piss and shit at us? That's what we have to deal with. You're a bunch of cowards."

I have no idea what she is talking about, or who she means by "you people."[29] What becomes abundantly clear, however, is that they think I am someone else, part of something that clearly threatens them, and this bust is their way of somehow retaliating.

I am charged with DUI, "Following Too Close," and "No Proof of Insurance." In the morning, after my prints clear federal BCI, I am released ROR on an I-Bond and informed by the booking officer that my driver's license has been "summarily suspended" because I "refused a field sobriety test."

It was only the beginning.

A PRIMER ON THE CHICAGO POLICE DEPARTMENT

In 2007 the Edwin F. Mandel Legal Aid Clinic at the University of Chicago Law School published a staggering condemnation of the Chicago Police Department. The formal study, *The Chicago Police Department's Broken System*, concluded that, compared to the national average, Chicago police officers are the subject of more brutality complaints per officer, but that the Chicago Police Department is far less likely to pursue any disciplinary action.[30]

This report by one of the world's preeminent law schools opened with an unforgettable story that tragically has become all too common throughout the nation's third largest police force:

In 2003 and 2004, Diane, a fifty-year-old African American school janitor and mother of three, was subjected to multiple acts of abuse by a group of Chicago police officers. These officers were members of an elite tactical [TAC] team that patrolled public housing on Chicago's south side. Known as the "Skullcap Crew" to local residents, they had a reputation for racist and sadistic behavior. Over the course of the year that they targeted Diane for abuse, they forced her, on two separate occasions, to disrobe and bare the most private parts of her body. They threatened her with a loaded gun, needle-nosed pliers, and a screwdriver, leaving her convinced that they planned to rape and kill her. They beat and choked her. They hurled racial and gender-based epithets toward her. They tore up her home. They desecrated religious objects sacred to her. They threatened to plant drugs on her and to falsely arrest her. They beat her teenage son. They brought a middle-aged African American neighbor into her home and forced her son to beat the older man for their amusement. Diane was subjected to these assaults on multiple occasions, despite initiating complaints with the Chicago Police Department (CPD). The officers denied any contact whatsoever with Diane, and the CPD failed to sustain any of her complaints.

The Mandel Clinic spent six years on the study, working closely with a local author/activist named Jamie Kalven and the residents of the Stateway Gardens public housing community where Diane lived. Their goal was to document the countless human rights abuses by the Chicago Police and offer an "advocacy and self-help program focused on issues of police accountability."

What they found was that poor blacks in Chicago experience "a different Constitution from that which we studied in our classrooms," one that made them subject to constant and unending "aggressive stop and frisks, street interrogations, and the searches of community members' homes." These abuses were justified (at least in the minds of the police) by the War on Drugs, which the report states, "created the context for human rights abuses on a grander scale" such that "police misconduct that would constitute a dramatic and newsworthy event in . . . many of the [predominantly white] communities from which we came was a routine reality at [housing projects like] Stateway." [31]

A year before they released their report, the Mandel Clinic filed a federal lawsuit against the CPD, resulting in a detailed federal probe. The investigation revealed that more than 600 officers had more than ten complaints filed against them during a five-year period. The number of police abuse and misconduct reports the CPD was fielding was astronomical, and soon there was such a backlog that it required hiring outside investigators to help catch up. [32]

In an attempt to placate growing public rancor, the CPD offered up its most egregious and least protectable offenders, an "elite" drug and gang unit called the Special Operations Section (SOS). The SOS were *already* under federal investigation on charges ranging from burglary, robbery, home invasion, and armed violence to literally *thousands* of false arrests.[33] It was easy for Daley the Younger to single them out as a "rogue operation" and use the old "bad apples" argument, but the move was so transparent.[34] The truth was becoming undeniable: the CPD was rotten to the core.

Of course, this ability to see and comprehend the truth about the CPD (or most other major metropolitan police forces) remains obscured and distorted at the class level. Most middle- and upper-income people, particularly if they are white, routinely express shock, disbelief, and outright denial of the exhaustively documented patterns of police brutality and misconduct. Most middle- and upper-income people are more than happy to have them around.

Such reactions of course make sense, even though they directly support the assertion that the police exist to protect private property and enforce the class system, rather than the naïve belief that police exist altruistically "To Serve and Protect." Even those who do join law enforcement out of a sense of altruism quickly discover the abuse, racism, and corruption that is endemic in the police state.

If there's one central theme here it's that challenging or maligning the police is seriously risky business. Although this critique is not meant as a blanket indictment of police, *writ large*, it's important, when reading through this, to keep in mind a few essential details.

Two generations of the American middle class have grown up with the omnipresent specter of crime as a central feature of the media landscape. This myth of the "dangerous city" relies on the constant inundation of black and Latino mugshots as symbols of this crime. Consequently, even though most cities are statistically safe when we look at crime as a whole, they are still considered violent and dangerous places. This media- and politician-driven myth is used to justify and excuse these unconstitutional police state policies.

The truth is that crime levels peaked in the mid-1970s and early 1990s, and have steadily declined since.[35] The only exception are nonviolent drug crimes, which have multiplied exponentially. By 2009 homicides in major metros like New York, Chicago, Los Angeles, San Francisco, Washington, DC, and Dallas were at their lowest levels since the early 1960s.[36] In most American cities the bulk of violent crime is either domestic or gang related, the latter concentrated in a few densely populated, disproportionately poor neighborhoods.

Nevertheless, ask your average single white female living in a big city what her #1 fear is and it is being assaulted while alone on the street. Ask her to describe her possible assailant, and odds are she'll point to some nearby homeless black guy.

There are also two strata of police in most major metropolitan departments: the regular uniformed officers, who handle beats, direct traffic, give speeding tickets, and answer domestic complaints; and the drug and gang tactical officers and detectives, who exist in a wholly separate culture. I have known many cops in my life, and they come in all shapes and sizes and belief systems, but the one commonality amongst virtually every Chicago TAC I have ever met or crossed paths with was a pronounced tendency for sociopathic behavior. In short, they lie, cheat, steal, manipulate, and torture and are often more violent and dangerous than the criminals they target. They are little more than a well-armed and protected gang, and as you will see, they will stop at nothing to cover their asses.

SOME LESS-THAN-FLATTERING HISTORY

Although they have never been considered choir boys in their hundred-plus years of existence, the contemporary image of the

Chicago Police Department begins in 1968 with Daley the Elder's "shoot to kill" order during the riots following the assassination of Martin Luther King Jr. Apparently, not enough rioting Negroes were killed to appease the rabid Daley, so he chided the police for what he considered "excessive restraint."[37] This public humiliation, along with a growing cultural schism, set the stage for the police riot at the 1968 Democratic National Convention that August. By any account this was a malicious and premeditated act of cultural warfare.[38]

That atrocity was followed a year later by the assassination of Black Panther leaders Fred Hampton and Mark Clark. Working at the behest of Richard Nixon and J. Edgar Hoover under the auspices of COINTELPRO, the Chicago police stormed Hampton's home and shot him and Clark to death while they slept. An FBI informant working in the Panther inner circle had drugged Hampton and Clark first to ensure they could not fight back. The police lied and claimed they were engaged in a "defensive gun battle" with Hampton, and then engaged, along with the district attorney's office, in an elaborate and thoroughly preposterous coverup.[39]

That was Chicago's darkest period. To this day the police have shown no remorse about the Democratic Convention riot. In fact, in the summer of 2009 a group of former cops on duty the night of the police riot held a 40th reunion (a year late) that was advertised on a website called ChicagoRiotCops.com. They portrayed demonstrators as "scum" and "Marxist street thugs" and told ridiculous tales of "bags of urine and feces, and bricks that were thrown at them, . . . heavy glass ashtrays dropped on them from hotel windows high above . . . nail-spiked rubber balls left behind their car tires and sometimes thrown at them."[40]

Thankfully, and almost shockingly, the media still manages to keep the record straight about Chicago '68 for one important reason: the police also turned on the press and beat them too, committing their fatal mistake.

Over the next 20 years, as the city struggled to recover its image, crime began its steady upward climb, as too did the struggle for justice within the black community. In response, the Chicago police would beat, torture, and falsely imprison hundreds of mostly African American men, abuses that eventually led to a case being brought before the Human Rights panel at the Organization of American States.[41] During most of those years, the police commissioner was the repugnant sociopath John Burge.

Burge applied to the almost exclusively African American group of murder suspects torture and interrogation techniques he had learned during the Vietnam War and were originally used on Vietnamese POWs. Electric shock applied to a man's testicles was his favorite method. Although Burge was forced into retirement in 1993 after the Illinois Supreme Court investigation concluded that he and his men had carried out years of "systematic torture," charges were never filed against him, and any attempts to bring him or his cohorts to justice were thwarted. He spent most of his retirement in Florida on a full police pension, courtesy of the taxpayers of Chicago, while the police union paid all of Burge's legal bills.

A 2006 report by the Special State's Attorney of Cook County, considered to be the definitive opinion on the Burge case, concluded that there were "some" torture cases for which they could justify seeking new indictments, and that Burge was guilty of such abuse, but the issue was moot since the statute of limitations had expired decades ago, and no prosecution could be brought legally.

On October 21, 2008, however, Burge was arrested at his home near Tampa on charges of perjury and obstruction of justice stemming from a civil case filed by a group of his torture victims. After avoiding the light of accountability for nearly two decades, he finally took the stand for the first time to answer those charges on June 17, 2010. He denied ever laying a hand on any suspect, and pumped out a few crocodile tears for fallen comrades.[42] Indirectly, the perjury conviction was a legal admission that Burge did in fact torture.[43] The following week, some measure of justice was finally achieved when Burge was found guilty on all counts. He was eventually sentenced to four and a half years of Federal time. He is now currently known in the Bureau of Prisons register as Federal Inmate #50504-018.

In the late 1990s, the Chicago police developed an interesting habit of shooting unarmed black motorists. An Amnesty International report issued in September 1999 states:

> In June 1999, LaTanya Haggerty, a 19-year-old passenger in a car pulled over by Chicago police after a short chase, was shot dead when officers mistook the cell-phone in her hand for a gun . . . A day after the Haggerty shooting, Chicago police officers shot dead Robert Russ, a former college football player, after he refused to get out of his car after a pursuit. He was shot when an officer smashed the car window and pointed his gun directly into the car . . . Both Haggerty and Russ were black.[44]

The year before the Amnesty report was released Chicago police officers shot 71 people, the highest annual total in a decade, despite a significant fall in homicides. The report went on to state that most of the officers committing these shootings or other similarly extreme abuses of authority either never faced charges, were acquitted, or had their sentences reduced after the fact, presumably when the incidents had faded from public memory.

Also in 1999, the Medill Innocence Project, based at Northwestern University's School of Journalism, exonerated death row inmate Anthony Porter, starting a chain reaction that raced through the entire American capital punishment system. Within a year then-Governor George Ryan emptied Illinois's death row and declared a moratorium on the death penalty. In dispute were many of the convictions highlighted in the John Burge case, whose trails led inexorably to former attorney general and then-Mayor (until 2011,) Richard Daley the Younger.

The intersecting issues that led to Chicago's culture of police brutality are the legacies of racism and segregation that have characterized this city since its founding, inculcated to multiple generations. So deep were the racial divisions ingrained into our collective psyches that they became manifest when Richard Daley the Elder bore the policy into the earth and laid out the new interstate highway system along racial boundaries, dividing the city into ethnic enclaves. Across the Dan Ryan Expressway from their beloved Bridgeport, in what used to be the vibrant Bronzeville strip, the Daley clan then watched as the behemoth Robert Taylor housing projects rose. Into these vertical egg crates were crammed more poor African Americans per square foot than anywhere else in the nation.

Over time, Chicago developed an institutionalized process of containing and managing poor blacks in what would become a majority African American city. In order for a new generation of developers to step in and begin rebuilding the bombed-out city with private capital, the current residents had to be viewed as an infestation to be removed. Crime and the War on Drugs were the justifying factors that set into motion a total retooling of the police department into a systematic brutalizing force. They would eventually grow to such a position of cocksureness that they would begin pushing the limits of their own credulity, as my case would quickly show.

▼

In the aftermath of my assault and false arrest, I was somewhat panicked. I didn't exactly know what to do, but one thing I did know was that I needed a lawyer. My friend and fellow activist Bryan Brickner recommended Peter Vilkelis, a Chicago criminal defense attorney who handled mostly drug cases. Pete was also a member of the legal advisory council of NORML, the National Organization for the Reform of Marijuana Laws. He was Chicago through and through, born and raised, and had a comprehensive understanding of the cops and the courts. In a milieu replete with sharks and cash-and-carry slimeballs, Pete was a refreshing breath of consciousness.

When we met to discuss my case, he figured out the deal quickly.

"Seems clear to me these cops were trying to teach you a lesson. They see you're connected to some activist group they got a beef with, and they decide to send a message through you. It's gonna be a tough one with your record, but it would be my pleasure to take this case, *pro bono.*"

Pete set about getting ahold of the police report. When the paperwork finally arrived in his office he called me and told me I had to see it myself to believe it.

The Latino officer who assaulted me was named DeJesus. In the original arrest report written on the scene, DeJesus states:

> Above subject stopped for a traffic violation. As A/O DeJesus was speaking to driver, A/O smelled a strong odor of alcoholic beverage on subject's breath. A/O instructed subject to exit vehicle at which time subject stated "Fuck You–You have no rights over me based on the Constitution." Subject then exited vehicle, stumbling as exiting. Refused field sobriety test. Placed in custody and advised of Miranda. Name check clear via computer—Has I.D.

The report also states that I identified myself as "Freedom Fighter" and then refused to volunteer any further information.

"You didn't seriously say your name was 'Freedom Fighter'?" Pete said, laughing.

"You don't seriously think I did?" I responded.

Pete continued. "The report initially stated that you did not resist arrest. Then, that was scratched out and 'Yes' was checked and circled."

"That's certainly interesting, and definitely bullshit."

"That's not all."

He pointed to a tiny, hastily scribbled line sandwiched in between two other lines. It read:

> Subject pulled away several times as A/Os attempted to place him in custody.

"It's pretty clear to me," Pete said, "when you look at the next report that that line was added later, and the box for 'resisting arrest' was changed then too. Here's what the next report states. It was written later at the station."

He hands me a much cleaner document, written in the same handwriting, by Officer J. DeJesus:

> Subject Following A/O's Vehicle too close breaking suddenly to avoid striking A/O's. Traffic stop ensued and subject had strong odor of alcoholic beverage on breath. Subject instructed to exit vehicle but refused and stated "Fuck You—You Have No Rights Over Me Based on The Constitution." Subject then exited vehicle falling down & stumbling. Refused Field Sobriety Test. Placed in Custody for DUI-Alcohol. Subject attempted to pull away several times. Subject began yelling "Hale had the Right Idea—You have no authority over me—Fuck the Government."

I looked up at Pete and could see he was visibly amused by this. *"Don't fuck with the Jesus, man,"* I mumbled to myself.

"It appears that with each successive report, you get drunker, and more dangerous," Pete said, "which I love because apparently this is you so drunk you can't stand."

He tossed me a copy of my mugshot, and just as I stated earlier, I'm staring at the camera, arms crossed in defiance, with a very clear expression of *This is total bullshit and you know it.*

"You were so drunk you couldn't stand, so they placed you

in custody, and *then* you tried to pull away in your car. But my favorite touch is the 'Hale' line."

"Yeah, what's up with *that*?" I said. "You mean like Nathan Hale? *I only regret that I have but one life to lose for my country?*"

"That's what I thought at first, but then I remembered something that happened the day before your arrest. I think they mean Matt Hale."

"You gotta be kidding me?"

"These guys are obviously not scholars."

There are but precious few moments in life when you hold in your hand proof that those with authority abused it and lied to cover it up. This was one of those moments. All those TACs needed to do was claim that they pulled me over drunk, and I refused a sobriety test. With my previous record of drug convictions, there's no way a judge would believe me if I disputed the charges. But for some totally unexplainable reason, they chose to fabricate this ridiculous tale, and in their ignorance of politics and current events, they set themselves up for one hell of an embarrassment.

Permit me to explain.

Matt Hale is a white supremacist and former Southern Illinois University law student who founded the white separatist "World Church of the Creator." In 1999 Hale was denied a license to practice law in Illinois when the Bar Committee refused to certify that he had the "requisite moral character and fitness to practice law in Illinois." It was clear his racist views were the reason he was denied.

Two days after the Bar ruling a follower of Hale's named Benjamin Smith went on a shooting rampage in the Chicago area, killing nine Orthodox Jews, a Korean student, and Ricky Byrdsong, the beloved African American coach of the Northwestern University men's basketball team. Hale used the subsequent media frenzy to cement his status as "one of the best-known leaders on the far right." He stated that America should be inhabited by only whites, and that there must be a race war to cleanse the continent.[45]

Around that time Hale had become embroiled in a trademark dispute with an Oregon church that bore the same name as Hale's church. The federal judge who presided over the case was Joan Humphrey Lefkow, a liberal judge appointed by Bill Clinton. Lefkow ruled Hale had to stop using the name "World Church of the Creator" and ordered the destruction of all their printed materials. Hale then counter-sued Lefkow, claiming her order violated the Constitution. While their case was pending, Hale solicited his bodyguard, an undercover FBI informant, to kill Lefkow.[46] Hale was arrested and charged. On April 26, 2004, two days before my run-in with the TAC squad, he was found guilty, and a year later was sentenced to 40 years. He is serving his term in a prison in Colorado, where he is prisoner number 15177-424.

"It's pretty clear to me," Pete says, "that these guys are figuring that any judge you go before will read what you supposedly said, that you support a Neo-Nazi who tried to have his judge killed, and they will drop the hammer on you."

"Hence the 'fuck the government . . . you have no rights over me based on the Constitution' nonsense?"

"I think so."

There is only one other TAC listed on the report, an officer "N. Isakson." The report does not indicate if this was the female, or one of the two other males. Two go unaccounted for, and we have no idea who they are.

"Was there anything left in your car when you got it out of impound? Any of those fliers?"

"No. It was cleaner than I left it."

"I suppose that's one small benefit of the grand it took to get the car out."

"I had an unopened bottle of champagne in the trunk and they took that too."

"Well, that doesn't surprise me."

"So what do we do?"

"At the very least, it shouldn't be too hard to prove you're not a white supremacist. Let's just hope the judge in this case doesn't share the same feelings about activists as these yahoos. "

▼

The police assault once again left me completely violated. The incident retriggered a deep post-traumatic response, and set my healing progress back a long way. The bogus police report was the *coup de grâce*. Whatever amusement I felt over the attempted Matt Hale connection was sufficiently exhausted by my rage at their arrogance and the way they flaunted and abused their power. What drove my blinding anger was that I was *innocent*. I was innocent, and it didn't matter. Every single word in that police report was a lie, and yet, the burden of proof fell upon my shoulders, and odds were I was going to lose, because I had a conviction record.

It wasn't just the specifics of my case that enraged me, either. It was our cultures' pervasive illusions about our justice system. I was amused that DeJesus included the line about having given my "Miranda warning," a legal advisement of rights. In all my experiences with police I have never once heard a cop say, *You are under arrest. You have the right to remain silent. Anything you say can and will be used against you in a court of law . . .*

The Miranda Law only exists on television series like *Law & Order*, and in paperwork like this. I very much doubt anyone has ever gone free because they did not receive their Miranda warning. Yet many middle- and upper-class whites believe this urban legend, which began with the vigilante films of the 1970s like the *Dirty Harry* and *Death Wish* series. These were popular with the "tough on crime" crowd, and the intention of these highly reactionary films was to create a climate of opinion that "criminals" had "too many protections" and were "getting away with murder."

The ultimate goal was to implement harsher and more punitive criminal justice codes, while steadily eroding basic constitutional protections. Not because "crime," per se, was out of control, but rather, the American system itself seemed to be crashing and burning, and there needed to be increasingly harsh measures implemented to maintain order.

In the 1970s crime was escalating as a result of desperate economic conditions—a stagnant economy and increasing inflation known as "Stagflation"—and an institutionalized culture of violence and criminality that was permeating society from the top down. It was those in the highest positions of power who had most abused the protections of the law. These were the people who, under a shield of legalese, murdered millions of poor people in Southeast Asia, fomented coups in Chile, Brazil, and Argentina, and assassinated dozens of political opponents at home, like Fred Hampton, Mark Clark, Martin Luther King Jr., and John and Robert Kennedy.

As the economy grew worse and worse (a consequence of official policies) the government took it out on the poorest sector of society, who were the worst affected, and the most angered. Things were bad all over, but we blamed the victims, who were increasingly destitute and turning to crime. Polite society quickly grew both tired of their plight and afraid of the rising crime wave. This was only too easily manipulated by a government that needed public support for harsher and harsher methods of containing this unruly, but justifiably unruly, underclass.

The same pattern repeated itself in the late 1980s and early 1990s, following the crack cocaine epidemic, where piecemealing low-level street dealers and gang members were portrayed as kingpins with endless resources. Once again policymakers, like Los Angeles City Attorney Kenneth Hahn, promoted the idea that offering these gang members any sort of legal protection "under the guise of upholding the constitution" would only result in "deadly blight."[47]

The truth about the police is simple enough to find, if you care to look. Psychologists will tell you there is little difference between the cop psyche and the criminal psyche, because when you strip away the labels of cop and criminal what you are left with is a collection of sociopaths. If that assessment seems harsh, after all you've read here about the Chicago police, perhaps the following may finally cement your opinion.

THE ASSASSINATION OF MAY MOLINA

On May 26, 2004, one month after my arrest, the activist community in Chicago was dealt a devastating blow when May Molina-Ortiz, a 55-year-old, wheelchair-bound diabetic/asthmatic grandmother, died in police custody after her home was raided by TAC Squad officers from the same Addison and Halsted station as the lovely Officers DeJesus and Isakson. Although Molina had no history of involvement with drugs or drug dealing, the police claimed to have found 80 tinfoil packets of heroin in her home.

Molina was an activist and founder of Families of the Wrongfully Convicted. Her son, Salvador Ortiz, had already served 16 years of a 47-year sentence for a murder he did not commit. In the month before she died Molina had opened an office on Chicago's West Side as part of a larger campaign she was launching to draw public attention to police misconduct and wrongful convictions.[48]

On the night of my assault by the police, among the fliers found in my car were those belonging to Families of the Wrongfully Convicted and Comite Exijimos Justicia (We Demand Justice Committee). These were what apparently caught the eye of the TACs. For several years these two groups had accused the Chicago Police Department of systemic brutality, misconduct, and the wrongful convictions of scores of innocent Latinos.

Following her arrest, protests ensued first outside the Addison and Halsted station and then outside the Belmont and Western lockup after Molina was transferred to await a bond hearing. Sometime within the next 28 hours she would die. Initially police and the coroner claimed her death was caused by "six undigested packets of heroin lodged in her esophagus, stomach, and small intestine." No one from the police or coroner's office could explain how someone in police custody for more than 28 hours could have had tinfoil packets of heroin lodged in her throat. A cursory study of anatomy shows that the esophagus is an involuntary reflux muscle, and things either go up or they go down, but do not remain stuck unless they were inserted *postmortem*.[49]

On June 16, 2004, Michael Ortiz, Molina's other son who was arrested with her, was released by a judge who said none of the tinfoil packets had tested positive for any narcotics. The alleged "heroin" was actually wax found amongst candle-making supplies, which police claimed they mistook for drugs.[50] The revelation was inconsequential. Molina was already out of the way, mission accomplished. A whole three months later a toxicology report conveniently surfaces claiming Molina was "intoxicated with heroin" at the time of her death, corroborating the bogus coroner's report. Her death is eventually ruled "an accident."[51] Everyone who knew Molina denounces any insinuation that she used heroin.

Family and fellow activists claim Molina died from police mistreatment. The implication is clear that the police, in their effort to cover up her death and support their heroin charge, forced the bags of heroin down her throat after she had been either killed or found dead. No charges were ever filed, and no one was ever investigated or reprimanded for what was done to her.

In late November of 2009 the Illinois Supreme Court ordered a new trial for Salvador Ortiz based on new eyewitness testimony. It was then revealed that in 2003 May Molina had discovered a new eyewitness to the crime.[52] Her fatal mistake was taking it public too soon. It was this that the police were trying to thwart when they stormed her home and later killed her. The best her family has been able to do is file a wrongful death suit in federal court. It remains pending.

May Molina's murder struck terror into my soul. I was absolutely convinced now that the police would stop at nothing to keep the depth of this scandal hidden. This meant that it was equally possible that they were going to do something drastic to me, to shut me up. So long as anyone had anything on them, they were vulnerable. This may be why they went to such ridiculous extremes as the "Freedom Fighter" story. What I did know was that I was scared, and I started to think it might not be such a bad idea for me to get out of Chicago for a while.

A BLUE JAY PERCHED ON THE FAR BANK OF THE RUBICON

I left Chicago and landed in San Francisco in late 2004 looking both to escape the Chicago police and for something to inspire me, since I had become thoroughly disillusioned as an activist after the two summer political conventions and the 2004 election. What I needed was a kind of reset, an ability to look at everything in my life from a fresh perspective. I could never have known that the "reset" I was looking for was just around the corner, headed towards me on a high-speed collision course, wearing a bird hat.

Through an acquaintance, I received an email invitation to a "Winter Solstice gathering," a private affair held at an undisclosed location somewhere in San Francisco. The acquaintance, named Anthony, was a friend of a friend, and he was taking me to the "gathering" as a favor, because I didn't know many people and was looking to meet some. When he picked me up he chided me because, in my hungover state from the night before, I smelt of alcohol.

"I don't think they'll let you in if they smell that on your breath."

"It's not on my breath, it's coming out of my pores. And what kind of party doesn't let you drink?"

"We're not going to a 'party.' We're going to a 'ritual.'"

Already I didn't like this guy, the pompous little shit. If only it had ended with him.

On our way to the "ritual" we stopped at a loft somewhere in the city to meet up with another group of people. As we're milling about the place, not really talking but everyone kinda looking-and-smiling at each other, the doorbell rings and in walks this huge bald guy with periwinkle blue eyes and a marble-slab physique, wearing a flamingo hat on his head, and toting a copy of a book titled *Crossing the Rubicon*. Next to him is a shy, slender brunette with a long French nose. They introduce themselves as Blue Jay and Beetle.

The host asks everyone to gather around for a "sharing ceremony." Everyone was asked to bring something to share with the group; naturally, I was unprepared. One by one, in soft tones, they read Rumi and Krishnamurti, quoted *The Celestine Prophesy* and *The Four Agreements* and the words of half a dozen Indian swamis with names I would never remember.

I was really uncomfortable; the whole exercise seemed so pretentious to me. I had on some antiwar T-shirt, and the cat who read from Krishnamurti picked up on my "activist vibe" and clearly disapproved by the way he looked at me, his eyes growing large and his head leaning back each time I said something, like someone had farted next to him.

Provocatively he tried to argue, through this Krishnamurti quote, that human beings are inherently violent, and thus, war is a natural part of our existence. I took issue, exclaiming that no human being wants to kill another, even in self-defense, and crimes of passion are rare and unnatural. War is most definitely unnatural, and anyone who's been through it considers it hell, a rich man's game where poor men die. The only reason war is seen as noble is because we reward people for thinking of it that way, and shame those who don't as "cowards."

Eyes wide, head reared. There's that stink again.

Blue Jay looks around at everyone, his expression half-bemusement, half-innocence. Suddenly he announces, "Hey! How about those war games going on during 9/11?! On the same day four planes are hijacked the Pentagon was also running three separate computer simulation and live-fly exercises involving hijacked planes? Is that a coincidence? No sirree!"

Most of the people in the ceremony circle look horrified. Some try to smile through it, but only manage a grimace. Someone in the group says, "thanks for that dark energy." I struggle to keep myself from laughing. *Dark energy?*

Oh man, I think, looking at Blue Jay unfazed. *This is my kind of guy.*

The "ritual" we attend is held in a private warehouse space. There are around a hundred people in attendance who call themselves a "spiritual community." They are mostly dressed in flamboyant clothing, lots of white robes and other types of ceremonial gear. They open the festivities with a ceremony of sorts, talking about "goddess" stuff, and then, while holding hands around the perimeter of the main dance floor, move through a series of three "Ohms." I must admit, the feeling of sonically oscillating at the same frequency with a hundred other people was pretty amazing.

Upstairs was a chill lounge with pillows and mattresses strewn across the floor, upon which were sprawled a writhing mass of e-tarded people clearly rolling on gobs of MDMA, giving massages, holding hands, and getting very deep with one another about their innermost fears, shames, and conflicts. Downstairs was the dance floor, where a string of DJs played house and trance all night. It was a trip. I had never been to a "ritual" like this; I thought they called them raves.

I also thought about all my activist friends and how much shit they would give me if they knew I was raving it up with a bunch of Bay Area New Age hippies. But one thing was for sure: these folks sure were having fun. And because it was a relatively small private gathering, everyone knew each other and there was a real intimacy to it all. I felt so out of place. I was convinced I stood out like the Village Idiot with a buzz cut.

I sat with Blue Jay and Beetle talking about *Rubicon* and asking questions about the scene. Blue Jay informs me that these types of "rituals" are a dime a dozen in the Bay Area.

"Dude, they're just raves with a prayer at the beginning," he says.

He asked me how I found my way to this particular gathering, since it was such a closed community, and in the process of explaining myself I end up dumping my whole story on him . . . crack, politics, Chicago Police, everything. By the time I finish, he and Beetle look exhausted.

Blue Jay reaches down inside his bag and produces a capsule of MDMA.

"I think you could use this, my good man."

I take it, and within half an hour, I feel my stress start to peel away. It's really potent shit, and soon I'm yapping away again like Blue Jay and Beetle are my personal therapists. I feel so much tension releasing as I get so much shit off my chest, shit I've been lugging around for years like a broke poet schlepping an old Underwood typewriter.

"Well, you told us how you got here," Blue Jay said. "But you haven't told us why."

"What do you mean?"

"Why are you here?"

"I guess because I'm running away from something."

"Hmpf. Sounds to me like you ran *to* something. What are you looking for?"

"I don't know," I said. "I just have a feeling I'll find it here."

"San Francisco's certainly a place for finding stuff."

We exchange numbers and he and Beetle leave. A week later, on New Year's Eve, Blue Jay calls and invites me to go out with the two of them. When he picks me up he explains that he has to make a few stops, but after that suggests we go to his place and take some LSD. I look at him with terror.

"Ahhhh . . . I'm gonna have to pass," I say. "You may not

know what I got stored up here," I say, pointing at my head, "but I do, and trust me when I say it ain't pretty."

Blue Jay *pshaws* me. "You'll be fine. I really think it will do you some good. When was the last time you had any?"

I think for a moment. "Probably thirteen or fourteen years. I really don't think it's a good idea, man. I'm really not interested in losing my mind."

He laughs and shakes his head. "You won't lose your mind. In fact, you just might find it again."

He produces another capsule of MDMA and hands it to me.

"I stuffed some extra colors inside for ya," he say, and shakes the capsule. I make out the edge of a small piece of blotter buried in the MDMA. "This way we'll guarantee you start off your journey in a good space, and stay there."

I hold it between my fingers, genuinely afraid to take it, still vividly remembering the one bad trip I had after my freshman year in college, when I was a wee 19. I never want to feel that way again. And I remember the last time I took LSD, when I was 21. It wasn't so much a bad trip for me, but I guess it was bad for my friends. It was at a barbecue with dozens of people, and I decided I would be the grill master, and effectively incinerated 15 pounds of chicken, then withstood people haranguing me all night about it. By the time the night was over, I felt like I had murdered the chickens myself.

But for some reason, on this night, with this stranger, I decide to trust.

"You promise you'll take care of me and not let me go nuts?" I plead.

"Dude . . . yer gonna be fine. We gotcha."

I swallowed the capsule, and awaited the onslaught of the wraiths.

Quite to the contrary, instead of flinging open my psychic dungeon and releasing all my collected demons, the LSD made my brain come alive. It was as if a fresh wind was blown through my cortex, and all this fetid, stale air was released. Most of the time my thoughts were so jammed up it felt like wading through molasses just to pop out a coherent sentence. Now, I was able to think so clearly. More than that, though, I found my sense of humor. I was such an intense dour fuck most of the time, I had literally forgotten what it was like to laugh, to be silly. But with those two, I let go, and laughed until I cried. And then cried more, from sadness, because I hadn't for so long, and the relief I felt was like the loosening of thumb screws. It was some good medicine.

The three of us engaged in hours of play and endless conversation. Beetle, who was a French Canadian from Montreal, explained she was a performance artist and showed me photos and videos of her work, which was astounding and intensely weird. Blue Jay told me some of his history. He was an Army brat, his father was a chaplain, and he had grown up on bases. He discovered psychedelics in his early twenties and realized that Christianity was a scam. He left his family and went off to travel the world. Now he felt his mission in life was to turn people on to "psychedelic medicine" as he called it. The two of them were so far removed from anything I had ever known, and they deeply inspired me.

At one point Blue Jay tosses a magazine in my lap. It's a copy of the monthly bulletin from the Multidisciplinary Association for Psychedelic Studies.

"Have you heard of these guys?" he asked.

"Yeah. Actually I have. But I don't know much about them."

"Dude, I think you might want to read this."

"How come?"

"Looks like ya got some crazy stuff you're workin' through. These guys help that kind of stuff, using psychedelic medicine. Maybe they can help you."

"You're not the first person to tell me that," I explain.

"Sounds to me like a message, brother."

When we parted ways he gave me the MAPS bulletin to take with me, and a DVD copy of a Peter Jennings's *ABC News* special on MDMA called *Ecstasy Rising*.

"Watch that," he said. "I think you'll find stuff in there for ya."

When I finally made my way back to where I was staying I felt cleared and reconnected to myself with a kind of renewed enthusiasm for my work. I was still without a home or a job, and I was wearing out my welcome everywhere. However, I came looking for a reset as I entered the New Year and I got it. Little may have changed, but I felt I was finally creatively unblocked, and that made all the difference in the world. More than that, I knew I had landed in the right place, and that 2005 was going to be the year that things were really going to change. I could feel it coming.

CHAPTER 7
It's 2005 . . . Now What?

Blue Jay's acid left me inspired to write during the first two weeks of 2005. I had been itching, somewhat out of misguided feelings of revenge and a desire to exonerate myself, to explore more police and drug war issues. With a renewed fervor and a feeling of impunity I began working on three new pieces: one about the Chicago Police Department and the rising police state, in which I had made the fateful decision to write about May Molina; one about the Illinois prison system that looked at the drug war from a local angle and accused the Chicago police of indiscriminate mass arrests; and a final piece that looked at the larger global issues of the drug war.

I felt emboldened in particular to write about the Chicago police because at the time I had pretty much decided never to go back to Chicago, and so I thought I was safe to do so from the West Coast. In researching the story, I got a few key members of the Chicago Coalition on War and Racism on the record, and they were all convinced Molina was murdered.

I was still debating whether or not to publicize my own story to draw the necessary connections between my assault and Molina's murder. My case was still pending, and I wasn't supposed to be saying anything to anyone. And in those few weeks, I had all but forgotten that I still had yet to face a judge on my charges. If I were to be honest with myself, I'd be forced to admit that I was intentionally ignoring it out of pure fear.

In the meantime, I watched *Ecstasy Rising* and was introduced for the first time to Rick Doblin, the director of MAPS, as he was interviewed by Peter Jennings for the program. I was surprised to learn that in the 1980s, before it was designated Schedule I, MDMA was not only used in PTSD therapy but also in marriage counseling because of its ability to help people lower defenses and open up to each other.

I was also appalled to learn that the claim that "Ecstasy puts holes in your brain" was a myth that arose intentionally out of a fraudulent government study in which rats were injected with ungodly amounts of methamphetamine, not MDMA. What really reached me was the testimony of a woman who had been raped and used MDMA to heal and start building love, trust, and intimacy again. It was as if the program were speaking directly to me.

This time, I got the message.

Two weeks later Blue Jay invites me to come over to his place for "a special surprise." When I arrive, he informs me that he has DMT (dimethyltryptamine) and "would like to send me on a journey." He explains that he'd been studying the work of a psychedelic researcher named "D.M. Turner" (Joseph Vivian) and that he was conducting an unofficial experiment with his friends on what he called a "K & D Cocktail." This was a mixture DMT and ketamine in a 60:40 ratio that was dissolved in solution and administered intramuscularly through a hypodermic needle, generally in the butt.

"I guarantee you it will change your life," he says softly, and with great reverence.

I will admit to being a bit fearful, but nothing was going to stop me. In the two weeks I had known this man he had managed to crack me open and help me regain some semblance of my true self, some desperately needed confidence and conviction. I trusted him. Moreover, he was gentle and sweet, and exceedingly generous to me.

Blue Jay knew a lot of people, but he was eccentric and socially awkward and something of a loner. Beetle was almost childlike, and the characters she created in her art were mythic, ripped, mixed and burned from fairy tales, and fantasy. That's why they were so good together. They were little kids trapped in adult bodies. Both deeply wounded at some point in their very young lives, they were seeking consciousness, transcendence, and healing. I wanted what they had, and they were offering it to me freely.

The room is prepared for me. They dim the lights and place a small mattress and a number of pillows on the floor. Blue Jay prepares the syringe, and holds it up to the lamp. A thin pink beam refracts through the magenta-colored liquid. They have me lie down and roll over on my side. I feel a prick in my butt cheek and then the sensation of pressure. I roll onto my back, and Blue Jay hands me a visor to cover my eyes. I put it on and settle back into darkness. Beetle lies down beside me, and my sweating hand quickly slips inside hers.

"It's OK," she says. "You are *so* gonna love this."

Most people experience DMT through smoking it, which is the most potent way to administer the drug, because aerosolized compounds cross the blood/brain barrier with lightning speed and rapidly flood the cerebral cortex. As a consequence, many describe the feeling of smoking DMT as "blasting off in a rocket ship" where they are hurled through a vortex into another dimension, and often lose all connection to their corporeal selves.

By contrast, intramuscular DMT comes on gradually, and the ketamine acts as a compressor to keep the DMT trip from racing into extreme hairiness, leaving you in a floaty, dreamlike state as you experience the DMT-induced visions. It was a few moments before I began to notice any effects, but once they came on, it was as if I were picked up by a slow-moving tornado and whirled towards the heavens, where I was gradually funneled into a magenta-colored vortex and flushed through to the other side.

When I emerged, I was floating above a giant magenta city of pyramids that stretched far out of view. The architecture style was ziggurat like the Mayan pyramids, with steps along the sides. On each block of the pyramid was an individual character of some language. The pyramids pulsed and glowed with effervescent energy, and the characters would rotate and move across the blocks like the Jumbo Tron signs of Times Square. It was as if the pyramids were processing units of some sort, and they were actively communicating.

Not a voice, but an awareness, inside me says, *this is where we come from . . . this is where you come from . . . we're the ones who made you . . . this is how we communicate with you, in this space.*

I somehow understand that they mean inter-dimensionally, though DMT.

I then have a simultaneous vision of all the pyramid cultures on Earth: Giza, Angkor Wat, Chichen Itza, Teotihuacan, Pyramid Valley.

Ours, the consciousness says.

Two strains of RNA wind before me, one color I understand to be from Earth, the other from them. They bond to form a helix.

Us.

An image of myself on either side of a mirror, the one side is corporeal, I am in my body. On the other side of the mirror, I exist as a glowing silhouette of energy.

Here.

That's where they exist, I think. *They're in the energetic dimension that's holding us together, they're the magnetic charge between atoms and molecules.*

Unbeknownst to me, I'm speaking and describing what I am experiencing in detail as it's happening to me. I don't realize this until Beetle's hand moves and she sniffs, and I'm suddenly jolted out of the vision and come crashing back down into my body. I'm suddenly aware I'm on the floor, with a visor on. I take a deep breath, and begin to float again, remaining in darkness, yet once again beginning to detach.

From out of the darkness, a song begins to play. Led Zeppelin's "Going to California." Picked up by the music, a synesthetic wave propels me into a new vision. As the guitar rings away, I am transported to the past and begin having a full sensory download of the 1960s and '70s. By "full sensory download" I mean that I am not only having a visual experience but I am also having the emotional experience along with it.

In my vision, I am taken . . . emotionally . . . through the idealism of the era, and the movements of the day. With painful clarity I see how they all begin with optimism and hope and the belief that a better world is possible. But somewhere along the way, dark forces arrayed. Shadows rise from within each of them, their projections and unrealistic expectations, their fears and prejudices and insecurities. I see greed and ego and little Abbie Hoffman action figures. I see some grasping at rings while others are pushed away.

I see them infiltrated, disrupted, and eventually neutralized. I feel the pain of everyone turning on each other in a fog of distrust and paranoia. I see populations divide and then divide again. A wall erupts out of the ground. On one side, people are crushed by stacks of dollars, on the other, copies of Marx and Mao. I feel children scream at their parents, and the old viewed with distrust. I feel burnout, disillusionment, and the seductive allure of oblivion, symbolized by Nixon waving goodbye, and a disco ball spinning in the sky.

The consciousness says, *They failed because they allowed themselves to become divided. Once divided, fear came from all directions. Do not follow this path.*

I see myself standing with raised fist, trapped inside a concrete box.

Old and young, red and blue, gay and straight, white and black, we are all constantly set against each other by a tiny minority who sits above us pulling the strings. To ever truly achieve the revolution we all dream of, we have to find a way to unite and look past the artificial differences put on us. The Sixties failed because it was a defiant revolution, a David and Goliath struggle, except that David forgot his sling at home and was crushed. His sling, in this case, was wisdom, and balance. Defiance and opposition lead to the same result. If we are ever truly to transcend, to evolve, we have to stop *fighting*.

You have to stop fighting.

Stop fighting.

The song ends, and the ketamine begins to kick in a lot harder, and I take off on a ride that feels like I'm body surfing the outer rim of the galaxy. When I finally come down, I'm filled with a euphoric sense of peace and forgiveness, and I feel liberated from the fear paradigm that had dominated my life. More sobering is my newfound understanding that I was an instrument of division, and by continuing this partisan activist path, I will only continue to act in this capacity. It is time to begin preaching unity, and love, not enmity, and hate. I'm ready to trade in my raised fist for a hug or two.

The real life-changer, though, was the revelation that there most definitely is a "God." I had seen it, felt it, heard it. Forty-five minutes earlier I was an avowed atheist who held nothing but contempt for anyone and anything religious or spiritual. But after I hung out on God's pimped-out balcony, and felt that divine consciousness within me, what could I say? Hallucination? Bullshit. It was more real to me than breakfast. It was the cipher that decoded everything else. The Pyramids, every religion, myth, and legend, the missing link? They all made sense now. They were all connected. They were all part of the same.

Seriously . . . *whoa.*

When I am able to focus my eyes, I write a few emails to people I have had falling outs with. The message I send is simple:

i'm sorry.

i was wrong.

a frienD helped Me To see.

BACK TO FACE THE MUSIC

Well, you can run, but you can never hide. The next day I received a phone call from Peter Vilkelis, my lawyer.

"Your hearing on the Summary Suspension and the DUI is in two weeks. I've put this thing off for as long as I can. You gotta come home and deal with this."

No sooner had I hung up the phone than I knocked a glass of wine onto my laptop, shorting it out. Anything of any value or importance to me was in that laptop; everything else I owned or knew was back in Chicago. I had no money, and I was alone, diving deeper and deeper down the rabbit hole. One inadvertent move caused a mass calamity and I began to panic. For the first time in my life I had a real live anxiety attack and I honestly thought I was dying. I called Edie and my mother in hysterics, and it took a few moments for me to even begin to make sense to them. They decided to split the costs between them to get my computer fixed and get me back to Chicago.

Yet again I was going home with my tail between my legs.

Edie picked me up from Midway Airport and took me back to our old place in Lincoln Square. The entire ride home I filled her

head with stories about the psychedelic conversion I had just gone
through in San Francisco. I gushed about how "changed" I felt,
how "different" I was, how much these drugs "helped me." I told
her she should try them too.

Although she remained mostly silent, I could tell she disapproved strongly, and could not really differentiate between these
drugs and cocaine, as she had no frame of reference. Her only
comment to me was, "do you think it's such a good idea to be
taking these drugs when you've got this court case looming over
your head?" Naturally, I dismissed her as "overreacting."

Within a week I had managed to track down a modest quantity of MDMA and LSD through a friend I had been introduced
to a year earlier who was a distributor of psychedelics, and who
for the purposes of this book and his and others' protection shall
remain anonymous (we'll call him "Albert"). Albert was sympathetic to my situation. He supported my activist work, and
was aware of my situation with the Chicago Police. He had also
been a consistent voice in favor of my experimenting with psychedelics, which he felt would give me the new perspective I had
been seeking. I had resisted him for a year, but once I returned to
Chicago, I told him of my escapades on the West Coast and how
my entire paradigm had changed. He smiled knowingly, but also
cautioned me to show restraint.

"These life-changing revelations do not necessarily resonate
with other people," Albert warned. "You gotta keep two feet on
the ground, and you still have to be careful what you say and do.
Chicago is *not* San Francisco."

I was having none of it. I had been converted, been saved, been
to the mountaintop and seen the promised land, and now I was
gonna scream from the peaks, *Here! Here! The answer is here!* I
wanted to turn everyone on. I begged Albert to give me a small
supply on credit that I could use for myself and to turn on friends.

"Charles . . . think very carefully about what you're doing here.
You've got a lot going on. You've got the police on your ass, and

because of what you do, you don't know who's watching you or listening to you. The last thing you need is to get busted with a quantity of anything."

I *pshawed* him. "I'll be fine," I said. "I'm over this activist crap. I just want to feel the love."

"Yeah, well, as you yourself know, Chicago can be a very un-loving city."

"Let me worry about that," I said.

"That's what I'm afraid of," he said.

Still, after enough nagging, he finally obliged me. He gave me about 20 capsules of MDMA and 10 hits of liquid LSD on sugar cubes. It was the largest quantity of illegal drugs I had ever held in my life. Even in my cocaine days, I nickel-and-dimed it, literally. Now, all I could see were endless waves of bliss before me. I was thoroughly, willfully, blind.

▼

In late February of 2005, on the day of my hearing for the summary suspension of my license (which was the foundation of the Chicago police's case against me, entirely predicated on my being too drunk at the time to even stand), I arrived at the Circuit Court building in the Daley Center with Tom Goforth accompanying me. I had asked Tom to speak on my behalf as a character witness to attest to the fact that I adhered to a political ideology that was diametrically opposed to that of white supremacist Matt Hale, whom the arresting officers had said I was praising during my arrest.

I had also appealed to the Steering Committee of the Green Party to write a letter on my behalf, and my friend and colleague Marc Sanson obliged me, describing my work for the party, and highlighting the party's key values, including diversity and non-violence, which, of course, were quite progressive by comparison to those of Matt Hale.

Peter had filed a motion to quash the arrest and suppress any evidence gathered during the traffic stop. Only one cop showed up, DeJesus, the officer who made the official arrest. He was dressed up in his full Chicago police uniform, as if he were a regular patrolman. He took the stand first and spun a tale in which I was pulled over by him and his partner, who he identified only as "Officer Isakson" during a routine traffic stop for "erratic driving," whereupon DeJesus smelled "a strong odor of alcohol" and asked me to step out of the car, whereupon I purportedly replied, "Fuck you, you have no rights over me based on the Constitution." I then apparently contradicted myself and voluntarily complied, opened the door, and in my attempt to exit the vehicle, I fell over, too drunk to stand, whereupon I refused a field sobriety test, began ranting about white supremacist Matt Hale, and was taken into custody.

Nowhere in his story did he mention the other two officers involved, or, naturally, anything else that happened that night, including their search of my vehicle, my refusal on Fourth Amendment grounds, and the beating they put on me. He repeated the story twice, verbatim, once for the State's Attorney, and then when Peter asked him to explain once again what happened.

Then I took the stand and told my radically different version. I explained that they were ahead of me in an unmarked TAC vehicle, and they almost caused an accident when they slammed on their brakes. That there were four officers present, that they demanded to search my car and when I refused, they physically removed me and began their search. When they turned up political material, they said, "Looks like we got one," and then proceeded to "teach me a lesson." I explained I was not drunk, and had demanded a field sobriety test. I suggested it was politically motivated.

The very young, very green State's Attorney, clearly blindsided by these revelations, shifted his tactic and began to focus almost exclusively on my arrest record. I was guilty, he argued, because I was a "violent convicted felon."

Peter objected, explaining that my crimes were simple nonviolent crimes, and that I had received only probation as a sentence.

The State's Attorney argued that my "attempted residential burglary" conviction was a violent crime, which Peter deftly dismissed.

"Mr. Shaw clearly had a drug problem, for which he received the prior convictions, but he's no longer engaged in those activities, and now works as a journalist and a peace activist. He is not a criminal."

Then Peter tore into DeJesus in cross-examination.

"You just told us you pulled Mr. Shaw over for erratic driving, and yet in your report you claim he was 'following too closely.' That would mean you were in front of him. Well, which is it? How could you have pulled him over if he was behind you?"

"Well . . ." De Jesus stammered, "he pulled up alongside us and tried to pass, and then we pulled him over."

"And, you claim this was a routine traffic stop. Were you in a patrol car?"

"No, we were in an unmarked detective's vehicle."

"Were you dressed in uniform?"

"No, we were in plain clothes."

"My client claims there was a woman present. A blonde with a pony tail. Who was that?

"That was Officer Isakson."

"Who were the other two men."

DeJesus paused. "There were no other officers present."

"It says here . . . that you claim Mr. Shaw tried to 'pull away several times.' How is this possible if he had already exited the vehicle and fell to the ground, apparently too drunk to stand?"

DeJesus had no answer.

"And if you look at your police report, the line stating Mr. Shaw tried to pull away is barely legible, sandwiched between two other lines, and appears as if it was added later. Why is this?"

DeJesus had no answer.

Peter grabbed the booking report with my defiant cross-armed mug shot and showed it to the judge.

"Does that look like someone who was so drunk he could

barely stand? It looks more to me like someone who is really angry at being falsely arrested."

Then Peter asked DeJesus exactly when I referred to myself as "Freedom Fighter." He had no answer. He asked when, precisely, did I state, "Hale had the right idea! You have no authority over me. Fuck the government!" DeJesus simply repeated what Peter had just said.

"That's right, he said, 'Hale had the right idea! You have no authority over me. Fuck the government!'"

When Tom Goforth took the stand he explained that he was a priest and a practicing psychotherapist, and had known me for about seven or eight years. When asked if I was violent or subscribed to these far-right-wing white supremacist views, he belly laughed and said, "absolutely not, that's ridiculous."

The State's Attorney tried to impugn Tom's testimony by alternately claiming he was a personal friend, and that Tom was "just some priest" and no expert on police matters, and his presence in the courtroom was inappropriate. Still, it was clear the judge had taken note of Tom's testimony.

In the end, Peter very calmly argued that I was a well-known peace activist who was acutely aware of the law and of his own rights, which was why I refused to comply with their orders in the first place, and that the series of events that DeJesus describes in his reports was highly implausible. He cited how many times De Jesus changed his story, and finally pointed out that the only case against me seemed to be that I had a previous criminal record.

By the time we were finished testifying, Judge Kennedy, a woman in her forties, looked exhausted. She shook her head a few times and then said:

"It's clear we have two widely divergent stories about what happened that night, and I don't know what the truth is, but in the end I do not believe the arresting officer's story. There are two many discrepancies. I don't believe you pulled him over, or that he tried to pass you; the story just does not add up. So the traffic stop and anything that happened afterwards is inadmissible."

That was it. It was over. I had won. I had actually won.

In a fit of hubris, as Tom, Peter, and I are leaving the courtroom, I say far too loudly, "Gentlemen, I think a civil rights case just dropped in our lap." I turn around to see DeJesus staring at me. He heard every word I said.

▼

Edie let me stay at our old apartment in her guest room, my old office, while I was trying to get myself situated again in Chicago. I wanted to head straight back to the Bay Area, but I was completely broke, and had used up all my "Get Out of Chicago Free" cards. I had moved cross-country three times in three years (four times in ten years) and every time it had been some form of disaster. There was no one I could ask for help on this one. If I wanted to move, I would have to arrange it all myself. Edie told me that the only stipulation to staying with her was that I had to find work.

The day after the hearing I got up to go look for a job. I made coffee and went to sit out on the enclosed front porch that overlooks the street. When I looked down into the street, a dark green unmarked TAC squad car was parked in front of my building, and two men were inside staring up at me. When I left my house about an hour or so later to hop on the El and ride downtown, the car followed me to the El stop and watched me go inside and up to the platform. They pulled into the alley that ran alongside the tracks, got out of the car, and scanned the platform. I did not recognize them. Once they saw I had spotted them, they got back into the car. The El arrived a moment later, and I got on board and left.

When I returned hours later, another unmarked silver-colored TAC car was parked outside my El stop. I turned right to head home, and it sped away in the opposite direction. However, as

I turned the corner a block away, the car had gone around the block and pulled up in front of my house. They just sat there, in the middle of the street, staring at me as I crossed and headed into my building. I couldn't tell if it was the same cops as earlier. As I mounted the steps, the car took off.

This went on for weeks. Not every day, and once a whole week went by without my seeing any of them. But fairly regularly they would park outside my building, usually in the morning and late at night, and follow me to the El stop. I knew they were trying to intimidate me, it was fairly obvious, but I just ignored them. I was mildly freaked out, though, but I didn't tell Edie. I didn't want to worry her, and I figured, they want me, not her.

I was growing paranoid and distrustful. I had been taking MDMA regularly. By day, I was the paranoid radical, by night, the warm fuzzy hugging everyone. This schism was bifurating my life and my personality, and the two halves were quickly becoming irreconcilable. Each day I had to get up again, in fear, and get through another day not knowing when I would find work again and get my own place, let alone get out of Chicago, not knowing what the cops would do, not knowing how this civil rights case I wanted to file would go, and feeling the generalized stress and anxiety brought about by the uncertainty of personal transformation.

I was changing, that was for sure, but I was overwhelmed by it, and not thinking clearly. I didn't have a framework into which I could insert this new person. I was still me, living my political world even after I had seen through it all. I was lost, and I was very lonely. I had isolated myself in an artificial bubble of entheogens once long-repressed emotions started to make their way out of me, loosened by the soft caress of the love drug.

I met with Tom Goforth and laid it all out for him. Like "Albert," he was happy that the entheogens had broken me out of my rut, but he feared I might be just as quickly falling into a new one. He understood what was happening vis-à-vis the loosening

of grief within me, and he felt I was not protecting myself by
going through it in a more structured therapeutic way with him.
He pointed out when I would ramble on about how perfect San
Francisco was that I was "idealizing" people and places I barely
knew. He suggested I was escaping, and even as my heart was
opening, my sense of reality was closing. All this ran the high risk
of backfiring and closing down my heart all over again.

My friends Bryan and Dianna Brickner echoed Tom's senti-
ments. When I went to visit with them, within ten minutes I proposed we all take MDMA together. It was ten o'clock on a Tuesday
morning. After demurring, they both scrutinized me with concern.

"What are you doing with yourself, Charles?" Dianna asked
me. "You need to be taking better care of yourself. I'm not sure
what's going through your head when you ask us if we want to
take a bunch of MDMA with you now, as if we both don't have
a thousand things that need to get done. What are you running
away from here?"

"I'm not running away from anything. I just want to feel the
love. I want to feel like I did in San Francisco."

"Well, you can't just force 'the love' on others and have an
artificial experience of intimacy," Dianna continued. "How real
and lasting is that? Explain to me how that is helping you."

I balked, I prevaricated, I rationalized, and I even shed a few
tears. They didn't understand! I had seen a glimpse of something
beautiful: it was me with the ability to feel love and happiness and
be secure in myself, and I didn't want to lose it. But they knew
that I had no idea how to hold on to it, that the only way I knew
how to get there was by prescription.

Back in 2002 I had seen an HBO documentary on MDMA. It
focused on the life of a man in his thirties named Scott. He had a
wife and three kids, and his 19-year-old son had turned him on to
Ecstasy and rave culture. Scott became enchanted. He explained
plaintively in the film about how he never got to experience his

youth because he and his wife got married and had children so young. Now, he was getting a chance to "have fun" with his life. I remember sympathizing with him, because I had missed out on that culture too during my twenties, as I roamed the ghetto in search of another hit instead.

Then Scott took it too far and gave his 15-year-old daughter and 10-year-old son MDMA *on camera* and very quickly lost custody of his kids. Suddenly his perfect fantasy world collapsed around him. Yet, he was still unable to let go. He continued to go to raves, only now by himself, fervently trying to maintain the thin porous membrane of his escape bubble. By the end he just looked pathetic, and HBO made sure to yank all sympathy for him.

Scott's plight would be somewhere in the forefront of my mind as I continually tried to manufacture artificially intimate settings with friends. I just wanted them all to feel the way I did, but I never paused a moment to recognize that everyone was coming from a different place, and that what I needed and sought was different from what other people needed, or sought.

I was love-starved, and so desperately lonely. My family was incapable of showing love, I didn't have close enough friends to get love that way, and the only person in my life to really give it to me unconditionally was Edie, and I couldn't connect with her intimately or receive her love. Of course, underlying all of this, still buried from view, was the glaring reality that I did not yet love myself, that I still harbored toxic shame and self-judgment and the internalized voices of every detractor, denouncer, and disciplinarian. Sure, MDMA was opening me up, but it was only awakening the potentiality. I still had no practicum. I was confused and disoriented by my awakening senses, but it was clear that there was now a light in the distance and I would soon be able to make sense of it all. One thing was for sure, I was definitely on my way.

In an instant of piss-poor judgment, it would all vanish, and I would be sent hurtling back to the proverbial Square One.

THE PORTAL SLAMS SHUT

On the evening of Good Friday, March 26, 2005, I left Edie's apartment and met a woman named Natalie and a friend of hers for dinner in the Wrigleyville neighborhood. Edie was in Florida on vacation with her family, and she had left Milhouse with me, making me promise her before she left that I would take very good care of him and "not do anything stupid." I was cherishing the precious time I was going to be able to spend with my hounddog, who I had missed so terribly when I was away from him in San Francisco, and would have to leave again once I got enough money to move back to the West Coast.

I had just met Natalie at a restaurant that had hired and fired me within a week. She was my wait-service trainer, a 21-year-old, beautiful, blond, and blue-eyed girl from Alabama, the virgin daughter of a pastor. Seriously. No, *seriously.* We had already gone out on one very affectionate date, which was for me like a godsend at the time. We had plans to eat dinner, hit an improv show at the Playground Theater, and then the whole lot of us were going to get together afterwards and have us a good old-fashioned MDMA party.

I had stashed inside a secret pocket of my backpack a small canister with a total of 14 capsules for the eight to ten people who were expected to attend. When we arrived at the Playground, I set my backpack down and headed out the back door to smoke with Natalie and another guy named Matt.

Once outside, I stood for a minute, and then was seized by this mild panic that I shouldn't have left my backpack unattended, so I went back inside to grab it. But instead of taking the whole pack with me, I took the MDMA out of the secret pocket and put it in the breast pocket of the jacket I was wearing. I also grabbed my overcoat, and headed back outside.

No sooner had I exited the rear of the building, sat down, and reached inside my overcoat for my cigarettes than a dark green unmarked TAC squad car comes screeching up right in front of us, two male TAC officers jump out of the car, and one yells at me, "What have you got in that pocket!? Get up, let me see!"

The cop immediately grabs me and begins searching my overcoat, and he pulls out a glass marijuana pipe that was deep inside the lining.

"Trying to hide this, were you?"

I remember breathing a mild sigh of relief that all he found was the pipe, but that relief disappeared into a sickening rush as I remembered that I had just placed the MDMA canister in my front pocket. I broke out into a hot sweat and the world spun, and I thought for a second I was going to puke. The cop pushed me back against the wall and began searching me, and within 30 seconds he found the MDMA.

"Bingo," was all he said. "Call 'em and let 'em know."

I was cuffed and placed into the back of the car. Within a few moments, three other TAC squad cars pull up and a bunch of TAC officers get out and are conversing behind me out of sight. Then, this massive six foot six or larger bald cop comes walking up to me seated in the back seat and smiles.

"We gotcha now," he said. "You can bet that. You ain't goin' *nowhere*."

He reaches inside his vest pocket and pulls out one of the capsules of MDMA.

"I know what this is. This is crystal meth. I know these capsules, I know this shit. You're going to tell us who you get this from, or you're going to pray you were never born."

I heard one of the other cops say, "Oh you sure don't wanna make Lieutenant Stasch, angry," then they all cackled with laughter.

"It's not crystal meth," I say.

Lt. Stasch reels around and says, "It's whatever I goddam well say it is."

I am once again transported to the TAC office at the Addison and Halsted precinct house, the same room DeJesus and his crew took me to a year earlier. The two arresting officers—their names were Suleiman and Haro—handcuff me to a bench in front of them.

I begin to panic because I realize that Milhouse is locked up at home, alone, and Edie is out of town, and there is no one to let him out or feed him and give him water. I also have the only set of keys to her apartment. I ask the cops if I can make my phone call now because I need to get word to my sister about my dog, and have her come pick up the keys from me. At first, they tell me, "OK" and ask for the keys. I tell them they are in my pocket, and they come and take them from me. When I then ask again to make the call, they tell me, "Sorry, can't do that."

"But you just told me you'd let me make my call."

"Phone calls are made after booking is complete. In about four or five hours, maybe more."

I plead again with them. "Look, I know I'm not going anywhere but at least let me get my dog squared away."

"We can't do that," one of them says. The other one then says, "Tell us your address, and give us permission, and we'll go take care of him."

Just at that moment, another TAC officer in the room says really loud, "Oh yeah, they'll definitely *take good care* of your dog. We're all animal lovers here, you know," and they all start laughing again.

Obviously, there was no way I was going to give them permission to go to my house, I knew they'd shoot Milhouse and do god knows what else. So, they begin asking me if I've got anything in my house I shouldn't, and that I "might as well tell them before they have to get a warrant." The ploy is transparent, so I simply ignore the question.

"Give us your sister's number, we'll call her," they say. I remain silent.

They sit and watch me for a few more minutes, and then they

both get up and leave. About half an hour later they return, with Natalie, in handcuffs. They lock her to the bench next to me. She looks utterly terrified, on the verge of tears. She looks at me with total disgust.

"They said you're a drug dealer. They want to know if I've ever seen you sell drugs or if I've ever seen drugs in your apartment."

"They're lying to you," I said. "They're trying to trick you."

"You shut the fuck up!" one of them yells at me. Then he turns to Natalie, and points at her. "You're gonna tell us if you've seen what we asked you about, or we're charging you too!"

"I swear I've never seen anything. I barely know him," she pleads.

"It's OK, you can tell us," they say to her. "He won't be able to hurt you."

Hurt you!?? her face radiates as she turns back to me.

"Oh very fucking clever," I say.

"Do you want to talk to us," they continue, then unlock her and walk her out of the room. They are gone for another half an hour, then return with *another* person who was outside with us, this guy Matt, whom I barely knew. They grill him the same way, with the same result, and let him go. Eventually, they give up and start back in on me.

"OK, you don't have to tell us anything. We've got enough right now to go kick down your door, shoot your fucking dog, and then what will we find? Tell us where you got this and we won't have to do that."

I remain silent.

"You know, if you tell us, if you give us someone higher up on the food chain, we can take that into consideration."

"You mean rat someone out?"

"Well, not exactly. Call it self-preservation. What choice do you have? Are you ready to go to prison?"

"I tell you what," I say, knowing they won't do it. "Put it in writing and have it signed by a judge."

"Sorry, it doesn't work like that. You give us a name or an address, we go there, and if we come back with someone or something more than what we busted you with, we'll tell the judge to go easy on you."

I can't help but laugh.

"You guys must think I'm an idiot," I say.

"Yup. Pretty much. You're the one in handcuffs."

"I learned my lesson with you guys once already. I ain't sayin' shit to nobody."

"Oh no, my friend," one of them says. "You most definitely didn't learn your lesson, that's why we got you now. Eventually, you're gonna tell us what we want to know. Remember, we still have your keys."

▼

I was led away to booking and spent the next 24 hours in the police lockup at Addison and Halsted before I was transferred to Cook County on Easter Sunday. Blessedly, I managed to get ahold of my sister with my one phone call, since my sister had a landline. I told her to call Edie immediately and let her know what had happened so she could see about Milhouse. I wouldn't know for days whether the cops had gone to my house as they had threatened.

At County I sat for another day inside an overcrowded holding cell in the basement before I was taken before the "video bond court." It took another day and a half to process me through County, and it was the longest 36 hours of my life. I didn't sleep and bit my fingers bloody worrying about Edie and Milhouse. At one point, I had an anxiety attack that I had to suppress with all my strength, and I just wanted to die.

When I finally got to my tier, I called my sister again, and she told me Milhouse and the apartment were OK. Edie had contacted Milhouse's dog walking service, which had a set of keys, and they retrieved him safely. Knowing he was safe, I went into my cell, and passed out for a whole day.

I expected to be in County for a while but less than two days later they offered me EMU/house arrest. Since Edie was still in Florida, she could not approve my transfer, so I called my sister and she reluctantly agreed to let me stay with her, despite the fact that she shared her apartment with another person she didn't know that well.

NO EXIT, REDUX

Jean-Paul Sartre's haunting play *No Exit* tells the story of three people trapped together in a hotel suite who cannot connect with one another. The three characters are a man and two women, imprisoned in a bizarre love triangle, each desiring the unrequited affections of one while rebuking the advances of the other. Each party schemes and manipulates the others to try and get what they want. Each is also guarding secrets for which they fear disclosure. By the end of the play, you realize that these characters are trapped in Hell, and that "Hell is other people."

For the next two months I was stuck in my own version of *No Exit* in my sister's apartment in Logan Square. I had a monitoring band on my ankle and I couldn't go anywhere. I was completely dependent upon Suraya, Edie, and the few friends I had who stuck by me, like Brian Allemana and Bryan Brickner. "Albert" also tried to be supportive, but he was not happy that I had been busted, and he feared that contact with me might compromise him, which is understandable, if lamentable. As a consequence, many other people in this social circle also decided I might be too big a risk to associate with, and I found myself mostly isolated.

It took a few weeks for the dust to settle. I contacted Peter Vilkelis and asked him to represent me. He was not happy with me at all. After putting his name on the line by defending me in as volatile and potentially dangerous a case as my run-in with the Chicago police, the least he expected me to do was to stay out of trouble. He didn't know any of the details of what was going on in my life, but I'm not sure it would have mattered even if he did. This bust made both of us look stupid.

Peter agreed to represent me, but we very quickly found out that it didn't matter. When I appeared for my first court date, he met me at the doors to the courtroom and pulled me into an adjacent conference room and closed the door.

"I talked to the State's Attorney to see what kind of play we could get on this case, and he told me that he had strict orders from those above him that 'this guy gets no play, he does time.' In all my years of defending people, I've never had the State's Attorney be unwilling to negotiate or hear my argument. You definitely pissed off the right people."

"So what does that mean?" I asked, already knowing the answer.

"It means that you gotta do some time. How much depends on you. I mean, you can fight it if you want, but it's going to cost you, and I can't do this one for free. And if you lose, you're going to get the maximum. The bottom line is, you know what you got caught with, and you really don't have much of a defense."

I took a moment to let it sink in. *Prison.* I still wouldn't believe it was real.

"Can't we prove I was set up?" I asked him.

"Set up means they planted drugs on you. Did they plant drugs on you?"

"No. They were mine."

Pete just shrugged, his eyes communicating, *You're gonna have to be a man on this one.*

After a moment, Pete said, "I don't want to make this any worse for you, but you should see something."

He dropped a collection of papers on the desk in front of me. It was the arrest report. In it, the two arresting officers—Suleiman and Haro—claimed they approached me because they saw me smoking pot outside the back door of the Playground Theater.

"Were you smoking?" Pete asked?

"No. Honestly. I mean, I was going to . . ."

Pete shook his head. "You should have known better than that."

"You're right," I said.

"One other thing," Pete said. "This you really won't like."

"What's that?"

Pete pointed to the arrest report. There, staring me in the face, was confirmation of everything I suspected. The report listed the other officers who were present that night, the ones who came racing over after they heard I had been picked up. Among the names was "N. Isakson," the female cop who was DeJesus's partner, present the night of my assault.

She was there to confirm it was me, that they got the right guy.

▼

Pete got me a continuance for a month to think about what I wanted to do. Slowly I let word out to selective people that I had been busted again and was headed to prison. In the beginning people expressed shock and sympathy, but that was soon followed by silence; no more calls or emails or visits but for a few activist friends who began imploring me to consider writing about my experience, explaining to me just how unique an opportunity I had been presented with.

One of my most ardent supporters in this regard was a writer friend named Guy Herron. He called me often from his home somewhere in the remote regions of Utah to offer support and to lay out for me all the reasons why I shouldn't be afraid to bare my soul. He told me that is what it takes to communicate complex and difficult situations to a larger audience, to bring major social and political issues to light and humanize them so that others could connect to them. But so long as I let my fears rule me and I hid behind my Shadow, the reality of our drug laws and our prison system would be kept hidden from the people most capable of bringing about real change, which was the vast American middle-class electorate.

Guy was the first to make a solid argument to me that drug prisoners like me were political prisoners, because we had committed victimless crimes that were little more than violations of a strict moral code. A code that did not respect the inherent liberty of citizens to make their own personal and ostensibly private lifestyle choices.

To help me understand that way of thinking better, he sent me a copy of *Borstal Boy*, a prison memoir by a former IRA soldier named Brendan Behan. The Irish-Catholic Behan was held by the British as a political prisoner, and the book charts his journey from naïve idealist to political pragmatist as he discovers, after being locked up with Protestants of his own class, that the differences between them were superficial, and imposed upon them by their respective power structures.

After considering everyone's input and mulling the decision over and over in my head for weeks, I decided that I wouldn't fight the case. I was guilty, and I had avoided this for long enough, twice escaping all-but-guaranteed prison sentences. It was time to pay the fiddler and face the consequences of my actions. I would allow myself to be guilty but talk about the extenuating circumstances, in the hopes that it might raise the question, *Is it fair to send someone to prison for possessing something that proved of great benefit to his life?*

I am grateful for the time I was able to spend with my sister, even though it was terribly challenging for both of us. My presence made her relationship with her roommate awkward, even though her roommate was decent to me about it and never protested or complained. More complex was how my arrest brought up years of resentment about the things I had done when I was still deep into my addiction. My sister always loved me and was always a huge support even in my darkest days, but what I had done had hurt her deeply, and she was ambivalent about how she felt about me. At times, we got along great; others, I could tell she regretted letting me stay there.

My sister was also going through her own deep and dark existential crisis related to her heritage. Unbeknownst to me, when she turned 21 she had gone to the agency that had handled her adoption and pulled the file on her birth family. I don't know what Suraya expected to find, or what ideas she had built up in her head about her Native American heritage, but I can easily imagine that, without any real contact or understanding of that world, all she knew were romanticized portrayals of beautiful, exotic, noble Indians living in harmony with the Earth on reservations. When she discovered the truth, it nearly destroyed her.

Suraya showed me the files that described how both of her parents were migrant workers who were living in Chicago in the early 1970s—there was still a big fishing industry on the Great Lakes, —and they worked in a cannery. They were incredibly poor, and Suraya's biological father was a chronic alcoholic who often was homeless and indigent. She also had an older sister, who was already a huge burden on her biological mother, so when her mother discovered she was pregnant with Suraya, she hid her pregnancy from the father and gave her away in secret once she was born.

The shock of this revelation threw my sister into a tailspin. It did not matter that she had been adopted by a safe, loving, and affluent family, and no matter of discussion about it would convince her. She was deeply and profoundly ashamed of her roots, a theme she shared with our mother, except that my sister was not like my mother.

Suraya has always been a very sensitive and shy person. She did not have the kind of obsessive drive our mother possessed, she was always more like our father, simple and quiet and into her own things. The net result was that she repudiated all things Native American, refusing to have any interest in them whatsoever, and she dove deeper and deeper into the same strain of alcoholism that had destroyed her family.

My sister blamed me for much of her substance abuse problems because I had introduced her to most of the substances she abused, and we had spent much time using together. But more than that, just like our brother, Zachary, she resented me for not providing a better example, for not realizing or reaching my potential, and for making the decisions I had made that had inexorably led me to where I was in life, now biding my time before I was shipped off to prison.

I felt like a complete failure, and no manner of pep talk about fighting injustice, writing a great book, or being a martyr for the cause made any bit of difference. My brother and my sister needed me in life, and I wasn't there for them, endlessly swimming circles in the septic tank of my own manufactured dramas. I knew my days of this kind of irresponsibility were over, that I had no choice but to get it together, start providing a positive example, and be there for them, or else I was certain that I would lose my sister to alcoholism, and my brother would simply drift away and I'd never see him again.

I made arrangements with Pete to appear in court on July 1, 2005, to accept a plea for a two-year sentence: one year in prison, one year on parole. That gave me a month to put my affairs in order. I petitioned the County to allow me to transfer my house arrest to Edie's and was utterly shocked when they approved it. I was able to spend the last month in my own room, with my dog and my best friend, in a comfortable space that let me prepare myself for everything that I was soon to face.

On July 1, I appeared in court with a shaved head, wearing a white T-shirt and jeans, and accepted a plea for one year in custody, and one year on parole. In the courtroom for support were Edie and Brian Allemana. Holding back tears, they both forced a smile as I was led away into the back to begin my journey into the underworld. I made sure I smiled back to let them know that I was OK, and I would be fine. My path to redemption led through that door, and I had ceased resisting. I was in a place of total calm and acceptance, and I took great comfort in knowing that they were the last people I looked upon as a free man.

1 Thanks to the drug war, women are now the fastest-growing prison demographic (see "Women Behind Bars" by Silja Talvi, *In These Times*, February 8, 2008).

2 Steve Mills and Maurice Possley, "Cook County Jail Beatings: Mass Jail Beating Covered Up," *Chicago Tribune*, February 27, 2003.

3 Stephen Lendman, "The US Gulag Prison System," Centre for Research on Globalization, www.globalresearch.ca/index.php?context=va&aid=2113

4 The Tactical Unit (TAC) is Chicago's drug and gang cops. They are special detectives who wear plain clothes and bulletproof vests and drive around in unmarked cars. And as you will read later in this book, they are as crooked as the day is long, and largely operate above the law.

5 A "hype" is a crackhead in Chicago street parlance.

6 "Schwing" is slang for smoking crack.

7 Supermax prisons require additional levels of security equipment and personnel, which adds substantially to the cost per inmate. Additionally, Supermax inmates are not put to work in the prison economy, thus eliminating whatever cost mitigation they might have incurred through their labor.

8 Charles Shaw, "A Sorry Excuse for a Decent Living," *The Next American City*, April 2005. Study by University of Illinois Champaign-Urbana College of Agriculture.

9 Ibid.

10 Ride is an obscure idiomatic expression for "homeboy" or "partner" usually indicating participation in a gang milieu.

11 Television is widely available in prison. It's a cheap and effective

tool for maintaining control, as TV serves to occupy and pacify inmates. So each tier has at least one or more unit sets, and many inmates either rent or purchase their own through the commissary.

12 "Edie" (name changed) is my best friend and former girlfriend. We lived together for the first half of the decade, and were separated but living in the same apartment at the time I was arrested. [Edie] was the only person in my life I completely trusted.

13 Both the ALF (Animal Liberation Front) and the ELF (Earth Liberation Front) have since had members imprisoned as domestic terrorists, with ongoing cases as of 2011. A great source for following the progress of this movement, and those cases, is Will Potter's "Green Is the New Red" (www.greenisthenewred.com).

14 This was written before the introduction of The Violent Radicalization and Homegrown Terrorism Act of 2007 (S.1959 / H.R.1955), a bill that accomplishes precisely the measures described in the above paragraph.

15 This idea is discussed in great detail in Christian Parenti's brilliant and exhaustively researched book. *Lockdown America* (London: Verso, 1999). It is the single greatest resource available for understanding police and prisons.

16 BCI in any law enforcement agency is the Bureau of Criminal Information where criminal records, fingerprints, photos, and DNA are kept.

17 COINTELPRO was an FBI counterintelligence program initiated under the Nixon Administration to infiltrate, disrupt, and ultimately neutralize the antiwar and militant black movements. COINTELPRO had a particularly devastating impact on the Black Panthers, imprisoning, murdering, or forcing into exile most of the leadership. Nixon's tapes reveal the extent to which he considered these two groups Public Enemy #1. The tapes also reveal how he first concocted the idea of using federal drug laws to attack these two groups, since drug use was considered a part of the "revolution." That template continued in force once Reagan took office in the 1980s and cocaine flooded the inner cities.

18 John Edgar Wideman, introduction to *Live from Death Row* by Mumia Abu-Jamal (New York: Harper Perennial, 1996), p. xxxiii.

19 Mumia Abu-Jamal, *Live from Death Row*, pp. 143–144.

20 Mumia Abu-Jamal, *Death Blossoms: Reflections from a Prisoner of Conscience* (Rifton, NY: Plough Publishing House, 1997), p. 11.

21 http://news.bbc.co.uk/2/hi/programmes/this_world/5241988.stm

22 www.democracynow.org/2005/9/27/after_the_hurricane_where_have_all

23 William Van Dusen Wishard, "The Heart of History," *The Jung Page*, May 7, 2007, www.cgjungpage.org

24 Fortunately, this was not the same David Addington as the conservative ideologue who was Dick Cheney's chief of staff and architect of the "unitary executive" theory.

25 "Southern Partisan: 'Setting the Record Straight': Attorney General Nominee Praised White Supremacist Magazine," FAIR: Fairness and Accuracy in Reporting, January 12, 2001.

26 "Critics Call Radio Hosts' Trip Propaganda Mission," Fox News, July 6, 2005.

27 Harry Atwater, "Are You a Yippie or a Yuppie?" *The Tech* (Boston: Massachusetts Institute of Technology), February 12, 1985.

28 *The Century of the Self, Part Three*: "There Is a Policeman Inside All Our Heads: He Must Be Destroyed" (BBC, 2002).

29 One thing that becomes immediately noticeable if you spend any time in the direct action world is the prevalence of tales of "bags of urine and feces" that seem to proliferate in police departments around the country. These tales are told about protestors in the 1999 WTO protests in Seattle. They have become as apocryphal as the tales among city doctors and nurses of fat women showing up in the ER complaining of abdominal pain who were unknowingly pregnant and in labor. These are crude attempts to demonize all demonstrators, as I would experience myself over the years as this bugaboo kept popping up wherever the protest movement would go.

30 Craig Futterman and Melissa Mather, *The Chicago Police Department's Broken System*, Edwin F. Mandel Legal Aid Clinic, University of Chicago, November 14, 2007.

31 Ibid.

32 David Heinzmann and Steve Mills, "Cop Agency Seeks Outside Help to Deal with Backlog of Complaints," *Chicago Tribune*, January 16, 2008.

33 Libby Sander, "Chicago Revamps Investigation of Police Abuse, but Privacy Fight Continues," *The New York Times*, July 20, 2007.

34 "List Documents Chicago Police Complaints," Associated Press, July 18, 2007.

35 FBI Uniform Crime Statistics 1960–2008, www.disastercenter.com/crime/uscrime.htm

36 "Many US Cities Record Lowest Homicide Totals Since 1960s," City-Data.com, January 6, 2010 (cites multiple news reports).

37 "Chicago Examined: Anatomy of a Police Riot," *Time*, December 6, 1968.

38 The 1968 Democratic Convention riots were exhaustively documented in David Farber's book *Chicago '68* (Chicago: University of Chicago Press, 1994) and in Haskell Wexler's film *Medium Cool*, shot on location at the Convention protests. Much of Wexler's outtake footage ended up in Brett Morgen's 2007 documentary, *Chicago 10*, which shows incontrovertible footage of police attacking peaceful demonstrators.

39 Jeff Cohen and Jeff Gottlieb, "Was Fred Hampton Executed?" *The Nation*, November 30, 2009; *The Murder of Fred Hampton*, DVE, directed by Mike Gray and Howard Alk (1971; Chicago; Facet, 2007) Chris Steele, "Panthers: The Truth About Fred Hampton's Murder," *Denver Progressive Examiner*, February 11, 2009; "The Murder of Chairman Fred Hampton Sr. by Chicago Police and F.B.I.," RGB Street Scholars, February 2010.

40 "Chicago Cops from 1968 Convention Hold Reunion," Associated Press, June 27, 2009; Murial Kane, "1968 Chicago Riot Cops Set to 'Celebrate' Mass Beatings," *The Raw Story*, June 18, 2009.

41 "Probe Demanded into Alleged Chicago Police Torture," Reuters, August 29, 2005; "Chicago Cops Tortured Blacks, Human Rights Panel Told," Associated Press, October 14, 2005.

42 "Repeated Denials—and Sobs—As Burge Finally Takes Stand," *Chicago Tribune Breaking News*, June 17, 2010.

43 "Burge Found Guilty of Lying About Torture," *Chicago Tribune Breaking News*, June 28, 2010.

44 "United States of America: Race, Rights, and Brutality," a report by Amnesty International, September 1999.

45 "Matt Hale Found Guilty of Soliciting Murder," ADL Extremism Updates, April 27, 2004.

46 Jodi Wilgoren, "White Supremacist Is Held in Ordering Judge's Death," *The New York Times*, January 9, 2003.

47 *Whiteout: The CIA, Drugs and the Press* (London; Verso, 1998), p. 77.

48 Nicole Colson, "Chicago Police Brutality," *ZNet*, June 4, 2004.

49 Ibid.; Charles Shaw, "The Creeping Police State," *Newtopia*, February 2005; Gerald Emmett, "Did the Chicago Police Murder May Molina Ortiz?" *News & Letters*, July 2004, www.newsletters.org

50 "Did the Chicago Police Murder May Molina Ortiz?"

51 David Heinzmann, "Activist's Death Tied to Heroin," *Chicago Tribune*, September 2, 2004.

52 Steve Schmadeke, "New Trial Ordered for Man in 1992 Lakeview Slaying: Inmate's Late Mom Crusaded for Conviction's Reversal," *Chicago Tribune*, November 20, 2009.

ACKNOWLEDGMENTS

THE AUTHOR would like to honor and thank the invaluable assistance of James Sainsbury and the Tedworth Charitable Trust, Andrew Harvey, Ken Jordan & Johnathan Talat Phillips of *Reality Sandwich*, Laura Mazer at Counterpoint, Tony Curzon-Price and Julian Stern at openDemocracy, Anthony Lappé, Neva Welton, Carrie Mapes, Ronnie Pontiac, and my partner Sonia Lub, who all put love, belief, and lots of critique into *Exile Nation* to make sure it found a home.

ABOUT THE AUTHOR

CHARLES SHAW is an award-winning journalist and editor, and director of the documentary *The Exile Nation Project: An Oral History of the War on Drugs & The American Criminal Justice System.*

Shaw serves as editor for the openDemocracy Drug Policy Forum and the Dictionary of Ethical Politics, both collaborative projects of Resurgence, openDemocracy, and the Tedworth Charitable Trust.

Shaw's work has appeared in *Alternet, Alternative Press Review, Conscious Choice, Common Ground, Grist, Guardian UK, Huffington Post, In These Times, Newtopia, The New York Times, openDemocracy, Planetizen, Punk Planet, Reality Sandwich, San Diego Uptown News, Scoop, Shift, Truthout, The Witness, YES!,* and *Znet.* In 2009 he was recognized by the San Diego Press Club for excellence in journalism.

Printed in the United States
by Baker & Taylor Publisher Services